My Life in Indian Politics

Advance Praise

For me, Mohsinaji has always been a motherly figure, an inspirational person with exemplary conduct in public life. She has been a woman of courage, who invariably identified and promoted meritorious and ideologically strong leaders in the party. I have been like a family member having known her, Khalil sahab and others since the mid 1970s when I was NSUI president. I vividly recalled how once she and her family had come to Shimla for a personal holiday when Irum was very young. She played a role in looking after my future wife in Delhi who had come from South Africa, having studied in London and then at the AIIMS. She looked after her very well and introduced her to Indiraji. There are so many fond memories and good times we have had. Mohsinaji's success at Azamgarh where I had slogged as a young political worker and subsequently, at Chikmagalur turned out to be a turning point in Indian politics resulting in our great comeback. I find her memoir to be fascinating simply because of her courage of conviction, ideological clarity and honesty.

—Anand Sharma, former union minister

Mohsina Kidwai belongs to a fast-fading tradition of politicians—genteel, soft-spoken, graceful, and yet no less pugnacious. Much before women came centre stage in the way they have in contemporary Indian politics, she made her presence, championing gender equality and fighting for the marginalized. Forged in the crucible of a newly independent India and witness to every momentous event that has shaped its destiny, she is still going strong … Her memoir is a much-needed account of the journey of a remarkable woman, while also providing an up-close and personal history of the making of a nation.

—Sharmila Tagore, actor and social activist

Mohsinaji was, in 2007, my choice for President and I felt that she should have been elevated to the highest office in the country. I still feel strongly about it. The elegance and grace that she displayed at work and home is worth emulating by all women. Her selfless work and commitment to the ideals of the Congress party and dedication to the Constitution of India are exemplary. I had the privilege of being a co-worker and an admirer of Mohsinaji. She held the people of the then united Andhra Pradesh with great affection as do we, the people of the state. I wish her good health and call upon the Almighty to bless her with all that will give her joy and happiness.

—Renuka Choudhury, former union minister

I have pleasant reflections of Shrimati Mohsina Kidwai when she was union minister of Health and Family Welfare, Government of India. She was always positive and receptive to suggestions to bring greater quality healthcare for our people. In 1995, she brought a transformation by inaugurating the innovative Health Insurance Initiative—Family Health Plan (FHP) by Apollo Hospitals group for the first time in the country. This enabled access to quality healthcare to people in the rural areas, farmers in Karnataka and Police unions in Andhra Pradesh and Maharashtra. This was the forerunner of private healthcare insurance in the country. Mohsinaji is a true visionary.

**—Dr Pratap C. Reddy, Chairman,
Apollo Group of Hospitals**

Mohsina Kidwaiji is one person about whom whatever one may say or write, would always fall short ... because she is such an amazing person, affectionate, down to earth with remarkable effective intelligence, one of the finest creations of God almighty. Though she held many portfolios and offices, her commitment to the health and family welfare sector is second to none. Kidwaiji's heart is not confined to expansion of medical advancement in every nook and corner of the country but the very best and the state-of-the-art technology being available for one and all. This visionary approach of the medical care system consists of mercy, empathy, integrity, ingenuity, nobility, ethics and technology itself requires a volume. I have been fortunate in knowing her well and often I found her to be an ideal, role model patient too!

—Dr Purshotam Lal, chairman and director of Interventional Cardiology, Metro Group of Hospitals

Mohsina Kidwaiji has a magnanimous personality. She is very sharp and intelligent and very active in her responses and reactions. This was evident when on various occasions, I witnessed her interactions with people at large who thronged at her residence every morning to meet her and appeal to address their problems. In the mornings before leaving for her office, she would attend to every individual and instruct her officers to take necessary actions. Everyone had free access to her residence and this was always evident, especially at Iftar parties at her residence when Late Rajiv Gandhi and other dignitaries used to mix free with all guests. She still carries the old charm and grace and has a great following. My family will always remain grateful for her blessings. May Almighty give her long life and good health. Ameen.

—Dr Mohsin Wali, eminent cardiologist and honorary physician to many Presidents of India

I had met Mohsina Kidwaiji in 1973 and since then, we have developed a deep bond of mutual respect. I always viewed her as someone who was close to Indira Gandhiji. She has all qualities that an ideal Congress person should be having—progressive outlook, clarity of thought and action, and a resolve to stand by the downtrodden, weaker sections, women and the poor.

We were together during Assam assembly polls of 1983, when Indiraji had deputed Pranab Mukherjee, me, Mohsinaji, Narayan Dutt Tiwari and many others. This was a difficult phase in Assam as, for four protracted and strife-torn years, the prickly 'foreigner' issue in Assam had mushroomed into a big agitation, often threatening attempts of compromise or mediation. Indiraji had decided to gamble on winning through the ballot. There were all sorts of threats and challenges but the Congress won, netting ninety-one state assembly seats.

In the subsequent years, Mohsinaji and I had several opportunities to interact. She was general secretary in charge of Kerala where I was amazed by her ability to unite various factions and groups with ease. She is always attentive and selfless, and has kept the party's interest above everything else. In the Congress Working Committee (CWC), too, I marvelled at her clarity of thought and candour. In fact, each time she spoke, everyone in the CWC used to hear her in rapt attention. Her commitment to the country and the Congress has been unwavering, admirable and worth emulating. Her memoir is a living testimony of it.

—A.K. Antony, former Defence Minister and ex-Chief Minister, Kerala

Mohsina Kidwai saheba has been a senior public figure in our political system. Her knowledge of situations and personalities has been of value to the political leadership. She has the uncommon, albeit unique, distinction of being among the few who express their viewpoint quietly yet softly. This wins her respect.

—Hamid Ansari, former Vice President of India

Mohsina Kidwaiji may have belonged to Uttar Pradesh, but we in Chhattisgarh consider her as one of us. In fact, she has a pan-Indian identity among millions of Congress workers spread across the country. I feel privileged and honoured to have been an associate of hers. It was a great learning experience. From her, I learnt how loyalty to the Congress and its leadership is paramount and unwavering under all circumstances. Her autobiography is a treasure trove. It is welcoming that a leader of her stature has penned in detail an analytical account of her role in crafting and executing government policies and strengthening Congress organization in a selfless manner.

—**Bhupesh Baghel, Chief Minister, Chhattisgarh**

Mohsinaji is an exceptional human being, an inspirational figure whose simplicity, courage of conviction and commitment to the cause of the Congress left a deep mark on me. I consider myself as part of her family, as my daughter studied with her youngest daughter, and she always displayed a lot of affection and warmth. My early memories of her is from 1978, when she won the Lok Sabha bypolls from Azamgarh. It had an electrifying impact on all of us who were feeling a bit dejected after the 1977 defeat. Probity, propriety, resilience and selflessness have been her constant companions. In nutshell, a role model for all of us.

—**Digvijaya Singh, former Madhya Pradesh Chief Minister**

While the role of women in Indian politics has been much celebrated over the past few years, the spotlight on Muslim women and their contribution has remained grossly understated. Mohsina Kidwai is the rare woman who broke many glass ceilings and remained a pioneer in generating politically sensitive gender discourse throughout her public life. Her poise, perseverance, value system and contribution has been immense. My father Kaifi Azmi referred to her as Mohsina Bahen, a term he rarely used for women who were not his direct siblings, and I should have called her Khala or Phupi but chance had it that I started addressing her as Mohsina Apa and she has been an elder sister to me, warm and nurturing. She has always steered clear of controversy or malice. and has earned the respect of all who have known her over the years. Congratulations, hugs and best wishes for Mohsina Apa's health and happiness.

—Shabana Azmi, actor–activist

For us, Mohsina Kidwaiji has been a role model and reference point in all matters of the Congress organization. We view her as a close associate of all members of the illustrious Nehru Gandhi family: Indiraji, Rajivji, Soniaji, Rahulji and Priyankaji. Her political life has taught me that moral authority comes from following universal and timeless principles like honesty, integrity and treating people with respect. Her memoir is worth reading and reflecting upon, as it covers the most decisive phase of contemporary Indian politics.

—Dr C.P. Joshi, Speaker, Rajasthan Assembly

Mohsina Kidwai's autobiography is an important account of Indian politics. This is unmissable for anyone with interest in knowing about the working of the world's largest democracy. As a prominent Congress leader, she is an authority on her party and the changing political culture in India.

—Yashwant Sinha, former Minister of Finance (1998–2002) and Minister of External Affairs (2002–2004)

Mohsinaji's life epitomizes the nation-serving lifelines of the Indian National Congress. Selfless, committed to the cause of the poorest of the poor, the downtrodden, minorities and women, Mohsinaji has left a deep impression on my concept of secularism, constitutional democracy, service, transparency and accountability in public life. I have had the privilege of interacting and working closely with her during the government formation in Bihar. She was always fair-minded, measured and accommodating towards coalition politics. I greatly value her contribution to public life and recommend everyone to benefit from her memoir.

—Lalu Prasad Yadav, former Chief Minister, Bihar, ex-Union minister

Mohsina Kidwai is a voice of probity in public life … exemplary in her conduct since her days in Uttar Pradesh politics. For our generation, she has been a reference point of the life of Indira Gandhi, the true spirit of the Congress and the principles for which it stood. Her memoir is a testimony of this.

—Nirmal Pathak, Editor, PTI Bhasha

Mohsina Kidwai exudes old-world charm: being one among those who has kept her dignity alive, even in politics. In that sense, she complemented Mrs Indira Gandhi, with whom she was closely associated for years. I do remember her narrating interesting anecdotes about Mrs Gandhi, including the one where she broke a Marie biscuit into morsels to feed to her driver because he had been driving long hours, or when she kept the then President waiting because she took the time to switch off all the lights in her study before she took his call. Mrs Kidwai embodies a class of politicians which is extinct today and one from whom there is a lot to learn.

—**Kumkum Chadha, author of** *The Marigold Story: Indira Gandhi and Others*

Mrs Mohsina Kidwai is a distinguished and accomplished politician who had the rare, if not unprecedented, distinction of being fielded in a daunting Lok Sabha bypoll from Azamgarh in 1978, when her party, the Congress, was down and out. It was a measure of the trust and confidence reposed by Mrs Indira Gandhi in Mohsinaji, who won the election and in a sense, marked the Congress's revival in the heartland after the Emergency. Victory and defeat are embedded in electoral politics and Mrs Kidwai accepted both in her life and career with singular equanimity.

—**Radhika Ramaseshan, columnist–journalist**

My Life in Indian Politics

Mohsina Kidwai
as told to
RASHEED KIDWAI

HarperCollins *Publishers* India

First published in India by HarperCollins *Publishers* 2022
4th Floor, Tower A, Building No. 10, Phase II, DLF Cyber City,
Gurugram Haryana – 122002, India
www.harpercollins.co.in

2 4 6 8 10 9 7 5 3 1

Copyright © Mohsina Kidwai 2022

P-ISBN: 978-93-5629-200-0
E-ISBN: 978-93-5629-206-2

The views and opinions expressed in this book are the author's own and the facts are as reported by her, and the publishers are not in any way liable for the same.

Mohsina Kidwai asserts the moral right
to be identified as the author of this work.

All rights reserved. No part of this publication may be reproduced, stored in a retrieval system, or transmitted, in any form or by any means, electronic, mechanical, photocopying, recording or otherwise, without the prior permission of the publishers.

Typeset in 11.5/15.2 Bembo Std at
Manipal Technologies Limited, Manipal

Printed and bound at
Thomson Press (India) Ltd.

This book is produced from independently certified FSC® paper
to ensure responsible forest management.

This book is dedicated to my husband,
Late Khalil Ur Rahman Kidwai,
who always encouraged me to fly towards my dreams,
serve society and the nation.
Khalil, your soul has always been with me.

Contents

A Special Note by **Sonia Gandhi**	xvii
Foreword by **Manmohan Singh**	xix
Foreword by **Shashi Tharoor**	xxiii
Preface	xxv
Introduction by **Rasheed Kidwai**	xxix

SECTION I: The Narrative Begins

1. Azamgarh: Not Just Another By-election	3
2. Turning Point	5

SECTION II: Flashback to the Future

3. Meeting with Nehru	17
4. Political Debut	22
5. Uttar Pradesh Congress Committee Chief	29
6. Determined to Bring Indira Back	35
7. The Government Strikes	42
8. A New Party Office at Lucknow	52
9. Road to Parliament	58

SECTION III: How It All Started

10. My Roots	69
11. A Political Phase	81
12. The Congress Splits	86

SECTION IV: Daughters and Other Reminiscences

13. A Mother's Confession — 93
14. Life Lessons — 99
15. The Premonition That Proved Right — 106
16. As Union Minister in Rajiv Gandhi's Cabinet — 112
17. My Foreign Visits — 119
18. The Breakaway Congress Experience — 122

SECTION V: Indian Politics (1947–2022)

19. Hope, Turbulence and Tragedies — 129
20. Rise of Divisive Politics — 148
21. Political Economy: Continuity with Change — 155
22. Inclusive Growth and Economic Milestones — 160

SECTION VI: Milestones Along the Journey

23. Meerut: My Parliamentary Karma Bhoomi — 175
24. My Organizational Role — 184
25. Chairperson, Central Haj Committee — 193

SECTION VII: Memories and Impressions

26. Colleagues and Opponents — 203

Acknowledgements — 235
Notes — 239
Short Bibliography — 243
Index — 245
About the Authors — 261

A Special Note

Shrimati Mohsina Kidwai's life story is one of great inspirational, historical and educational value. I am, therefore, very happy that she has decided to write her memoir.

Mohsinaji has always been a figure of exceptional ability, dedication, dignity and warmth. Her sixty-plus years of active participation in the nation's public and political life mirror so many aspects of the social change and development that India has seen during this period. Her memoir provides eyewitness descriptions of so many significant moments in our nation's political, social and economic history, as well as her impressions of the leading figures in national life. Her wealth of experience in the Congress party, as a minister in the state and central governments and as a parliamentarian, are reflected in this book, as are her close relations with Indiraji and Rajivji who held her in high regard—a regard I too share.

Mohsinaji has a remarkable ability to establish a warm rapport with people from across the political spectrum as well as from all walks of life. These qualities, together with her integrity and gentle candour, her deep concern for the more vulnerable sections of society, her personal charm and her abiding belief in the principles of democracy, pluralism and social justice are reflected in her memoir. No wonder, she is a much-loved and respected figure in our national life. She is a cherished member of the Congress party whose rich experience and wise counsel we value greatly, and also a cherished personal friend.

I congratulate her warmly on the publication of her memoir and hope it would be widely read.

Sonia Gandhi, President of the Indian National Congress
August 2022

Foreword

THIS BOOK IS AN INSPIRING account of Mohsina Kidwai's entry into the Congress party in 1960 and her life-long commitment thereafter to the ideals and values associated with the Indian National Congress.

In a way, her association with the Congress party began much earlier. Her father-in-law, Jameel Ur Rahman Kidwai, was actively involved in the pre-Independence and post-Independence affairs of the Congress in Uttar Pradesh (UP) and was well known to Pandit Jawaharlal Nehruji. In February 1954, a few months after Mohsinaji's marriage, Jameel sahab took Mohsinaji to call on Panditji at the Teen Murti House of the prime minister in New Delhi. There, they met both Panditji and Indiraji. As skillfully narrated in Mohsinaji's memoir, after blessing her, Panditji turned to Jameel sahab and asked him, 'When are you introducing her [Mohsinaji] to the political world?' Her father-in-law smiled and said, 'she has just got married; too new even to think about it'. Little did they know that she would plunge into the political life very soon.

The opportunity came in 1960. Jameel sahab, who was a sitting member of the UP Legislative Council, fell ill and had to be hospitalized in Lucknow. Fresh elections were due shortly and the

Congress leaders were not sure whether he would be able to stand for re-election to the council. After consultation, district Congress party leaders came to the conclusion that the Congress ticket should be given to Mohsina Kidwaiji. She contested and was duly elected, and at a young age, became a member of the UP Legislative Council. Thus began a long and eventful political career that was to last for over sixty years and to the benefit of all of us.

Mohsinaji's first six-year term as a member of the Legislative Council (MLC) ended in 1966. Fresh elections were called, but this time, the Congress party in Uttar Pradesh was a divided house, with various factions supporting their own candidates. It was a fierce political battle and Mohsinaji lost by 250 votes. Feeling hurt by the nature of the political campaign, she went to Delhi to share her anguish with Indiraji. As she describes in this engaging memoir, after patiently listening, Indiraji told her, 'Mohsina, this is politics. You have to have a very thick skin to take it all in and live with it. I bear the brunt of so much opposition angst; should I take the refuge in my emotions and forego the service to my party and my nation because of the Opposition attacks?' With Indiraji's encouragement, Mohsinaji fought her third election and won.

Mohsinaji's career graph in politics rose steadily thereafter and she became a minister in the Uttar Pradesh cabinet. In 1974, Shri Hemvati Nandan Bahugana was the Congress chief minister of Uttar Pradesh and Mohsinaji was made minister of state for food and civil supplies. Sometime later, impressed with her performance, Bahuganaji gave her independent charge of the social welfare department. She also served as a cabinet rank minister for small scale industries. In 1976, when she was a cabinet colleague of Shri Narayan Dutt Tiwari, the then chief minister of Uttar Pradesh, Mohsinaji was appointed president of UP Congress Committee by Indiraji.

A landmark event of the subsequent period was the Lok Sabha by-election of Azamgarh in 1978, which was won handsomely by Mohsinaji, pitted against many odds as a Congress candidate. This by-election changed the mood of the electorate and was a turning point for the Congress and Indiraji. It was Azamgarh where I met Mohsinaji for the first time. The Azamgarh verdict was followed by the Congress' great comeback in the parliamentary election of 1980 under the leadership of Indiraji.

Mohsinaji first served in the union council of ministers under the leadership of prime minister Indira Gandhi in September 1982, as minister of state for labour. She also served in several departments in the cabinet of Shri Rajiv Gandhiji. The transport portfolio, for instance was particularly weighty. She had three ministers under her—Madhavrao Scindia, Rajesh Pilot and Jagdish Tytler. Before moving to the transport ministry in September 1985, she had handled the ministry of health and the ministry of urban development. This wide range of portfolios Mohsinaji handled over the years, gave her remarkable range and depth of administrative experience and wisdom.

Mohsinaji's eventful life and career is the inspirational story of a woman who has dedicated her life to the service of the nation. There is a great deal to learn from it.

Manmohan Singh
Former Prime Minister of India
August 2022

Foreword

SMT MOHSINA KIDWAI IS ONE of the Congress party's most senior and distinguished leaders. Beginning her involvement with public life by winning election to the Uttar Pradesh Legislative Council in 1960, aged just 28, she went on to dedicate her life to politics and public service. Becoming a member of the state legislative assembly and then the Lok Sabha, she rose to serve in senior cabinet positions first under Indira Gandhi and then under Rajiv Gandhi, gaining their trust through her tireless work at every level of the party. She continued to sit in the Rajya Sabha until well into her eighties, her age proving no barrier to her commitment and her active involvement in public service.

My Life in Indian Politics recounts her personal life as well as her fascinating career, from her early years in Barabanki to the scrappy battles of local politics to the corridors of power. I got to know Mohsinaji rather late in her political career, and at the (belated) start of mine, and found that her gentle, soft-spoken manner reflected both her decency and her determination to ensure the right results were achieved. All through her memoir, one is struck by the themes that seem to consistently characterize Mohsina Kidwai's work: humility, dedication, integrity and a fierce determination to do the right thing. Her identities are manifold: a staunch Congresswoman; a loving mother of three daughters; a proud Muslim; and above all, an Indian, dedicated to the well-being of her country.

Rasheed Kidwai, the co-author, writes in his introduction that Mohsina Kidwai's career was marked by the fact that 'she was never shy of speaking her mind or sharing her candid thoughts'. This has to be one of her most admirable qualities, and it is one that shines through clearly in this book. Her willingness to express herself directly, without rudeness or cant, and assess things as they really were, is a gift to the reader, and was no doubt an important part of her success. When I worked closely with her, she was the Congress General Secretary in charge of Kerala, and from her quick grasp of uses, her responsiveness and her effectiveness, it was easy to see and to understand why she was held in such enormous respect by her colleagues in a state so far away from her own. The trust she enjoyed from the party President also contributed immeasurably to her clout and effectiveness. As Rasheed Kidwai notes, her assessment of the Congress was clear-eyed and her approach was always restless, always seeking to improve the party's prospects. It is no wonder that the party was a natural home for her. Her commitment to Nehruvian and Gandhian philosophy is unwavering, and this has coloured her approach to policy, ideology, religion and life at large. As she drew so much inspiration from those who served before her, we would all do well to draw inspiration from her career of work and service, and the manner in which she conducted it.

As an author, Mohsina Kidwai writes with passion, clarity and memorable detail, recounting her decades at the frontline of politics and expressing with unwavering strength her firm belief in democracy, freedom and the politics of inclusivity. At various times, her memoir is moving, funny, and entertaining, but always intriguing—a treat for any historian of Indian politics. This book is a fitting marker of her long and dedicated career, and of the legacy that she has bequeathed to Indian politics: one of principled service, visionary selflessness, and all-embracing tolerance. I am pleased to commend it to the general public.

Shashi Tharoor
Author, former union minister
August 2022

Preface

I HAVE DECIDED THAT NOW WHEN I have retired from active politics and have time at my disposal, I should pen down my life's journey. When I look back, I realize that I have gone through so many phases and experiences in the pace of time that require a relook, documentation and commentary. Gautam Budhha said, 'Health is the greatest gift, contentment the greatest wealth, faithfulness the best relationship', and I have been lucky to experience all of it.

But there are two major regrets in my life which I would like to mention. Much like my passion for badminton and singing, I wanted to attain higher education. Though I did go to the Aligarh Muslim University, I repent not opting for academic excellence. The second regret is more of a pang of guilt or conscience—that I did not look after my parents enough, though some would say I did a lot. I seek forgiveness from the Almighty on this count too.

My late husband, Khalil Ur Rahman Kidwai, was keen to assist me and kept me motivated to write. Alas, he is not around to see his wish finally get fulfilled. The 'directive' to pen my memoir kept coming from Seema, Farida and Irum, my daughters, who are my life to me. In fact, the list of those who kept compelling me is rather long. I would just like to say a big thank you from the bottom of my heart.

I have lived through interesting, crucial and momentous times. In some ways, my story dating back to the pre-Independence days is also a tale of free India that faced insurmountable challenges, achieved far more than expected, yet remained a proverbial 'glass half-full or half-empty'. All I can say is that it has been rather satisfactory to live through those moments and a delightful experience to be writing them down.

For over six decades, I have been in public life. It's been like being a witness of the nation-making process, in which, my party, the Indian National Congress (INC) was and is a catalyst. Essentially and fundamentally a nationalist and Congress leader, I have tried writing my autobiography, which I now happily present to the readers. Since 2014, the Congress may not have been at the helms of affairs at the Centre, but its commitment to democratic values remains awe-inspiring.

As a child, I was schooled in the ideas of and ideals set by our great freedom fighters and the first-generation leaders of independent India who guided the Congress' notions in governance. I joined politics to serve the society well and for ensuring the greater common good. At no point in my political career did I think of using power for meeting any personal goals. Looking back, I am extremely thankful to my family and friends who helped me sustain my resolve to keep to those pious elements of idealism and lead a selfless existence in political life.

India's former prime minister and the most decisive leader, Indira Gandhiji, inspired me immensely. I owe a deep sense of respect for her in my individual capacity and as a citizen of India—for her cause-based politics in the national interest. She led from the front and set a benchmark for leadership in Indian politics. Since 1947, we have travelled a long way as a country. We all should take satisfaction in the fact that our democracy has ensured it instills a sense of fairness within our institutions.

Hence, under tumultuous applause, it is not appropriate on the part of the ruling BJP under the leadership of Prime Minister Narendra Modi to belittle India's glorious strides, taken between 1947 and 2014. The quest for a 'New India' is grossly misplaced and inappropriate. I accept the argument that change is continuous but effectively and positively, it should be taken forward only in tandem with historical continuance. This calls for encouraging a much more accommodative politics than what we are seeing now. Unfortunately, of late, we are witnessing without the provision of delegation, consultations and freedom of expression, our democracy, which is the world's largest, destined to being cut off from its aims.

In my memoir, I have tried presenting my understanding of the nation, its institutions and its people. At the crossroads, it is painful to see how politics is being polarized today. It should be in our reckoning that the key collective strength is our belief in non-violence, respect for diversity and an inclusive orientation for national development. We can't do with a 'Congress-mukt Bharat'; the Congress is more than a party—it is a movement that was started to end the colonial rule and chart out a new future for India without any biases. Irrespective of a few electoral losses, I am quite satisfied with the way my party has upheld its core principles and belief in the 'Idea of India'. In the government or as Opposition, it shall always strive to serve the mass interest and fight the tendencies which are detrimental to our diverse national culture.

My book is an effort to unite the various streams of ideas and should be seen as a document produced by someone who has spent a lifetime in Indian politics following the visions and ideals of our founding fathers. I am from that school of politics where the grand idea of mass welfarism triumphed over any lesser considerations, and this should continue. The games of agenda-setting, smear campaign and narrative distortion are no longer puzzles for the keen observers of the Indian politics to indulge in. Those who are looking for 'masala'—'witch-hunting' scandals, gossip, innuendos and bad blood, will certainly be disappointed with contents of my memoir. Like in my personal and public life, I have made conscious attempts not to venture into areas where I would not be myself.

I am quite sanguine about the prospects of the Congress; the party has not lost its way.

Irrespective of how vicious the politics in India has become today, the party will struggle through democratic means. As the citizens of this great country, we should think about our democracy and the national interest. Our Constitution should guide us, no individual can have an upper hand.

Jai Hind.

Introduction

Hazāroñ saal nargis apnī be-nūrīperotīhai, baḍī mushkil se hotā hai chaman meñ dīda-var paidā

(For a thousand years the narcissus has been lamenting its blindness, with great difficulty, the one with true vision is born in the garden)

A CURSORY LOOK AT THE ELECTED representatives to the Indian parliament reveals a telling yet largely glossed-over fact—barely twenty Muslim women have made it to the Lok Sabha so far, from among nearly 9,000 Members of Parliament (MPs) voted since 1951. Out of the seventeen Lok Sabhas constituted till May 2019, five times, the lower house of parliament did not have a Muslim women member. Equally shocking is the fact the number of Muslim women elected to parliament never crossed a mark of four in the 543-seat lower house of parliament.

According to noted French scholar Christophe Jaffrelot, Muslim women face a double bind—they are discriminated against both as women and as Muslims. His sentiments find echo in Gilles Verniers, a political science professor at Ashoka University, when he observed, 'In terms of cumulative discrimination—being a Muslim and being a woman—there is a compounding effect for sure. The usual barriers to entry that apply to all women, apply even more strongly to Muslim women.'[1]

Mohsina Kidwai, hailing from a conservative, aristocratic Muslim family of Avadh, holds a distinction of winning in Lok Sabha thrice—in 1978, 1980 and 1984. Her parliamentary credentials are remarkable, having won from Azamgarh (the Lok Sabha bypoll which marked the great comeback of Indira Gandhi) in Eastern Uttar Pradesh and Meerut in the western side of the state. Anyone remotely connected with the socio-economic conditions of Uttar Pradesh and caste matrix, or observing the related fundamentals, would vouch that finding acceptability in these two diverse regions is a rather insurmountable task. In addition, during the course of her long and illustrious political life spanning from 1960 to 2016, she was elected to Uttar Pradesh Assembly, Legislative Council and the Rajya Sabha, besides serving as the chairperson of up congress and cabinet minister in the Uttar Pradesh Congress government.

In the list of women Lok Sabha MPs such as Sajda Ahmed, Mamtaz Sanghamita, Nusrat Jahan, Masoomnoor, Noor Begum, Kaisar Jahan, Tabbasum Begum, Begum Abida Ahmad, Begum Akbar Jahan, Mahbooba Mufti, Rubab Syeda, Mofida Ahmed, Maimuna Sultan, Chavda Zohraben Akarbai, Nafisa Ali and Ranee Narah, Mohsina Kidwai holds unique distinction, not only in terms of duration spent in office as the elected representative, but the high positions she held in Indira and Rajiv Gandhi's cabinets. At one point in 1987, Rajiv Gandhi had toyed with the idea of making Mohsina Kidwai Vice President of the Republic. She was sounded but the quest to serve as a public representative reportedly prevailed upon her, and she did not accept the high office. The post went to another illustrious son of India, Dr Shankar Dayal Sharma, who rose to serve as president.

Throughout six long decades, Mohsina Kidwai has been a picture of service, sacrifice, integrity and probity in public life. As someone who is well-acquainted with her personal life, I have no hesitation in sharing a few thoughts that she may not have penned or would have struck down on grounds of the low and earthly profile she has maintained. However, in my modest view, the fitness of things in the present context demand that an independent—rather, unauthorized—account of some of these issues find a place in her memoir. After all, 'a memoir is the backstairs of history,' and a politician's account is far more delectable because it tells the readers what could have gone right, instead of the numerous wrongs.

In May 2016, when Mohsina Kidwai ceased to be MP, she felt a sense of fulfilment. But it also came with a worry. The former housing minister for the rest of India did not have a house of her own in the national capital or anywhere else, except for ancestral, joint-ownership property in Badagaon. For those wary of the political class, one should get a sense of what probity in public life means for a person who has been the country's transport (including railways, civil aviation and surface transport), health and housing minister for a decade, and a cabinet minister in Uttar Pradesh. Despite leading such a Spartan life, neither Mohsina Kidwai—nor any of her close relatives—ever felt like they were doing something extraordinary.

On the political front, what distinguishes Kidwai from many others in the Congress, is that she was never shy of speaking her mind or sharing her candid thoughts, without crossing the Lakshman Rekha (or rubicon) of party discipline. A lot has been written about the Shah Bano Begum judgment and Rajiv Gandhi government's move to overturn it, Ayodhya imbroglio, Congress ties with the Samajwadi Party, Bahujan Samaj Party, communal riots, Mamata Banerjee, tackling issues of probity, and other momentous events in post-Independence India. I can share with confidence that had the political leadership heeded to the sound advice tendered by Mohsina at many of those points, the course of the country's politics and contemporary history would have been far better and fruitful.

If Mrs Kidwai's thrust on virtue and integrity has been exemplary, her religiosity also warrants special mention. Like Maulana Abul Kalam Azad and Maulana Hussain Ahmed Madani, she remains wedded to the idea of composite nationalism and inter-communal unity. Mohsina strongly, rather passionately believes that Muslims could live as observers of their faith in a multi-religious, multicultural, pluralistic, society as full citizens of an independent, secular India. In this endeavour, she wants present and future generations of Indian Muslims to fight against both Hindu right wingers and Muslim separatists, giving intellectual and scholarly basis to her line of thinking. For Mohsina Kidwai, in independent India, there should have been a central law to curb communalism and religious fanaticism. Among her numerous and valuable suggestions, Kidwai advocated reforming textbooks by including descriptions of the various cultures and living conduct of all religions of India.

The real strength of Mohsina Kidwai's memoir lies in her assessment of the Congress. This is one institution she really cared about and she played a pivotal role in its rise and great comeback in 1978–79. When everything looked bleak for Indira Gandhi after the party's 1977 defeat, she would often restlessly ask, '*aakhir kab hamari wapsi hogi?*' Mohsina Kidwai paved the way with her spectacular electoral victory at Azamgarh in 1978, when she became Uttar Pradesh Congress Chief.

The future of present-day Congress looks bleak. But after going through her autobiography, it becomes clear that if the Grand Old Party gets 'back to basics', its revival is very much possible. The Congress needs the self-belief of 1978, and renewed confidence in the party's core ideology, liberal ideas, inclusive thinking. Secularism, for instance, has been an integral part of the Congress ideology, implying a clear separation of religion from politics. In the Indian context, the Congress' definition of secularism meant equal respect for all faiths and protection of the security, identity and interests of all religious minorities. The concept of equal respect for all religions was first highlighted in the Nehru Report of 1928 and by Mahatma Gandhi at the Second Round Table Conference in London in 1931, where he showcased the Congress as India's most nation-oriented and secular organization.

Successive Congress resolutions kept proclaiming that the Congress would translate into reality the guarantees given in the Indian Constitution. Jawaharlal Nehru had pronounced the bottom line of the party's secular creed at a meeting in the Ram Lila grounds on Gandhi Jayanti in 1951: 'If any man raises his hand against another in the name of religion, I shall fight him till the last breath of my life, whether from within the government or outside.'[2] Can anyone in the Congress today claim to be following Nehru's words in letter and spirit?

Theoretically and historically, the Grand Old Party has taken upon itself a duty to lead the nation. Successive AICC political resolutions crafted and drafted by in-house wordsmiths such as Dr Pattabhi Sitaramayya and U.N. Dhebar to P.V. Narasimha Rao, Pranab Mukherjee, Arjun Singh and Vithal Gadgil, have insisted upon the Congress' role. Speaking at Jaipur in 1948, P. Sitaramayya had equated the Congress ideology closely with the Indian nation. He told AICC delegates, 'The Congress is the service station of the life-giving ideology of the nation. The life-sustaining doctrines are pumped through the arteries of the government of the nation, where they become somewhat sullied in implementation and are returned to the Congress for purification. The ideology constantly discussed by the populace and constantly renovated as public opinion, is once again canalized by the Congress through the government in a renovated form. That is how the Congress and the government act and react upon each other.'

In 1955, U.N. Dhebar had stated with a poet's flair,

> What is the Congress? It is a tear, fallen from the sufferings and agonized heart of humanity in bondage, coming to life. The tear was destined to become a stream, the stream a river and the river a mighty Ganga or a Brahmaputra, which was to wash off its sins and weaknesses of ages, to weld her people together, breathe new life and new spirit into their heart, and carry them afloat, united, purified and strengthened by their cherished goal.

The Congress ideology and policies were suited well to the situation of the country then. For instance, there were issues of the abolition of Zamindari, bonded labour and untouchability—issues that Gandhiji had taken upon himself to address. His resolve formed the basis of the Congress ideology.

The Congress's duty to lead the nation was tweaked a bit in 1998, when the party, under Sonia Gandhi's leadership, officially opened its doors to coalition. However, in its successive political resolutions, it kept refuting the claim that days of single-party rule were over, and that a conglomeration of regional parties at the centre could reflect the adequate federal character of the polity. The Congress at Pachmarhi Conclave had insisted that its concept of stability of ideas, policies and programmes was superior to those of regional parties, which it claimed, could never evolve past local/ethnic/linguistic considerations.

After finishing the book, readers would perhaps agree with me that if the life lived and practised by Mohsina Kidwai is emulated by some Congress workers and leaders today, there is no reason why the Congress cannot find the lost plot and revive its past glory. Jean-Jacques Rousseau had said in his *Confessions*, 'I have resolved on an enterprise which has no precedent. And which, once complete, will have no imitator. My purpose is to display to my kind a portrait in every way true to nature, and the man I shall portray will be myself.'[3] Mohsina Kidwai's autobiographical account is successful in its simplicity, originality and uniqueness, even as she consciously avoids being self-righteous and often expresses herself in modest diffidence.

Rasheed Kidwai
August 2022
New Delhi

SECTION I

THE NARRATIVE BEGINS

1
Azamgarh: Not Just Another By-election

It was the summer of 1978. The stage was set for an electoral contest that was particularly crucial for Indira Gandhi and her Congress (I) in the wake of the party's new-year split. The Emergency had been lifted the previous year and the April–May by-election in Azamgarh, a little over thirteen months since the Congress had been routed in the Lok Sabha elections of 1977, was a challenge, politically as well as personally.

The Congress's main rival in the parliamentary by-election was the Janata Party, which headed the ruling coalition at the Centre and was determined to defeat the Congress again in this humid, eastern district of Uttar Pradesh, around 260 km east of the state capital, Lucknow. The bypoll had been necessitated by the resignation of Ram Naresh Yadav, who had defeated the Congress's Chandrajit Yadav in the 1977 elections but had since taken over as the chief minister of Uttar Pradesh, an appointment that had the blessings of Union Home Minister Choudhary Charan Singh. A victory for the ruling party would mean that the strains within the coalition at the Centre had not yet dented its support in the heartland, the country's most populous and politically important state and the

Janata Party's main stronghold in North India. For the Congress, another defeat would mean Mrs Gandhi was still a long way off from regaining for her party its lost legitimacy.

Charan Singh was the most active in this contest—and targeted Indira Gandhi and Sanjay Gandhi. The Janata Party's election race got off the ground, centred on its one-point 'Hate Indira Campaign', supported by Prime Minister Morarji Desai. That the government was bent on weakening any opposition had been evident at least a year back, when on 18 April 1977, about a month after coming to power, it formed the Shah Commission to go into the excesses of the Emergency. By 15 August 1977, P.C. Sethi and Yashpal Kapoor, two of the active Congress leaders apart from R.K. Dhawan and K.D. Malviya, had been arrested.

It was in such a situation that Mrs Gandhi chose to field me for the election, although I was technically an 'outsider' from Barabanki, nearly 250 km away from Azamgarh. It would be a tough battle, but I prevailed, defeating Ram Bachan Yadav of the Janata Party, my nearest rival. The rest, as they say, is history. The by-election would herald Indira Gandhi's return to power in 1980.

2
Turning Point

THE AZAMGARH ELECTION, I THINK, was a turning point for the Congress, after the gloom of defeat from the previous year. A side story to the party's resurgence is how Indiraji launched the Congress (Indira) with the 'hand' symbol against the previous one—cow and calf—after the 1977 split. But in this chapter, I shall focus on the battle the Congress (Indira) faced in Azamgarh, at a time when most veteran leaders were on the other side of the intra-party divide and politically against Indiraji. Jagjivan Ram, too, had left the party in 1977. In Uttar Pradesh, the only leader who remained with Indiraji was Kamalapati Tripathi. Leaders like C.B. Gupta, H.N. Bahuguna (who had won from Lucknow in 1977) and Charan Singh—all had left. Even leaders like Chandra Shekhar had turned against her and left the party. As things stood, only Congress workers were with Indiraji, while most of the big leaders were with Morarji Desai and the Janata Party.

The elections in Azamgarh, then an impoverished corner of Northeastern Uttar Pradesh, had been necessitated after Ram Naresh Yadav vacated his Lok Sabha seat following his appointment as chief minister of Uttar Pradesh. In the 1977 Lok Sabha elections, we had drawn a blank in all the eighty-five parliamentary seats in

Uttar Pradesh. I was an unusual choice on many counts. It was supposedly a caste election, where the Janata Party had fielded a seventy-year-old leader, Ram Bachan Yadav, an avowed chela (follower) of Charan Singh, who was the all-powerful home minister of the country then. The UP chief minister's prestige was also at stake as it was the constituency he had vacated.

Interestingly, there was lot of posturing and internal politics within the Congress prior to the announcement of my candidature. Some powerful regional leaders were unhappy that I had been made the Uttar Pradesh Congress Chief. There was a Hindi newspaper, *Santap*, which had published some rather uncharitable comments about me. I, however, remained polite and smiling when the editor of the daily met me. After some conversation, he, all of sudden, began apologizing and confessed having written the piece without meeting me. He also blurted out some names of my party colleagues who had 'planted' the disinformation. I refrained from reporting this matter to Indiraji.

The choice of a woman nominee, that too a Muslim, was a gamble of sorts that Indiraji had taken. True to her political instincts, she was perhaps testing the home ground of Uttar Pradesh to check if her electoral successes in the Karnataka and Andhra Pradesh Assembly elections in March 1978 could be counted upon as indicators in her bid to stage a comeback in the cow belt.

But winning elections in the Hindi belt was not easy. Prior to the Azamgarh Lok Sabha bypolls, there were by-elections in Haryana and Bihar, where my party collegues Balram Jakhar and Tarkeshwari Sinha had lost.

Also in the fray was Chandrajit Yadav, the breakaway Congress candidate who poured more resources into the Azamgarh election than I or the Janata Party nominee had done. Perhaps, his stakes were personal. Elected twice to the Parliament from Azamgarh, this was his swansong: one last, now-or-never fling to establish his own political credibility and that of the floundering faction of those who had deserted Indiraji.

Azamgarh had a population of over 11 lakh, of whom 6,37,394 were voters. Approximately 20 per cent of the electorate were Dalits; another 10 per cent were Brahmins and 28 per cent were an assortment of Thakurs, Bhumiyars and other non-Yadav backward communities. Muslims constituted about 16 per cent of the electorate.

When I contested from Azamgarh, the Janata Party was at its peak. At that time, the district magistrate (DM) was a Mr Gupta, and the district's police chief (SSP), a Mr Sinha, both wonderful officers whose first names I don't recollect. The chief minister had asked them about the upcoming election, and they had briefed him, saying they were both neutral officers who wanted only to ensure that there was no law-and-order problem. They were asked to be transferred but when we protested to the Election Commission, the transfer orders were stayed. Things were quite different then; although we were in the opposition, the rules were observed.

As stated earlier in this chapter, Azamgarh was a big district but mostly underdeveloped then, in terms of civic amenities, such as roads, water and electricity. In that difficult environment, Indiraji was with me for five full days. The Janata Party regime did not even provide a room for the then prime minister. I had booked a room in one of the rest houses a week before her arrival. At noon, in the month of May, when we reached the rest house, an old security guard told us all the rooms were locked. It was hot and humid. When we asked him about the room I had booked, he said he could not open the lock as it was occupied by the public works minister, Masood sahab.

'Do you know for whom I am asking about the room?' I asked the guard.

He seemed a little taken aback. 'For whom?' he asked.

When I told him it was for Indiraji, he opened all the three rooms in the rest house. There was no sign of any personal belongings of any minister.

We rested for a few hours and it was afternoon by the time we stepped out to attend a scheduled meeting in a village. But with no motorable road, our car was unable to proceed, so we opted for a Jeep. The meeting had been well-organized and a full crowd was waiting for us. In fact, a large crowd greeted Indiraji wherever she went. The organizers of the meeting had arranged for snacks—locally made samosas and sweets, and tea in earthen pots. I noticed Indiraji taking the snacks on a plate and walking up to the drivers, asking them to eat. And people called her arrogant! What misconceptions they had.

Another facet of Indiraji's that I saw then, was how well she could adapt to any situation. City-bred people, used to all the amenities of urban life, would have balked at using the village washroom that only had a cloth curtain for privacy. Not Indiraji.

She drew water with the handpump and used a corner of her sari to wipe her hands. It was a learning experience to watch a prime minister doing all these things without a hint of irritation, not even raising an eyebrow.

I digress here a bit before coming back to the election. A number of youths from Azamgarh studied in Aligarh Muslim University (AMU), whose students had invited Indiraji to visit the campus. An invitation had also come from an influential local Congress leader, Mushir Ul Hasan Sherwani, whose daughter was getting married. Mushir sahab was a man of real Ganga–Jamuni tahzeeb, or our famed composite culture. He had a big white house next to a temple. Behind the scenes, Mushir sahab planned the visit in such a way that Indiraji could attend the wedding, too. We came by train to Aligarh and the crowd of onlookers stretched right from the station to the university guest house. Mr Sharma, the SSP, kept running alongside our cavalcade, providing good escort. Indiraji's personality commanded respect from all, including policemen. We would travel by an open Jeep and even the policemen were prompted by the crowd to say, 'Indira Gandhi zindabad!'

I told Mushir sahab to conclude the wedding first. But as Indiraji reached the marriage venue, people seemed to forget that they had come to attend the wedding.

These are snippets that I thought I would narrate just to give the reader an idea of Indiraji's personal magnetism.

Coming back to the Azamgarh election, wherever I went, every Muslim I met said their vote for the Congress (I) would be because of me, not Indira Gandhi. I told them if they did not want to vote for Indiraji, they might as well not vote for me too. In the end, I was able to convince the Muslims.

One day, when George Fernandes was addressing a meeting, Indiraji's car happened to pass by the venue. The entire crowd came over to our side. Even women would wave at her, wherever Indiraji went, conveying their support for me and the Congress. It was a wonderful time for Indiraji and me, and also for the party workers.

Among those present in Azamgarh then was the legendary chief minister of Karnataka, Devaraj Urs. Mark Tully covered the campaign for the BBC, while journalists like Sunil Sethi and Arati Jerath wrote glowing pieces in credible publications such as the *India Today* magazine. Here is an excerpt:

> For the first two weeks, the message was clear. As both, a woman and a Muslim, Mrs Kidwai reserved her mother-figure image for the 20 per cent Dalit population and her personal faith for the 16 per cent Muslims. Equally, she was relying heavily on the women of the region, who constitute about 50 per cent of the 6,37,394 registered voters. Mrs Gandhi's projections worked successfully on all three counts. Mohsina Kidwai obtained the

bulk of both Dalit and Muslim votes and caused a sudden and unprecedented spiralling in the number of women votes polled.⁴

I was quoted as saying, 'You see, being a woman helps. I just walk straight into village homes and call for the women of the house. 50 per cent of our electorate are women. And, of course, all the Muslims are with me.'

Political analysts and those who covered my campaign could see that I was working against the grim disadvantage of not belonging to the area, unlike the candidates of the Janata Party and the breakaway Congress. The septuagenarian Janata candidate, Ram Bachan Yadav, was recovering from a cerebral stroke. Very much the benign, unpretentious elder statesman of the region with twenty years of active state assembly politics behind him, Yadav was probably not concealing much when he analysed why I had been fielded by Indiraji.

He was quoted as saying in the *India Today* issue:

> What she [Mrs Gandhi] is trying to do is to test her own position. If Mohsina Kidwai can make it in UP, so can she. Mrs Kidwai might be her dummy but she won't get anywhere. And anyway what's the use of a candidate who does not belong to the area? Since Mrs Kidwai comes from Barabanki near Lucknow, people here are saying that they will have to spend ₹100 each time they travel to her and back if they want their passport papers signed, for instance.⁵

Ram Bachanji, perhaps, did not realize that passport papers were farthest from the minds of the general populace battling for clean drinking water, food and jobs.

The media, however, continued to praise me. After my victory, it was stated, 'But there was yet another feature in the potent caste polarizations in Azamgarh that clinched the deal for Mrs Gandhi. And that was the unexpected shift of upper class—Brahmin and Thakur—sympathies to her side.'

Regarding the crucial caste factor in Azamgarh, it was observed that caste question in this belt of North India had always been a burning issue, fanned by political leaders and the privileged class alike. But Azamgarh saw both upper castes and Dalits voting in tandem along with Muslims. The anti-Indira wave of the 1977 elections was fading.

George Fernandes and Atal Bihari Vajpayee had both been pressed into action against me. Vajpayeeji, the foreign minister then, delivered a speech that was high on rhetoric and quick-witted, but without populist slogans. The speech was a classic fragment of Vajpayee's oratory.

I have many fond memories of Azamgarh polls fresh in my mind even today, after four decades. There was a person called Tilakdhari Pandit, whose house was the election office of my political opponent, Chandrajit Yadav. One day, I was asked to visit that house. I was apprehensive, considering it was the election office of my rival. But the person who had approached me, insisted. When I reached, the entire household of women was there to greet me. They accorded a traditional welcome, offered snacks and kept telling me that regardless of the political affiliation of Tilakdhari Pandit, they would be voting for me. The lady of the house then handed me twenty rupees for the election fund, a big amount in those days. Genuine and true love can easily be understood through gestures. When I encountered it there, I instantly sensed that wonderful warmth and I cherish it even now.

It is said that sometimes the smallest things take up the most room in your heart. I experienced it in Azamgarh on another occasion, when, one day, a paanwallah, barely metres away from where I was staying, asked me why I do not leave for campaigning in the morning like my political rivals who go in cars. I hesitantly told him that we did not have much funds to spend on petrol and diesel. He quietly handed ₹20 to me, perhaps more than a day's earning for him then. He, however, told me that it was his 'bohni' that he considered it auspicious for me! I was so deeply moved and touched that I could not return it.

A word about district officials. Nowadays, it is generally assumed that the district administration would side with the ruling party or the establishment. Azamgarh was the home district of the then Uttar Pradesh chief minister, Ram Naresh Yadav, but both, the district administration and the election commission officials, remained neutral, vigilant and upright throughout the election period. There were many challenges before them. This was the time when manual voting used to take place and ballot papers were used, which were kept in ballot boxes.

Since nineteen candidates were in fray, the ballot paper was longish and the ballot box could not accommodate many. I later learned, to my astonishment, that the local authorities had reportedly used cotton bags to collect the ballot papers. This quick-fix solution was reportedly approved by both poll authorities and the political representatives. Within minutes, some of my rivals, sensing defeat, objected and sought repoll but the district collector and the election commission officials overruled, pointing how political representatives belonging to all candidates had unanimously agreed to the idea of using cotton bags. I reliably learnt that even calls from the chief minister had been ignored.

A word about my friends and colleagues. Azamgarh town did not have proper hotels and the circuit house was out of bounds for us. N.D. Tiwari was seen sharing a room with Buta Singh and many others. Buta Singh would walk up to a well to take bath in the open. Kamalapati Tripathi had instructed all Congress leaders not to leave Azamgarh till the campaigning ended, and everyone, including Dr Shankar Dayal Sharma, Kedar Pande, Devaraj Urs and Jaganath Mishra abided by it. Dr Shankar Dayal Sharma was, in fact, the overall election manager of my constituency. His dedication, commitment, sincerity, effective intelligence and hands-on approach was a great learning experience for all of us.

I won the election by 36,000 votes and was the first candidate to win an election with the Congress (I) hand symbol that Indiraji had chosen.

One day before the counting, Indiraji's younger son, Sanjay Gandhi, was arrested in Delhi on politically motivated charges. In fact, throughout 1978–79, Sanjay was jailed six times in various criminal cases and spent five weeks in prisons in Delhi, Dehradun and Bareilly. In one case, he was sentenced to two years' jail but got bail. These cases slowly slid into obscurity, thanks to a series of witnesses turning hostile and the tardy nature of investigation.

In May 1978, when Sanjay was arrested for the first time, Indiraji was on a train to Benares (Varanasi) on her way to Delhi when she heard the news, and also learned that he had suffered injuries in a police baton-charge. As soon as she could, Indiraji rang up someone in Azamgarh to say that no party leader should come to Delhi or leave me to fend for myself. The political vendetta was so grave that often, her trains were delayed.

Interestingly, it was my sister who called me from Canada to say that news had been broadcast about my victory in Azamgarh, the party's first in the entire North India since the Congress's Lok Sabha defeat in the 1977 elections. It was a crucial, morale-boosting triumph and the Congress did not look back—all because of Indiraji and the real Congress workers at the grassroots, who stuck with her despite the split. A year and a half later, in early 1980, the Congress (I) would storm back to power with a thumping majority. The Janata alliance, a loose coalition of many parties, had already come apart by then.

Azamgarh was a personal triumph for me but it might not have happened at all. For that I would forever be indebted to an elderly gentleman—my father-in-law, Jameel Ur Rahman Kidwai, a former freedom fighter who had worked with Jawaharlal Nehru and gone to jail many times.

It was December 1977, still a few months away from the by-election. My father-in-law was admitted in the Balrampur hospital in Lucknow, Uttar Pradesh, for a heart problem. At the same time, in Delhi, a meeting had been called to declare our party the Indira Congress. I was the Congress's Uttar Pradesh chief, but was reluctant to travel to Delhi because of my father-in-law's condition. But he insisted I go. 'You are the president of the UPCC. Indiraji belonged to UP and, if you don't attend the meeting, it would be a setback to her,' he told me.

I consulted Dr Saxena, who was looking after my father-in-law. He told me that Jameel Ur Rahman sahab might be shifted from the ICU the next day; although nobody could say for sure what might happen because he was a heart patient, after all. He said my father-in-law was insistent that I go to Delhi for the meeting.

The meeting was on 2 January, in the Mavalankar Hall of the Constitution Club, and I was all set to go, when I learnt, in the early hours of the morning, that Jameel Ur Rahman sahab had passed away.

SECTION II

FLASHBACK TO THE FUTURE

3
Meeting with Nehru

My father-in-law, Jameel Ur Rahman Kidwai, introduced me to the Indian political tradition and was instrumental in my joining the Congress in the year 1960. It would be the journey of my life, one that called for giving everything to the profession I had embraced and, eventually, immersing myself—just as pilgrims commit themselves to the long road of their faith.

But before I delve further into my years in the Congress, I need to go back a few years. It was the February of 1954, a couple of months after my marriage, when Jameel Ur Rahman decided to travel to Delhi to meet Jawaharlal Nehruji and introduce me to him as the newest member of his family, his daughter-in-law. I had never felt so nervous. Here was I, a newlywed woman, with little knowledge of the world at large, waiting in the living room of Teen Murti House, the residence of not only the Prime Minister of India, but a stalwart figure of the freedom movement, who was respected for his politics as well as for his liberal erudition.

While we waited, Nehruji's daughter, Indira Gandhi, came down the staircase that led to the living room. She walked up to my father-in-law, greeted him respectfully and then looked at me. 'Is this pretty young woman your daughter?' she asked my father-in-law.

'Daughter-in-law,' Jameel Ur Rahman sahab replied. 'My eldest son's wife. They got married just two months back.'

Indiraji congratulated us and then sat down beside me. That was my first meeting with Indiraji and the beginning of a bond that would last thirty years before her untimely death at the hands of her own security guards. We were, perhaps, destined to meet because, over the next few decades, we would together fight many political battles and ideologies, to forge a relationship that would survive two generations of the Nehru-Gandhi family.

Indiraji left the room a little while later. Pandit Nehru then entered. After he had welcomed his two guests, my father-in-law introduced me to Nehruji. The prime minister blessed me, then turned to Jameel Ur Rahman. 'When are you introducing her to the political world?' Nehruji asked.

My father-in-law smiled. 'She has just got married; too new to even think about it,' he replied. But the seed had been sown and the answer to the question—casually tossed around though, it seemed at that time—would play out in the affirmative in the years to come.

Neither my father-in-law nor I had ever thought that politics would be the chosen path for both of us. We returned after having tea. I became Indiraji's admirer from that very day. Both father and daughter oozed charm.

Jameel Ur Rahman was already in politics at the time and my debut was still six years away, in 1960. Jameel Ur Rahman would fall ill and have to be hospitalized in Lucknow for treatment then, at a rather inconvenient time. The Legislative Council elections were close and Congress leaders weren't sure whom to field in place of my father-in-law, who was the sitting party member of the council from his area.

They didn't have to wait too long to find out. Jameel Ur Rahman and some of his colleagues came up with the solution. Since my father-in-law was not sure if he could contest, they suggested that I be given the ticket, as the Congress would then have a better chance of retaining the seat.

Jameel sahab's commitment to the party was absolute. Some memories stay forever, no matter how old they might be. It was sometime in 1942 that Jameel sahab had been given a ticket by the Congress to contest an election to the Constituent Assembly against a strong Muslim League. Most Muslims in the political arena had joined the League and only a few had chosen to remain with the Congress, inspired by its progressive and secular approach to nation-building. Jameel sahab's Muslim League opponent was Jamal Mian, a strong leader who belonged to the Firangi Mahal school of thought.

When Jameel sahab's elder brother learnt who his opponent was, he tried to persuade his younger sibling not to go ahead with the contest. He needn't have tried. Much to his brother's disappointment—and displeasure—nothing could sway Jameel sahab. It was not for personal gain, he told his elder brother, and his party's decision was sacrosanct. Whether his opponent was from the Muslim League or any other party, it didn't matter to him, he said. His party had asked him to contest and, being a Congressman, he could not let his party down in any way.

Needless to say, the brothers did not have a very cordial relationship after that.

As the day of the election drew near, many leaders joined in to campaign for Jameel sahab, among them a few maulanas, too. When these religious scholars visited Jameel sahab at his home, he received them with utmost respect, but refused to commit to a date whenever they would ask to join him for campaigning. This happened a few times and the maulanas were clearly not pleased. Jameel sahab lost the election.

Later, when he went to Delhi to brief Nehruji on the election and his defeat, Panditji said he had heard that some maulanas had wanted to campaign for Jameel sahab. 'Yes, they did express such a desire,' Jameel sahab had replied, but added that the maulanas didn't actually get to campaign for him. The electoral arena, he said, was neither a place for maulanas, nor was the battle about a religious issue where they could have helped him. Not only was Jameel sahab dedicated to the party, his commitment to the party's ideals was exemplary.

Look at the plight of politics today. Every candidate seems to want to invite this maulana or that pandit to deliver a speech in their favour. I don't believe in all this and feel out of place seeing, hearing or experiencing the blatant misuse of religion in politics. There was a time when nationalist Muslims like us were almost considered untouchable in our community. It was because a sizeable number of Muslims supported the Muslim League.

Jameel sahab's elder brother was a staunch Muslim League supporter. In the 1942 election, he had openly supported his younger brother's opponent. The two brothers were not even on talking terms for the rest of their lives because of their political differences. Such was my father-in-law's commitment to the Congress ideology.

Another episode comes to mind too, from sometime before Independence. Jameel sahab was then the president of the zila (district) Congress Committee. Once, when a membership drive was on (in those days, the membership fee was 25 paise), he got a postcard from Nehruji that said Mahatma Gandhi had received a complaint from a party worker in Haidergarh tehsil (administrative division) that a new member was a contractor by profession. The membership form clearly stated that no contractor could become a member of the Congress. In the postcard, Nehruji had written that Gandhiji wanted the zila committee chief to travel to the tehsil concerned and personally investigate if the party worker's complaint was true.

Jameel sahab, for some reason, could not prepare for the trip, which would have meant taking a bullock cart, as motor vehicles were not readily available then. After fifteen days, Jameel sahab received another postcard from Nehruji asking if the matter had been investigated. Nehruji had also written that Gandhiji wanted to convey, if the zila committee chief was not capable enough to travel to the tehsil, Nehru himself should go and investigate the complaint.

Jameel sahab made immediate preparations to travel to Haidergarh, where he found that the party worker's complaint was genuine. The new member was indeed a contractor. His membership was scrapped with immediate effect.

That is what the Congress stood for—transparency and an unwavering commitment to its lofty ideals that laid the foundations of an independent India. The only goal was freedom from alien rule and the party symbolized that collective aspiration which transcended manmade divisions of caste, creed or religion. The Congress led this struggle against the might and force of the British empire and, in the process, became a force in itself, a sweeping non-violent impetus that would unveil India's tryst with destiny on a midnight in August 1947 and rewrite the country's history.

In 1960, my personal destiny nudged me towards the party, an accidental tryst that has now lasted sixty years and more. The next chapter dwells on the initial days of that extended involvement.

4
Political Debut

THAKUR MAHANT JAGANNATH BAKSH DAS was a freedom fighter and a heavyweight leader of the Congress in Barabanki. One day, he called at my home and spoke to me; I still remember what he said. 'Mohsina Bibi,' he said, 'you have been given the ticket from the Congress party to fight the next Council election. Now prepare yourself mentally to take on the challenge.'

I was stunned. Confused, and somewhat disturbed, I told my husband, Khalil Ur Rahman Kidwai, what Mahantji had said. He too was puzzled. Neither of us could figure out why the party had chosen to field me. Finally, both of us decided to wait for my father-in-law to return home from Lucknow, for only he could explain this unexpected development. To my disbelief, Jameel sahab said that what Mahantji had told me was true; I had to fight the upcoming Council election.

My memories of those early days in politics are still vivid. I distinctly remember the day in 1957, Ramsewak Yadav had come over to meet Jameel sahab. Ramsewak, a socialist leader, was contesting from the Barabanki parliamentary seat as an independent backed by socialist leaders, and had come to seek my father-in-law's blessings.

'Look, Ramsewak, personally, I wish you all the success and a long life,' Jameel sahab had told him. 'But at the party level, I cannot bless you to succeed. When our party is in the field, why are you contesting from another party?'

Ramsewak was a lawyer and had a roaring practice. He was a nice person, had a great following within his Yadav caste, and kept on winning from 1957 to 1971. But his successive victories spawned and then furthered caste politics in Barabanki, ensuring that the Yadavs in the constituency divorced the Congress forever.

There was another politician, Anantram Jaiswal, contesting from our district. He too was in the Socialist Party. Jaiswal had worked as an advocate prior to joining politics and had served as both Member of Legislative Assembly (MLA) and MP. Between the 1960s and 1970s, Jaiswal was imprisoned five times on various counts. Both Ramsewak and Anantram combined their forces.

Then there was Ramchandra Singh of the Communist Party. He had served as an MLA once, though his party did not have much of an influence in the area.

There was a time when the Congress would dominate in all the seven Assembly constituencies in the Barabanki region. But in the 1967 Assembly election, the Congress could retain only two seats—one that my father-in-law won and the other that went to Ghanshyam Singh, a Scheduled Caste candidate.

Since then, the allegiance of voters turned from political parties to castes. Among Yadavs, only those within the Congress would vote for the party. Some other backward classes, such as kurmis, stayed with the Congress. The upper castes, Muslims and the Scheduled Castes were overwhelmingly with the Congress. This combination always favoured the party in the elections. But growing casteism proved deleterious for the Congress's prospects. Even then, we did not let the BJP strike roots here.

This is not to say that caste and religion were not factors in politics earlier, but that they became more pronounced after 1967. I mean, when Ramsewak Yadav became an MP from our constituency, caste became a decisive factor. The Bharatiya Jana Sangh, which was still struggling for identity in the region, started using religion and religious symbols more aggressively, just as socialists were counting on caste. The JP Movement in the seventies metamorphosed politics. It opened the floodgate for political upstarts. Those who didn't deserve to become even councillors were elected MPs.

The Congress in Barabanki owed its first victory in the region after Independence to freedom fighter Thakur Mahant Jagannath Baksh Das, who was incidentally the first to break the news of my candidature to the Uttar Pradesh Legislative Council. He belonged to the Mahadeva religious sect. In the 1967 elections, his sister-in-law, Bindumati Das, lost the Assembly election to a Jana Sangh candidate. This contest had an interesting background. Thakur Mahant Baksh Das was the district board chairman. Some of the board's decisions had angered teachers. In revenge, they had fielded a teacher on a Jana Sangh ticket against Bindumati Das, who won.

The biggest challenge in the initial years was the development of Uttar Pradesh. The issues fifty or sixty years ago were different from the ones we are confronted with today. There were no roads, no wells, no power, no tubewells. Wherever we went in the constituency, people would demand digging of tubewells and roads. This demand might look small today but in the 1960s and the 1970s, road connectivity was a big issue.

Coming back to my own elections in the Uttar Pradesh Legislative Council, from the day Mahant Baksh Dasji had broken the news to me, I remained nonplussed for a few days. My mentor and father-in-law was recuperating in a hospital in Lucknow.

I consulted with my husband, Khalil, and he was extremely supportive. Although I got the ticket, I was not very pleased. My priorities were different. I had children to look after.

As the days passed in a whirlwind of meetings and strategic campaign sessions, as enthusiastic party workers toiled hard on the ground, I too got deeply involved. I won the election and at the age of twenty-eight, became an MLC. The irony was hard to miss. There was no curtain to stand behind for this hesitant and shy young woman, who had so long preferred to remain in the background. My place was now in front of hundreds of people at a public meeting or in the Assembly and, eventually, the Indian Parliament.

Election to the council meant frequent travel to Lucknow, and with it, the twin challenges of staying away from home for long hours and my children's upbringing. The positive side to that—politically, at least—was that now I could associate faces with names, most of whom I knew as my father-in-law's colleagues who would often visit Jameel sahab at his house. They were now my colleagues too, and started to recognize and encourage me as I slowly merged with the flow of life in politics.

As for my father-in-law, he remained a mentor and guide, while my husband was always by my side, never once grudging the spotlight that naturally came my way with my entry into public life. He remained a caring spouse in private and a shield outside. Spared the biting acrimony of domestic discord—often the case when wives get ahead in life—I eased into the new role that had been thrust upon me.

Then one day, I delivered my first speech in the Assembly on the budget. I had been extremely nervous and unsure of how I had performed. When the Speaker adjourned the House, I started moving towards the exit, when suddenly my senior colleagues came up and congratulated me, saying they had liked my speech. That made my day. At times, though, it was still hard to adjust to colleagues who were many years my seniors in age, as well as experience. Usually, during lunch time, all the women members would gather in the retiring room for ladies. They would discuss current issues, the happenings inside the Assembly, and comment on each other's performances.

I found it difficult to be around women who were so much older than I was. I had started wearing khadi, since that was the accepted fabric of my work space and also a way of the Gandhian life my father-in-law had embraced; one that I had started to accept and adopt as well. My older colleagues would ask why I wore such pale-coloured saris. I avoided answering such questions. I knew what I was doing—this was the only way I could look older and integrate myself better with the House ambience.

Not long after I entered the House, I focused on community service, using my political reach to make a difference in the lives of those less privileged. It soon turned into a pursuit, a compulsion to help those in need who approached me. It was a gratifying thought—the realization of being part of a system that worked towards social development, mainly at the grassroots, and being the channel to convey their concerns and problems to the people in-charge, who could take decisions that could change their lives for the better.

My first six-year term as an MLC ended in 1966. Fresh elections were called but this time, the Congress was a divided house with several factions deciding to field their own candidate independently. I was a contender from the group headed by C.B. Gupta, a former freedom fighter. As I was the sitting council member, I was fielded against a party heavyweight, Muneshwar Dutt Upadhyay. It turned out to be an ugly contest, where the election was communalized against my candidacy. I lost by 250 votes, but what really hurt me was the mud-slinging, which I experienced for the first time. Also, this was only the second time I had ever contested an election.

Hurt and let down, I went to Delhi to meet Indiraji at her Jantar Mantar residence. All my anger and hurt poured out as Indiraji listened patiently. After I had finished, she spoke. 'Mohsina, this is politics, you have to have a very thick skin to take it all in and live with it. I bear the brunt of so much opposition angst; should I take refuge in my emotions and forgo the service to my party and my nation because of the Opposition attacks?'

I understood what Indiraji was trying to tell me. She had taught me something important, very gently.

In August 1966, another election followed. Guptaji felt that I should be fielded again, but advised me to meet Indiraji and ask her opinion. This time, too, the Congress was divided on whom to give the ticket to. While Guptaji had made it clear that I was his candidate, Dinesh Singh wanted Sultan Alam Khan to be fielded. I went back to meet Indiraji. While I was with her, an aide came in and told her that Bahugunaji and M.R. Sherwani were waiting outside. Indiraji asked me to wait in her dining room while she met the others in the living room.

As I sat in the dining room, I couldn't help overhearing Bahugunaji's loud and agitated voice, insisting that Indiraji should not consider me as a candidate. He said I had just lost an election in May and it was too early to field me again. It would set a wrong precedent, he said, if a candidate who had lost less than three months back was fielded again so soon.

When Bahugunaji's voice rose even further, Indiraji cut him short. 'Bahugunaji, the record of your supporters winning in recent elections has been rather dismal. How many Muslim women come out to fight elections? The ones that brave it, you make their election so communal and dirty that they do not stand a chance.'

Indiraji stood her ground, saying that women from such communities and families don't come out often in the open and only more so in the political field. 'We must and should support and encourage such endeavours, and develop and cultivate their leadership in every respect. Mohsina is going to be our candidate.'

With Indiraji's support, I fought and won the election and went back to the House for another six-year term—to the surprise of many and the disappointment of some.

5
Uttar Pradesh Congress Committee Chief

My life as a politician had settled into a familiar rhythm of House sessions and social work. The initial days of hesitancy were over. Politics, like any other profession, does toughen you up. I was now nearly a decade and a half into my new career, a veteran seasoned enough to handle the unexpected. Or so I thought.

It was sometime in 1976 when one day, Narayan Dutt Tewari, the then Congress chief minister of Uttar Pradesh, came up to me after a cabinet meeting in Mathura. I was then a minister in Tiwariji's cabinet. 'Mohsinaji, you will have to come with me to Delhi,' he said. 'Indiraji wants to see you.'

I was surprised. This was rather sudden. 'I am sorry, Tiwariji,' I told him, 'but I am afraid I can't accompany you to Delhi. I need to take care of a lot of things in Lucknow once I leave Mathura.'

Tiwariji smiled. He was not giving me an option, he said. 'You have to accompany me.'

We travelled by car to Delhi. About four hours later, as the car pulled into the front porch of 1, Safdarjung Lane, the prime minister's residence, Tiwariji turned to me. 'Indiraji wants to appoint you the president of the Uttar Pradesh Congress Committee (UPCC),' he said.

I was taken aback. Not only was this unexpected, the responsibility was huge. All this while, he had kept quiet about the purpose behind the visit. 'Tiwariji, we travelled for so many hours together in this car and you did not even mention once why you brought me here during the whole journey,' I told him.

I didn't get a chance to say anything more. The car had stopped and we were escorted inside Indiraji's residence. She seemed pleased to receive us and came to the point directly.

'Mohsina, I want to appoint you as the president of the UPCC,' she said, looking at me.

'I don't think I am capable enough to handle such a post,' I replied, hands folded. 'Indiraji, please take back the offer. After seventeen years of a blemish-free political life, why do you want to scatter unknown and unintended blemishes on it that I presume will come with this office?'

Indiraji smiled. 'I have full confidence in you and your capabilities,' she said. 'You will be just fine being a minister and the state congress president, trust me. So go, start your work.'

Before I left, she asked me to meet Sanjay Gandhi. When I met Sanjayji, he told me a few things and then said, 'Mohsinaji will you be able to fight Kamlapati Tripathiji?' I asked him what kind of a fight he had in mind. I said if it was going to be a personality-oriented smear campaign, I could not do it. But if it was political, aimed at strengthening the Congress organization, I shall gladly do it and I will, in fact, try my best.

Now when I look back, I think it was rather adventurous of me to have said all this. This was the time when Sanjay's word was considered final and often went without questioning. It was gracious of him to have taken my point of view well.

And thus began a new innings for me—at the helm of the Uttar Pradesh Congress—at a time when the political environment in the country was like a charged wire held taut with tension. The Emergency was still in force and the Congress was preparing to launch its 20-Point Programme that focused on the poor and farmers. But the male sterilization drive propagated by Sanjay Gandhi had left hundreds of families, mainly in rural India, seething. Many strong leaders of the Congress, among them some of Indiraji's trusted aides, had left the party and joined hands with the opposition, the Janata Party because of this move.

Urban India, too, was disappointed with the Congress and the Emergency. Clearly, Indiraji had not anticipated the backlash. Loved and revered once, she had, overnight, turned unpopular among vast swathes of the country's population. The Opposition tapped into this discontent, portraying her as an incapable representative of the people and then unleashing a penetrating propaganda against the 20-Point Programme.

The programme's main areas of focus were eradication of poverty, alleviating the lot of farmers, empowerment of women through self-help groups, increasing the reach of education and health, employment, providing energy and roads to villages, land reforms, drinking water and water for irrigation. It was a strong vision for a prosperous India. The Janata Party, too, had realized the programme's potential—if this unparalleled vision was launched and implemented on the ground, it would spell the death knell for the opposition party and it might as well abandon any thought of dismantling the Congress for generations to come.

So, with the web-like infrastructure of the Rashtriya Swayamsevak Sangh (RSS), the Janata Party targeted the family planning programme that was part of Sanjay Gandhi's 5-Point Programme that had been incorporated into the government's initiative. The 5-Point Programme included extensive planting of trees, adult education, eradication of the caste system and family planning. But while it looked promising on the whole, it was the family planning part that overshadowed the other components of the plan.

What the Opposition did was seize on this component and projected it as an incursion into the personal lives and decisions of citizens. The Opposition spread fear among the people, especially in the villages, taking advantage of the lack of literacy and general awareness in rural India. Rumours and misconstrued information swirled while endless repetition ensured that the panic was total. The Opposition milked every drop of misinformation and succeeded in rallying hatred as they leveraged the emotional trauma endured by the citizens. Since there was an unprecedented ban on the press, there was also no way for the right information to reach the people.

In retrospect, the initiative to restrict the number of children to two per family was not as wise as it looked on paper at a time when India was struggling to provide food and shelter to its poor. All the more so, as it was badly implemented.

Indiraji could sense the growing discontent and social disgust and realized she would have to pay a heavy price for imposing the Emergency in 1975 and the misuse of power that had followed. Still, she chose to announce the general elections, which were held in March 1977, just after the Emergency was lifted. The Congress suffered a crushing defeat at the hands of the Janata Party in these elections. Both Indiraji and her son, Sanjay Gandhi, lost their parliamentary seats and the party ended up nearly 200 seats down from its 1971 tally of 352 MPs. It was a massive blow to the party. For the first time in independent India, the Congress was not at the nation's helm.

In Uttar Pradesh, the Congress drew a blank in all the eighty-five Lok Sabha seats in the heartland, a frustrating and morale-shattering result for someone who had just taken over the reins of the party in the country's most politically important state. Not only that, Indiraji herself had lost from Raebareli.

I decided to meet Indiraji and hand in my resignation as state party chief. 'Indiraji, I feel I am incapable of carrying out my responsibilities as UPCC president. It is under my presidentship that the party has suffered such a major defeat [in the state],' I told Indiraji when I met her.

'What is the point of carrying on as UPCC chief when I couldn't ensure even your victory?' I told her. 'I don't wish to hold any office. I will work with you but will not remain the UPCC president.'

Indiraji appeared disillusioned but still refused to accept my resignation. 'Mohsina, my defeat has nothing to do with your presidency. It was not your fault as the president at all. My defeat is not because of you in any way. You go ahead and take care of your work,' she said.

A huge task lay ahead for the Congress and its leaders. They had to put the humiliation of defeat behind them, reach out to the people at the grassroots again and work extremely hard to regain their trust and goodwill. It was an uphill battle taking along all the hundreds of disillusioned party workers and leaders at every level, and especially Indiraji, who seemed a shadow of her confident self by now compared to when she had first entered politics.

As time passed, there was a sense of general regret among the people of Raebareli for voting out Indira Gandhi. They realized that Indiraji had nursed her constituency and its people for eleven years like her own. Anger was also building up against Raj Narain, who now represented the constituency.

The mood was changing again but the road ahead was long and difficult. Most of the heavyweights in the party had deserted Indiraji and left the Congress—either to form their own outfits or to join the Janata Party. There were only a few leaders who still stood by the party in Uttar Pradesh. The major support came from the large number of loyal party workers on the ground. They helped me shake off my dejection: if they could hang on, so could I. And with this determination, I went back to do what was expected of me: getting the party back on its feet in the state.

There was another silent promise I had made to myself at this point: I would help ensure Indiraji was brought back to power.

6
Determined to Bring Indira Back

ADVERSITY, THEY SAY, IS THE best teacher. Sometimes, it's the best motivator too, especially when one sees people close to them retreat into a shell of lonely disillusionment. Something similar had happened to Indiraji and I couldn't bear to see our leader in that state. A feeling akin to frenzy took over me as I hit the road again, determined to bring her back to power—back into the hearts of the people who were used to seeing her majestic stride, had once embraced her as their leader but had now summarily rejected her.

Uttar Pradesh had rebuffed Indiraji, so Uttar Pradesh would have to bring her back, I told myself, as I travelled the length and width of the state, often at a stretch, non-stop for several days, my driver Shafi behind the wheel and I in the back seat. At every place I stopped, party workers would join in as I spoke to villagers, farmers and ordinary citizens. Indiraji, however, remained cooped up in her home, unable to shake off the heavy burden of defeat and the feeling that she had let her people down.

Back in Uttar Pradesh, the Assembly had been dissolved and fresh elections were announced in June 1977. I met Indiraji to try and convince her to come out and motivate the large majority of party workers, who were still too demoralized to campaign. Indiraji refused.

I persisted. 'I don't want to listen to your reasons, please come out and see how the workers want your support,' I pleaded with her. But Indiraji wouldn't be swayed.

'We will arrange meetings with small groups of workers, you need to just come out,' I said.

'No,' she replied.

'Why not?' I asked her.

'Mohsina,' she said, 'I have been told that if I go among the people, the Congress will suffer. I have already caused so much loss to the party—I don't want to hurt its prospects any further.'

I asked Indiraji who were these people who had been able to make her believe such trash. Indiraji refused to name anyone.

'Indiraji,' I told her, 'whoever has managed to bring this wrong notion to your mind is, in my opinion, not your well-wisher—neither yours, nor the Congress party's.'

It was like speaking to a wall. Indiraji wouldn't budge from her decision not to come out in public; so deep was her disappointment. I got up, took her leave and went back to Uttar Pradesh.

A large amount of election material had already been printed, including party flags, posters and badges. One candidate, however, refused to accept the campaign material since they had Indiraji's photograph on them. I was furious and told him I will field another candidate in his place.

'The election will be fought under Indiraji's name and only her name,' I said.

'You don't know and you don't understand,' the candidate snapped.

'I don't want to know or understand anything,' I retorted. 'If you don't want to fight this election, return the ticket now. The election will be fought under this name and this banner—you decide what you want to do.'

Eventually, he took the material and went ahead with his election. Since Indiraji had refused to come out and campaign, the Assembly election was fought without her. She, however, extended her support in every other possible way that she could.

The party had no finances to fund its candidates. So as the state party president, I broke a fixed deposit of ₹90,000 I had saved and sent whatever little amount I could to the candidates.[6]

Struggling for finances and still hurting from the defeat earlier that year, we mobilized whatever resources we had. The Congress won forty-eight Assembly segments of the 425 in the state, and emerged as the single largest opposition party.

The next step was whom to elect as the leader of the Opposition. Indiraji sent Swaran Singh to Lucknow to help us decide. He spoke to all the party MLAs. The majority of the elected MLAs wanted Narayan Dutt Tiwari to be the leader of the House. Tiwariji had faced much opposition during the 1977 defeat and the Congress, as a party, was not sure if he was the right choice. But with the majority of the MLAs extending their support, Tiwariji was unanimously elected the leader of the opposition in the House.

Tiwariji and I had different ways of functioning and did not agree on every issue or decision, but both of us had realized how important it was to keep the party together and strong, and that this was no time to tolerate any kind of factionalism. So we stuck together and worked as a team.

Not everyone, however, saw it that way. Kamalapati Tripathi and some of his close aides didn't want me to remain the state unit chief and tried to create a rift between me and Tiwariji. When I visited Indiraji in Delhi, she seemed to have received some complaints about the functioning of the party. I told Indiraji that if at this juncture, there was disunity between me and Tiwariji, it would have been disastrous for the party.

'When the time is right, I will let you know if there is any hindrance in our functioning,' I added.

Days passed. Despite all the challenges, including opposition from within and attempts to destabilize my tenure at the helm, Tiwariji and I, with the help of party workers across the state, managed to get the Congress back on its feet, slowly but steadily.

Once the Congress appeared to be on the road to recovering its lost ground, I again asked Indiraji to resume her contact with people. It was October now, seven months since the humiliating defeat in the March general election. Indiraji too was ready to step out again and tour the heartland. So the state unit organized a tour of Western Uttar Pradesh, starting with Ghaziabad.

As our twenty-five-vehicle convoy neared the venue of a rally, I told Indiraji that the first few meetings might be tough to handle since this was her first tour of the state after her defeat. There was still some lingering anger in the people—some of it engineered—and it was better that she remain prepared for any kind of reception. Indiraji nodded. She knew that the road ahead was far from smooth. Exactly how uneven, we would soon find out.

Huge crowds of party workers and the general public had lined the streets as the cavalcade entered Ghaziabad. A few among the crowd waved black flags at Indiraji. Then suddenly, without warning, some people armed with iron rods smashed the windshield of the car Indiraji and I were travelling in. Luckily, none of us in the car was hurt and we managed to reach the meeting venue unscathed.

When Indiraji went up on the stage and was about to start her speech, someone from among the crowd snatched the microphone from her. Not one to be cowed down, she spoke to the gathering without a mic.

After Ghaziabad, we visited other places, meeting expected resistance, even occasional violence, but the number of supporters seemed to grow by the hundreds and thousands as we travelled from one city to another. In Meerut, people appeared to have come from every nook and corner to see and hear Indiraji speak. It had been so long and her defeat and absence had been a huge price to pay for their vote against her and the Congress. This was also the first time Indiraji was on a tour without any security cover, except for a man whose surname I remember was Dutt, her personal security officer.

Indiraji, Tiwariji and I climbed into an open-hood Jeep. The crowds swelled by the minute; they came on foot, in cars, on two-wheelers and on tractors. Every now and then, slogans would rise from among the sea of bobbing heads, a raucous spontaneous chorus that would go on for a while and then subside on its own. '*Aadhi roti khayenge, Indira ko layenge*', someone's voice would cut through the low buzz of excitement before another would come up with a matching clincher, '*Tufaan mein aur aandhi mein, vishwas hai Indira Gandhi mein*.' (An approximate translation of this slogan would be: amid all adversities and storms, we have full faith in Indira Gandhi.)

I felt sheer joy at the response of the crowd. It meant the party was recouping the losses it had suffered on the ground. It had taken months of hard work, from senior leaders to the junior-most workers, but now it was time to celebrate a little. Our patience and indefatigable toil were finally paying off.

The same month, in October, the party's Agra unit had organized an event in the memory of B.R. Ambedkar, the architect of the Indian Constitution. The MLA from the city of Agra, Gulab Sehra, had invited Indiraji and the rest of the state leadership to this event. With Indiraji's consent, I had made reservations in the newly inaugurated Taj Express for the journey to Agra. The seven of us—Indiraji, Tiwariji, Kamalapatiji, D.P. Singh, Dutt (Indiraji's lone security man), Chandra, a Sewa Dal worker who was always with Indiraji, and I—were to get off at Agra Cantonment station.

Word about the journey had spread fast and crowds gathered at every station the train passed through. Elsewhere, people came out on roads along the train's route while some appeared on rooftops to wave at Indiraji.

By the time the train reached Agra Cantonment station, a huge crowd had gathered there. I told Indiraji to wait for some time before getting off the train. She said that would delay us and got down. I was just behind her. Suddenly, the crowd surged towards us and Indiraji was nowhere to be seen. She had disappeared somewhere among the teeming mass of people. Nor could I see any of my other colleagues who were with me on the train.

The next few minutes were chaotic. People pushed and jostled, and I found myself moving with the crowd towards the exit. Then I lost consciousness. I have no recollection of what happened but when I opened my eyes, I heard someone telling me, 'Madam, get up, get into the Jeep.'

I looked around. 'Where is Indiraji?' I asked.

He didn't know. But he insisted that I get into the Jeep. I did, with the man's help, but made it clear that I wasn't going anywhere till I had found Indiraji. I could feel a pain in my ribs and blood oozing from my mouth. But I wouldn't let the driver move the Jeep even an inch till I knew where Indiraji was. Then, suddenly, I saw her, standing and waving from another open-hood Jeep. The others who had come with me on the train were safe too.

It was only after we reached the circuit house that I realized I had lost both my slippers. My ribs also hurt and I was still bleeding from the mouth. Indiraji had a doctor come in to take care of all the injured. She also sent someone to fetch me a pair of sandals.

Indiraji left to attend the meeting we had come for. I stayed back since I was in no position to move. 'Mohsina,' Indiraji told me later, 'there was no policeman in sight, the Sewa Dal workers themselves struggled to stay around me.' Luckily, Indiraji did not suffer any injury.

After our heartland tour, I stayed at my brother's place in Delhi. That's where I usually stayed when I visited Delhi, both on official work and otherwise. UP Niwas was another option but more often than not, I preferred to be at my brother's house. I was still in pain and since a doctor had advised complete rest, I had planned to extend my stay in the capital.

Little did I know that storm clouds were gathering—and all thought of rest would be blown away by one phone call.

7

The Government Strikes

The ring of the telephone sounded like an omen. I picked up the phone. Maneka Gandhi, Indiraji's younger daughter-in-law, was at the other end of the line.

'Mohsinaji,' she sounded frantic, 'please come home as soon as possible, the police are here to arrest Mummy (Indiraji).'

I was in unbearable pain, hardly able to walk properly. But there was no time to waste. By the time I reached Indiraji's new residence at 12, Willingdon Crescent, a huge crowd had gathered outside. Many party leaders too had reached the spot. We all followed the police car when Indiraji was finally arrested and escorted out. The police car swept through Delhi and drove towards the Haryana border.

When she realized where she was being taken, Indiraji refused to travel any further. She had the police officers stop the vehicle. She got down and sat on the pavement. Indiraji then accused the Delhi Police for taking her beyond the borders of Delhi, for which they had no warrant. The officers had to turn around and eventually, drove her to Tihar Jail. We followed Indiraji till the prison gates shut behind her.

The next day, I stopped at Willingdon Crescent on my way to visit Indiraji. Her elder son, Rajiv Gandhi, was getting ready to visit his mother in jail with a lunchbox. He asked me and Pranab Mukherjee, who was present there, to accompany him and then drove us to Tihar Jail.

My first meeting with Rajiv Gandhi had been brief but cordial, with neither of us aware of what the future held, but both destined to work together and share a relationship that would be built on a very strong thread from the past, an unspoken bond of trust and respect.

Indiraji's arrest only served to trigger an outpouring of support for her among both party workers and the people at large. Each blow by the Janata Party would prove more beneficial to her as well as the Congress, as time would tell.

I need to go back a little, here. Chaudhary Charan Singh, the home minister in the Janata Party government, was a close friend of my father-in-law; the two shared a relationship that remained unaffected by politics. Charan Singh left the Congress in the sixties to float his own party but his friend didn't join him. 'Chaudhary sahab, all of us cannot and will not part ways with the Congress party along with you,' my father-in-law had told him. 'Our paths are different.'

But they remained friends despite this and Chaudhary sahab saw me as his daughter. After the Janata Party came to power, I told Indiraji that since Chaudhary sahab was a family friend, I would call upon him. Indiraji had no objection. I had another purpose in mind, too; to find out what plans the Janata government had for Indiraji.

What I found out was not too pleasant. 'We will arrest her soon,' Chaudhary sahab had told me. I tried to reason with him but he was adamant. 'We will put her in the same barracks where she had put the Maharani of Gwalior (during the Emergency),' Chaudhary sahab added.

Later, when I met Indiraji, I mentioned to her what Chaudhary sahab had told me. Indiraji didn't seem too surprised. 'I have a suitcase packed and I am ready,' she had said.

Chaudharyji lived up to his intent. Indiraji was arrested on 3 October 1977. On that day, around 5 p.m., Sonia Gandhi was at 12, Willingdon Crescent, preparing tea for her mother-in-law, when CBI Superintendent of Police N.K. Singh knocked on the door.

What followed over the next few hours showed Indiraji at her imperious best. 'Handcuff me!' she roared at N.K. Singh. 'I will not go unless I am handcuffed.'

Sanjay Gandhi made frantic telephone calls to Congress supporters and, from another phone, Indiraji's trusted aide R.K. Dhawan called up the local media.

As I have mentioned earlier, I had received a call from Maneka Gandhi. She was part of *Surya* magazine, and had already conveyed to the magazine staff that if they rushed to Indiraji's house, a great copy awaited them.

Indiraji, meanwhile, kept delaying her arrest till the media arrived in great numbers. 'Where is the warrant of arrest and the FIR report?' she asked Singh. When the CBI officer struggled to produce the relevant documents, Indiraji's lawyer, Frank Anthony, chipped in, saying, 'Is that [then Union home minister] Charan Singh's new law?'

'I'll not budge until you handcuff me,' Indiraji kept repeating, 'bring the handcuffs and take me.'

Indiraji would eventually be released on technical grounds. 'Even Mummy herself couldn't have written a better scenario,' Rajiv Gandhi, who maintained an apolitical profile then, told a foreign correspondent.

Le Monde, a French newspaper, commented: 'Political prisoners are often regarded as martyrs in India, where prison, as was once the case for the majority of members of (Morarji) Desai's Government, can be an antechamber of power.'

Indiraji would be jailed a year later, in December 1978, when Morarji Desai managed to pass legislation to set up special courts to try her and Sanjay Gandhi. Soon after her expulsion and dramatic exit from Parliament, Indiraji was arrested and taken to Tihar Jail, where she was put in the same cell complex as George Fernandes had occupied during the Emergency. Every day, Sonia Gandhi would bring Indiraji's three meals from home.

It was a tough time for the party. But even as we struggled to stage a comeback, some senior leaders, including the then Congress president, K. Brahmananda Reddy, announced on 1 January 1978 that Indiraji had been expelled from the party. Reddy had the support of some veteran leaders such as Y.B. Chavan, Vasant Dada Patil and Swaran Singh. D.K. Barooah, who had famously coined the slogan, 'Indira is India, India is Indira' was nowhere to be seen.

The CWC met at the residence of Maragatham Chandrasekhar at 3, Janpath. Twelve members sided with Indiraji, but the AICC chief was not accommodating. In the absence of V.C. Shukla, Bansi Lal, Ambika Soni, Karan Singh and Barooah (who had deserted her by then), Indiraji found a new band of loyalists in Buta Singh, A.P. Sharma, G.K. Moopanar, Syed Mir Qasim, Chandrasekhar and Budh Priya Maurya, all members of the CWC. They marched to Reddy to challenge Indiraji's expulsion. Buta Singhji, who was formerly with the Akali Dal, spoke harshly to Reddy, demanding to know how Jawaharlal Nehru's daughter could be expelled from the Congress. 'She *is* the Congress,' Buta Singhji said, before walking out.

In this battle for survival of the Congress and Indiraji, Buta Singhji, Sharma, Maurya, Moopanar, Mir Qasim and others left on a nationwide tour to obtain the signatures of the 700-odd members of the AICC. They found majority support in the state capitals.

A convention was organized in New Delhi on 2 January 1978, in which Indiraji announced that she was floating her own party, the Congress (I) or the 'Real Congress'. Perhaps, Buta Singhji's assertion before Reddy that Nehru's daughter 'was the Congress' was still ringing in her ears. She fought back and returned to power in 1980, and most leaders who had left her in 1978 returned to her party, giving the Congress (I) the status of the 'Real Congress'.

When the AICC called for a requisition meeting on the second day of 1978, we elected Indiraji the party president instead of Brahmananda Reddy. For this, all the then Pradesh Congress Committee (PCC) members from every district had to sign papers and show their support for the proposed motion. The entire leadership of each state, including Uttar Pradesh, had been working hard to gather the signatures of the PCC members. Some of those who still opposed my continuation as the chief of the Uttar Pradesh unit tried to take advantage of this campaign and demanded my removal. Although Kamalapati Tripathi was not directly involved, five of his closest aides threatened to leave the Congress if I was not removed.

When I heard what was going on, I again met Indiraji in Delhi. I told her that since this was threatening to weaken the Congress in Indiraji's home state, I was willing to resign as the UPCC president, as the dispute was also sending across a misleading message to the entire country. I asked Indiraji to consider the name of whoever Kamalapatiji wanted to make the next UPCC president.

Indiraji listened patiently to what I had to say and then spoke. 'Mohsina, you go do your work—this should not concern you in any way.'

The five Congressmen resigned from the party. The requisition meeting was held in Delhi, after which the party split and the Congress (I) was formed, with Indiraji as its president.

Back in Uttar Pradesh, the state unit worked tirelessly to strengthen the party. We all knew that if the party was strong in Uttar Pradesh, it would make Indiraji's return to power at the Centre a lot easier. We organized a successful and high-impact PCC meeting in Kanpur. Indiraji agreed to stay for a night and a day, finding time for the meeting, although elections had been declared in some south Indian states.

My position in the party had strengthened, too, and my presence had become more sought after than before. The party was now my biggest commitment—possibly greater than any other concern. As the days passed, my schedule got more hectic. Public rallies and party meetings took up most of my time. Even when I wasn't travelling and was at home, there would be a steady stream of party workers who would come seeking advice or to take instructions on organizing meetings.

When I was UPCC president, we had organized a successful rally to protest the very unfair and low price—₹6 a quintal—the Janata government was offering to sugarcane farmers. The Congress, during its rule, had fixed the price at ₹20 a quintal and the farmers had been benefitting from these relatively high returns. Now many of them had started to burn full-grown crops since they were not being able to afford the labour costs at such minimal returns. The state government had imposed prohibitory orders under Section 144 to stop this rally and deployed a heavy police bandobast to ensure the blockade.

We had, however, secretly planned to go ahead with the rally on our route through Lucknow city. The police were caught unawares as they had not anticipated this move. Both sides of the road were heavily lined by police personnel who had been ordered to surround the rally. Some of my colleagues—Kamalapati Tripathi, Uma Shankar Dikshit and Narayan Dutt Tiwari—and I were in an open-hood Jeep. While the police were trying to stop us from moving further, I asked the driver to accelerate, which he did.

The police hadn't expected such aggression from someone known to be calm and poised, such as myself. Our vehicle managed to move through the police cordon but the vehicles behind us hesitated. That gave the police enough time to yank out the ignition keys and stop the vehicles. Many party workers were injured in the police baton-charge that followed. The police also used tear gas to control the crowd.

The then DM, Yogendra Narain, shaken by the turn of events, hesitantly told me and my colleagues that we were under arrest. We were then taken to Lucknow jail.

While my fight had been for a just cause, the one most affected by the circumstances was perhaps my youngest daughter, Irum, still a child then. It was natural that she would be affected since on the next day, at school, she was subjected to a barrage of questions from her schoolmates.

Why was her mother in jail? What crime had her mother committed to be put behind bars, they asked her. Too young to understand the real reason, the questions left her embarrassed and traumatized. Back home after school, she insisted on meeting me in jail.

When she met me, I showed her the surroundings and tried to make her feel reassured that her mother was comfortable and being taken care of by the jail authorities. I told her I was fighting for a better India, a fair and inclusive India, an India that would not discriminate against anyone, where everyone would be equal and where farmers, who contributed the most to the country's well-being by producing food for us, would be given a fair price for their hard work.

I told her that my fight—my 'crime' in the eyes of the authorities—was surely worth going to jail for. To fight for the less privileged was a fight to be proud of. The sugarcane protest was a fight for justice on the ground. Little did I know that a soon-to-be enacted midair incident would nearly embroil me in what could have been a long, legal tangle.

On 20 December 1978, two misguided and overzealous party supporters hijacked an Indian Airlines plane, Flight 410. The Boeing 737 with 126 passengers on board, including two former ministers of Indira Gandhi's Emergency regime, A.K. Sen and Dharam Bir Sinha, had taken off from Lucknow airport at 5.45 p.m. on the last leg of its journey from Kolkata (then Calcutta) to Delhi.

According to media reports, none of the passengers had initially taken any notice of the two young men, who rose from their seats in the fifteenth row and moved casually towards the cockpit fifteen minutes before the aircraft was due to touch down at Delhi's Palam airport. The two men, listed on the passenger manifest as Bhola Nath Pandey and Devendra Pandey—they were not related but both were in their late twenties—politely asked the flight purser, G.V. Dey, if they could visit the cockpit. Dey said he would communicate their request to the captain, M.N. Battiwala.

As Dey was about to enter the cockpit, one of the men grabbed an air hostess, Indira Thakuri's, elbow, while his companion tried to force his way into the cockpit. However, the self-locking mechanism on the magnetic door of the cockpit clicked into place. Undeterred, the two men threw their weight against the door until it flew open, and disappeared inside. By now, the passengers and cabin crew had realized that something was amiss.

Captain Battiwala later told *India Today* at his Park Circus apartment in Kolkata,

> From beginning to end, it was a horrible task explaining to those idiots that there was such a thing called an aircraft's range of flight. First, they demanded to be flown to Nepal. When I told them,

particularly the crazier of the two who kept pointing a pistol at my head, that we were not carrying that much fuel, they demanded to be flown to Bangladesh. I bet they had forgotten their schoolroom geography.

Back in the main cabin, the passengers had calmed down after the initial nervousness. When the two hijackers emerged, they asked the aircraft to be flown to Kathmandu, instead of Varanasi. The hijackers delivered speeches in Hindi, dwelling on Indiraji's arrest the day before and the 'vindictiveness' of the Janata Party. They proclaimed themselves as Youth Congress (I) members, a claim the Congress and I denied.

The hijack drama ended by evening, when the aircraft landed at Varanasi and taxied to a corner of the runway. The hijackers demanded to speak to Ram Naresh Yadav. The Uttar Pradesh chief minister was contacted but he refused to oblige. Later, after receiving instructions from Prime Minister Morarji Desai, he took off for Varanasi in a Cessna aircraft owned by the state government.

The hijackers had, in the meanwhile, informed the district authorities through the plane's wireless that they had four demands, the main one being the unconditional release of Mrs Gandhi from jail.

When the passengers complained that the aircraft was getting unbearably stuffy, the hijackers allowed them to open the rear doors. Inside the cockpit, Captain Battiwala pulled back the emergency chute-release lever. Seeing the chute drop down from the doors, a few of the passengers scrambled down onto the tarmac, followed shortly after by almost half the passengers on board. By then, the father of one of the hijackers arrived at Varanasi airport and spoke to his son over the wireless. The father's voice shattered their bubble of heroism. The two men meekly walked out of the aircraft, shouting pro-Indira Gandhi slogans, and surrendered to the waiting authorities.

Earlier, while the hijack drama was on, a senior government official had called me up. He said the two hijackers had told the authorities they would release the plane only if Mohsina Kidwai asked them to. I told the official I didn't know these people. Since my name had come up, some legal luminaries—I won't disclose their identities—advised me to apply for anticipatory bail. I may not have had a law degree, but common sense came to my rescue. I told my lawyers that an anticipatory bail plea would be an admission of guilt and would associate the Uttar Pradesh Congress with this incident. I was firm in my decision, which saved me endless rounds of courts and the stigma of an association with an incident of hijacking.

8
A New Party Office at Lucknow

When the opportunity arises, strike. And strike hard. Nothing epitomizes this better than politics. It doesn't matter if those at the receiving end were colleagues or comrades till the other day. All that matters is seizing the advantage. The swifter, the better. How else does one explain what our rival faction did to us, effectively locking us out from what had been our party office?

Of course, we found a new party office soon and this chapter is about how we did that. But first, I would like to hold up before my readers an example of how ugly faction rivalry can become.

I have already mentioned in an earlier chapter that my father-in-law, Jameel Ur Rahman sahab, who was instrumental in my entry into politics, passed away around the time Indiraji formed the Congress (I). His funeral was to be held in Baragaon, my home in Barabanki district (more on Baragaon in the family history chapters).

While in Baragaon, I received the news that the Uttar Pradesh Congress faction, which had opposed Indiraji ahead of the 1978 split, had claimed its right to the state party office in Lucknow and locked the premises. That this faction might do something like this, I had anticipated long before, and had moved all our valuables and assets—including cars and office equipment belonging to the party—to my official residence at 6, Darulshafa, the MLAs' residential hostel in Lucknow. As the name suggests, it was supposedly a hospital, or dispensary, built by Nawab Saadut Ali Khan, for the indigent sick, but was never used for that purpose.

With all the office equipment now at our house, I turned it into a functioning Congress office. Not a day's work was lost. The entire staff remained with me and stayed with the UPCC—committed and loyal to the party and Indiraji. I must mention here that I didn't own any property in Lucknow and the Darulshafa bungalow was a government accommodation I had been allotted as president of the state Congress.

There had also been an attempt to dislodge us from the bungalow. Many of my well-wishers were aware of the situation and of the low-key, sporadic attacks on my residence. One such well-wisher, a person called Shukla, approached me and said that a house was going to be auctioned in Lucknow. He suggested that I buy it so that I could have a permanent residence in the state capital. That evening, I told my husband what Shukla had suggested and we both agreed that we could afford the house, which was priced at ₹1.5 lakh, a big amount then.

Later, however, my husband had second thoughts about buying the house. 'The Congress is going through a very rough patch,' he told me. 'In such a situation, will it be appropriate for you to buy a house for our family?'

I realized what he was saying made perfect sense. Although we had the resources to buy the house, the Janata Party might insinuate wrongdoing; worse, it could even plant allegations accusing me of dishonesty when everything that I had was either hard-earned money or assets handed down to me as inheritance. We decided not to buy the house for private ownership. But another plan was already forming in my mind: why not buy the house as an office for the party?

I was at a party meeting at Tiwariji's residence when the news came in that the auction had started. I reached the venue with some of my colleagues and bid ₹2,000 over the last bid. To my surprise, it tipped in my favour. At ₹2.75 lakh, 10, Mall Avenue—the current UPCC office—was ours.

But now what? Where would the money come from? My husband and I put in some of our own money towards paying the daunting total amount. I then sent out an appeal in newspapers asking party workers to contribute. The response was overwhelming. People gave whatever they could, in coins, in ten-rupee notes, some even in notes of ₹100. Finally, 10, Mall Avenue was purchased and registered in my name.

When I next met Indiraji, I told her about the new party office we had bought. Indiraji seemed amused. 'Mohsina,' she said with a smile, 'I have heard that the house is registered in your name and people think you might not want to give it away.'

I had come prepared and handed Indiraji a blank signed paper I had brought with me. 'Yes, Indiraji, legally, no one has the power to take it away from me, but I don't intend for it to be that way,' I told her. 'I have, with all honesty, bought it for the party, and that is how and what it will be.'

Till 2018, the party office had been registered in my name. Indiraji never attempted to transfer it in her own name or the party's name or, for that matter, any other name.

I did not own a house till 2019. I vividly remember the expression of my party colleague Raj Babbar when I handed over the party office papers registered in my name with a degree of indifference and no sense of belonging. The words he spoke were to the effect of 'what you are doing? Nobody would do this and with such ease'. I was a little surprised as I always viewed 10, Mall

Avenue as the party's asset, even though I had paid for it and it remained in my name for over four decades.

As the UPCC chief, I faced many tricky intra-party situations, too. When I reflect on these, I feel personal ambitions have done the greatest disservice to the party, though I concede that it's too much to expect everyone to be like Thomas Merton, an American Trappist monk, writer, theologian, mystic, poet, social activist and scholar of comparative religion, who could easily say, 'When Ambition ends, happiness begins.'

For a politician, I would go by the famous words of Franklin D. Roosevelt, 'In our personal ambitions, we are individualists. But in our seeking for economic and political progress as a nation, we all go up or else all go down as one people.' Unfortunately, this fine balance is often lost.

When I headed the UPCC, Yashpal Kapoor was my esteemed party colleague and a trusted aide of Indiraji's. So when he filed his nomination to contest against Kamalapati Tripathiji for a lone Rajya Sabha berth, I was baffled. Tripathiji was not only a veteran but also a highly respected person within the Congress. Luckily, I checked with Indiraji. To my surprise, she was not aware of Yashpalji's candidature. I decided to assert myself and told Yashpalji to either withdraw from the fray or face disciplinary action. He was taken aback by my firmness but had to yield. In subsequent years, I saw how senior party leaders often plotted against their colleagues, resulting in the defeat and humiliation of official candidates. Civility prevents me from naming them, but all I can say is that in 1989, I too became a victim of internal sabotage in Meerut, where I had won twice in a row. The culprit is still around as a prominent leader of the party.

Coming back to the party office, I, my husband or our children never viewed 10, Mall Avenue as 'ours'. It was, in a way, a token acknowledgement of the contribution of the Nehru-Gandhi family and a small gesture on my part to honour the ideology I had subscribed to. Several newspapers and magazines, too, published reports of how I, in spite of being the owner, had a sense of complete detachment from the 'property'.

Take, for instance, the resolutions the Congress had passed before independence on issues like untouchability or the abolition of the zamindari system. All zamindars, including my father-in-law, had signed the resolution for scrapping the system. It was purely because of this ideological commitment that the Congress had come to power. Contrast this ideological mooring with that of other parties, and you instantly get the idea why the Congress remained in power at a stretch for so long. Political parties should have clear vision, and the strength to implement it.

Think of the Constitution. It was drafted by learned people who believed in a diverse India that would guarantee the rights of all its people, irrespective of their geographical background, history, religion or caste. Unity in diversity is our main strength and should never be compromised at any cost. Our elders had fought for freedom and had even gone to jail for that; we should respect their struggle. Rewriting textbooks or the history of a country hardly helps in nation-building.

Take the example of Nelson Mandela, who spent twenty-seven years in jail. His sacrifice, his struggle against apartheid, cannot be written off, just like that. When he was finally released from captivity, Mandela spoke of reconciliation and peace. If one sees documentaries on India's freedom movement, the first thing that strikes one is, again, the absence of violence. In 1922, after the demonstrators in Chauri Chaura had taken their fury out at policemen, Mahatma Gandhi had called off the non-cooperation movement as he was opposed to any form of violence. It is this ideological commitment that drove the Congress of the Mahatma,

Nehruji and Maulana Abul Kalam Azad, whose predictions about India and Pakistan hold true even today.

It is because of such a vision and the policies of the Congress that India could develop into a nation where the minorities are protected by the Constitution and are not merely vote banks, but enjoy equal rights and privileges as well.

My gesture of dedicating an office to the party was a small way of paying my respects to this ideology and to the departed leaders who built our country.

9

Road to Parliament

SARCASM IS THE SOUL OF mockery, but sometimes, it can backfire. To the extent that it can change the course of someone's career, taking them from a field of limited influence into a wider arena. My journey to Parliament, the country's august house of democracy, traced a similar path, at least in the initial stages. But before I go further into that, I'd like to take my readers into confidence.

Yes, this chapter is about the Azamgarh by-election, a topic I have dealt with in the early pages of this book, and why it was so vital to the Congress's scheme of things at a time when the party seemed down and out. Barely a year earlier, the Congress had drawn a blank in all the eighty-five Lok Sabha seats in the heartland, winning only one Assembly segment (Rampur) of the 425. However, this chapter is not so much about the election as it is about how I came to fight the bypoll in the first place.

The Janata Party, as everyone knows, came to power in March 1977 after defeating the Congress in the national elections. Janata Party leader Ram Naresh Yadav had won from Azamgarh, but had vacated the Lok Sabha seat after accepting the post of Uttar Pradesh chief minister, necessitating the bypoll so that a new member could be elected to Parliament from the constituency.

Being the president of the Uttar Pradesh Congress, I had visited Indiraji to discuss candidates whose names had been proposed as potential contenders of the by-election. But Indiraji herself wasn't too sure whom she wanted to field. She remained undecided and asked me to come back later with more names. I then suggested Kamalapati Tripathi's name, and Indiraji seemed to agree. She sent one of her aides, Kalpnath Rai, who was also close to Kamalapatiji, to ask the veteran leader if he was willing to take up the offer.

Kamalapatiji, who was much senior to me in age and saw me as his rival in state politics, was reluctant to contest, possibly more so after he heard that I had proposed his name. Instead, he came up with a counter: 'why isn't Mohsina,' he asked Rai, 'contesting this election?'

It was more sarcasm than suggestion but Indiraji took it rather seriously when Rai conveyed the comment to her. By the time we met again, she had made up her mind. 'Indiraji, I think you are scared of the Janata Party and don't want to field a candidate,' I told her when I visited her home, a few days later.

'Mohsina, you go and file your nomination from Azamgarh,' she responded.

I was taken aback. 'Me? I don't have a place there, and you have much better leaders than me for Azamgarh,' I told her. 'You have entrusted me with the responsibility of heading the UPCC and I already have a major task at hand,' I added. 'How will I be able to contest this election?'

Moreover, I had visited Azamgarh only a few times times, I said, and again suggested that Kamalapatiji be made the candidate. He belonged to Varanasi and was considered an influential leader in Eastern Uttar Pradesh. I also suggested the name of Mir Qasim, who was from what was then Jammu and Kashmir state. Indiraji said Mir Qasim might not be interested in coming so far from the

Valley. I suggested another name, Aziz Imam, a popular leader in the heartland, but he had had a tussle with Kamalapatiji.

I later learnt that as soon as the Azamgarh seat had fallen vacant, Indiraji had started gathering information from Congress circles as to who would be the right candidate. In fact, she had already made her decision before our meeting. There was no going back. I tried again, 'Indiraji, I am not sure if I can commit to such an immense and overwhelming responsibility. There are many people within the party who do not approve of me. So, who will I fight, my opponents from within my party or the Janata Party?'

Indiraji seemed surprised. I sensed this was my chance to wriggle out of the electoral tussle and handed Indiraji a letter from the editor of a journal. Before I come to what the letter contained, here's a brief background: the editor, in an issue of the magazine, had published a detailed article about me and which was extremely derogatory in nature. I had been furious but, in accordance with my habit of ignoring nonsense and the complexities of fighting defamatory suits, I had chosen to ignore the article and gone about my work.

I was preoccupied, too, with a lot of things. The upcoming by-election, for one, and the fact that the Congress was yet to finalize its candidate. That was one reason I had come to Delhi to meet Indiraji. What I hadn't known at the time was that the editor, too, had come to Delhi. He had wanted to speak to me and had sought an appointment for a meeting at UP Niwas, where I was staying. I had refused to meet him but he had been insistent. He had refused to leave till I met him. Finally, I had relented.

He started apologizing the moment he walked in. Holding his ears with both hands, he asked for forgiveness for the article he had published in his magazine. This was unexpected and I asked him what had made him change his mind. He said he had recently visited the Press Club and many journalists there had asked him if he had ever met me in person. When he had said that he hadn't, they had told him to go and meet me first and then decide whether what he had written about me could be true. That was why he had come to visit me and apologize personally.

The editor also disclosed the names of some people within the Congress who had sent him piles of distorted information about me, which they had wanted published. 'They gave me money and I went ahead and published it [the material],' the editor added. He then handed me a written apology with the names of the persons involved mentioned in the letter. It was this letter that I had given Indiraji to read and then take a call on whether she still wanted to field me for the Azamgarh by-election.

Indiraji read the letter and then looked at me. 'Don't worry,' she said. 'Prepare to fight the election, I'll take care of the rest.'

Indiraji kept her word. She sent Kalpnath Rai to Azamgarh to rally support for me and some other trusted aides, such as Priyadarshni Jaitley and Gufran Zaidi, to monitor the election situation on the ground. She herself oversaw the arrangements and strategy for the crucial by-election, and even stayed in Azamgarh for five days. By the time she left, Indiraji made sure that she had appointed reliable people for the work that lay ahead, and also for taking care of my security and well-being.

When I filed my nomination, leaders of all the political parties in the fray said the Congress would win the seat. They said I had been active on the ground and people had noticed my work since I had assumed charge as state Congress chief.

Indiraji's decision to ask Kalpnath Rai to organize support for my election had been a clear snub to Kamalapatiji—a message that she won't tolerate dissent within the party. To tell the truth, I never figured out why Kamalapatiji considered me a rival. I treated everyone with due respect, including my opponents. Politically, although I was not in agreement with Kamalapatiji, I had never misbehaved with him. I did what I thought was right, trusting my instincts while listening to my conscience, but had never once been impolite.

Eventually, Kamalapatiji shed his antagonism towards me. I called on him one day to consult him on some political matter. When we finished our discussion and I was about to leave, he suddenly said, 'Mohsina, when you come, it feels like a dense shade has taken over.'

I smiled and left. He had mellowed and finally accepted my leadership. The same Kamalapatiji had once told me, 'Mohsina, I cannot accept you as our UPCC president, so do not come to consult me.'

I had replied,

Kamalapatiji, as long as Indiraji wants to see me as the president of the UPCC, I will carry on with my work, with dedication and commitment. I will keep coming back to you again and again to ask for advice and consult you on issues that demand your advice, for you know better and more on some issues that concern the party. So you will have to see me often, unfortunately.

Indiraji, one day, visited our Lucknow home when I was away in Azamgarh, busy with the by-election campaign. The Congress was out of power but many people had gathered to meet the former prime minister, my daughter Irum told me later. She had not gone to school that day, staying back to meet her mother's 'friend'. I'll step aside for a while here and let my daughter narrate her experience of meeting Indiraji and the conversation she had with her.

Here is Irum's account:

I had stubbornly refused to attend school on that particular day and stayed home to meet my mother's friend. I had begun to think in my naive subconscious mind that she was a part of our extended family, since she had been omnipresent at all times in our lives—in conversations, references and many instances narrated by my mother.

When I did see her that day at home, Indiraji asked me, 'Why have you not gone to school today? Isn't it a school day?'

I replied that I hadn't gone to school because I had wanted to meet her. 'You could have met me any time but the day lost at school will not come back,' Indiraji told me. I was never able to get this out of my head. To be honest, at that moment, I felt a little offended and disappointed. As I grew older, I could make sense of our conversation. The thought and lesson behind this was so strong—a lady who was so busy and preoccupied with so many issues, had the mind space to pay such attention and show such concern towards me.

It has been forty years since the day when Indiraji had dropped by at our home. That Irum still has such a vivid memory of the visit only serves to underscore the effect Indiraji's presence had had on my daughter.

The by-election victory went a long way in restoring the Congress's confidence in Uttar Pradesh. It marked a new beginning for the party, as well as for Indiraji, who emerged triumphant in the Chikmagalur by-election, soon after. As for me, it marked a personal milestone. At the age of forty-six, I became the first party candidate to contest an election on the new 'hand' symbol.

After the results had been declared, I received a call from Indiraji. She wanted me to come to Delhi as early as possible, but it was already late in the evening. Indiraji said she had heard of a new train, the Gomti Express, that left Lucknow early in the morning; if I took that train, I could be in Delhi on the next day.

At the New Delhi station, I was welcomed with beats of drums and chants of 'Congress zindabad'. A victory reception had been organized at the AICC headquarters, which was packed with Congress workers, supporters and leaders. 'Now that Mohsinaji has become a Lok Sabha MP, her stature and respect would know no boundaries,' one of the leaders who was present said in a speech.

Indiraji spoke immediately after. 'With Mohsina now in the Lok Sabha,' she told the gathering, 'the respect of the House would rise with her presence.'

Nearly six months after my success in Azamgarh, my leader, mentor and role model, Indira Gandhi, stunned the Janata Party by bagging an impressive victory at Chikmagalur, Karnataka, where a Lok Sabha bypoll had been held. The moment Indiraji had decided to contest from Chikmagalur, all eyes had turned there. It was a historic election that turned the fate of the Congress around, and ensured its return to power at the Centre; its outcome decided the future of democracy in India. Opposing her in the fray was Veerendra Patil, a formidable Janata Party candidate, and twenty-five others, including someone claiming to be the great grandson of Tipu Sultan.

Indiraji projected herself as the champion of the downtrodden. Scheduled Castes form the single largest group in the Chikmagalur Lok Sabha constituency with about 1.25 lakh votes out of a total electorate of nearly six lakh. We worked tirelessly to ensure the victory of Indira Gandhi in this constituency. Pranab Mukherjee was a key figure supervising Indira's election. We had toured the entire state for eight to nine days, covering all the taluks from Bidar to Karwar. I had stayed put in the constituency for long. Indiraji had instructed me to focus on Urdu-speaking Kannadigas, who comprised over 10 per cent of the constituency.

Mir Qasim, Pranab Mukherjee, I and several others could sense that Indiraji was doing well. But it was a silent poll, in the sense that the voters had kept everyone guessing. George Fernandes was our main rival, targeting Indiraji at every public meeting. He had spread a canard that Indiraji's convoy had hit a girl, who had died. Fernandes, who was Minister for Industries in the Morarji Desai Cabinet at the Centre, was sent to Chikmagalur to lead the campaign for Janata Party candidate Veerendra Patil. Along with party workers, he had travelled to every nook and corner of the constituency and campaigned vigorously against Indira Gandhi. He connected well with the public as he could speak Kannada. In his speeches, he used to ask for one vote and a one-rupee note. There used to be newspaper photographs of Fernandes holding a bucket in his hand, seeking donations. The Janata Party had even tried to rope in Kannada matinee idol Rajkumar, but he had outrightly refused to get involved.

We had coined a slogan that had made it to the national headlines. The slogan '*Ek sherni, sau langur, Chikmagalur bhai Chikmagalur*' was a big hit with everyone. We used to campaign throughout the day and in the evening, we often shared some lighter moments. Vasant Sathe could sing well and once, in Indiraji's presence, he made me sing, too. Indiraji encouraged me to sing and even complimented me.

In close groups, Indiraji was not an introvert. She once showed me a magazine that had a feature on plastic surgery. She had asked how the model before and after the surgery was looking and somehow, both of us did not like the idea of plastic surgery to enhance appearance. Indiraji, in any case, did not believe in makeup except for applying light powder, occasionally, to better tackle sweating, but she did not carry any makeup material.

I remember when the Kannada New Year of Ugadi was celebrated, people in Chikmagalur and elsewhere consumed a mixture of neem leaves and jaggery, which, apart from its mythical health benefits, served as a tangy reminder that life was a mixture of the sweet and the sour.

Often dressed in slippers and a sari, Indiraji was addressed as 'amma' everywhere she visited. She was staying at the residence of Congress leader D.M. Putte Gowda in Mudigere area of Chikmagalur city. Like Pranab and me, Karnataka Chief Minister Devaraj Urs was a central piece of her campaign. She could often be seen asking, '*kahaan hain woh*' (where is yours)?

Interestingly, to woo the Tamil voters in Chikmagalur, we had forged an alliance with Tamil Nadu Chief Minister M.G. Ramachandran's (MGR) All-India Anna DMK. Though MGR had been supporting the Janata Party government at the Centre, he had allowed his party to back Indiraji in Chikmagalur with the sole purpose of isolating the DMK.

Throughout the campaign, I saw Indiraji putting her hand to her chest every time she passed the dargah, mosque, church and temples that dotted the constituency. In her speeches, she would promise industrialization and upliftment of the weakest of the weak.

On the day of the polls, the heavens burst forth in all their fury. But nothing was enough to prevent almost 70 per cent of the electorate—the largest recorded turnout till then in the constituency—from turning up to help her beat her opponent Veerendra Patil by 77,000 votes.

SECTION III

HOW IT ALL STARTED

10
My Roots

WHERE DOES A STORY BEGIN? Do stories have a beginning at all? Some might say that since all stories have an end, there has to be a point where it all began. The truth is, it is up to the narrator where to start; a convenient point, a key moment, or a point where a flashback meets the future. Azamgarh, for me, was one such point—an unexpected intersection where all the signals of my political destiny went green as I picked my way through, reluctant and hesitant at first but increasingly determined to pull it off, as the days passed. That is why I began this autobiographical book with the 1978 by-election, which ensured my entry into Parliament and into the thick of national politics. But it's time to pause now and rewind to where it started in the first place.

I'll begin with my father, Qutubuddin Ahmad Mulla, who belonged to an affluent family of zamindars and was the only son of his parents. His father, Waziruddin, owned a large estate in the centre of Ahmadpur. The village in modern-day Barabanki was founded during the rule of Emperor Akbar in the 1580s. He had intended to build a new, big house in the heart of the village, but had passed away before the plan could materialize.

Qutubuddin Mulla's mother, Ateef Un Nisa's ancestral home was in Daryabad, which enjoys a glorious past. Daryabad, also in Barabanki district, played a crucial role in the freedom struggle and was well-known as a scholastic and literary hub before 1947. My father was the nephew of one of the greatest Quran commentators in the Indian subcontinent, Maulana Abdul Majid Daryabadi. Daryabadi's grandfather was Mufti Mazhar Kareem, who had been sentenced to the Andaman Islands (Kala Paani) for issuing a fatwa against the British Raj.

Daryabadi was actively associated with the Khilafat movement, Royal Asiatic Society, London, AMU, Nadwatul Ulama and several other leading Islamic and literary organizations. In addition to contributing an extensive commentary on the Quran in English, Daryabadi also wrote an independent 'tafsir' in Urdu, published as *Tafsir Majidi* by the Academy of Islamic Research and Publications, Lucknow. He also authored the book *Hakeem-ul-Ummat* in 1950 and authored a biography, *Muhammad Ali Zati Diary*, an engaging account of a great son of India, the late Maulana Mohammad Ali Jauhar, in 1943. Majid Dada, as I would affectionately address him, was highly influenced by Maulana Ashraf Ali Thanwi and Maulana Hussain Ahmed Madani. I can say with pride that my religious orientations have been shaped by Majid dada.

Unfortunately, my grandmother died during childbirth, leaving my father orphaned very early in his life. My dadi's sister, Iffat Un Nisa, who lived in her maternal home in Daryabad with her father, decided to adopt the little boy. My father grew up in his mother's maternal home, unlucky at birth but fortunate to have found a foster mother who made sure that he didn't add to the numbers of the dismal child mortality statistics in that age. In 1880, the mortality rate in India for children under the age of five was 509 deaths per thousand births. This means that more than half the number of children born that year did not survive beyond the age of five. Nothing changed till the turn of the century. The situation has improved since and, in the year 2020, the child mortality rate had fallen to under 4 per cent.

The years passed and Qutubuddin, now a young man, enrolled in AMU, once known as the Oxford of the East. He studied law, as it was considered a respectable profession for the landed class. He was also good at tennis and had even been selected to play for the official university team. After completing his law course, Qutubuddin started his practice under the guidance of his uncle, Masood Uz Zaman, at the district court of Banda. However, he soon left his law practice and took up service in Fatehgarh as the manager of the Court of Wards, which was considered a respectable Revenue post. In 1939, he was transferred from Fatehgarh to Aligarh and finally settled there.

My mother, Zahra Khatoon, was the daughter of Hasan Ur Rahman Kidwai, who belonged to a distinguished family of zamindars, settled in Baragaon village, District Barabanki. Her mother, Mukhtar Un Nisa, was the daughter of the Raja of Gandara (Barabanki), Hafiz Shaikh Asghar Ali.

But before I proceed further, a word about the Kidwais. The Kidwais claim their origin from Qazi Qidwai, whose descendant, Nawazish Ur Rahman Kidwai, a zamindar, had settled in Baragaon. After his death, his property, along with the house, came to his four sons, Nisar Ur Rahman Kidwai, Maghfoor Ur Rahman Kidwai, Basheer Ur Rahman Kidwai and Fazal Ur Rahman Kidwai. Members of the wider family have since branched out to different towns and cities, some even settled abroad; but a descendant of each brother still lives in the Baragaon house to look after the property. I am a direct descendant of Nisar Ur Rahman Kidwai, the maternal great-grandfather of my parents.

The bloodline goes back many centuries to a transcontinental country that bridges Europe and Asia—the rugged highlands of Turkey. Qazi Qidwa, or Muizuddin Kidwai, lived during the Sultanate of Rum or Rum Seljuk Sultanate, a Turko-Persian Muslim state established across major cities and territories of Anatolia, conquered from the Eastern Roman or Byzantine Empire.

Muizuddin had arrived in India along with Khwaja Ghareeb Nawaz Hazrat Moinuddin Chisti (1143–1236 CE) during the reign of Shahabuddin Ghori. He was one of the seventy-two companions of Qazi Qidwa, mostly scholars and Sufis, who had migrated to India then. Qazi sahab belonged to a princely family of Rum (Turkey) and, in India, he was looked upon as a Syed or a noble person. Syeds are incidentally the most honourable, respected, educated and high-ranking individuals among Muslims. In Islamic societies, the title 'Syed' is generally used as an honorific that denotes descent from Muhammad, the prophet.

From Ajmer, where he had reached first, Qazi sahab was asked to proceed to Awadh. Designated as the chief justice of the province, he settled in Awadh. That was how the Kidwais made the region their home as they spread through fifty-two villages of this area, their Sufi influence visible to us even as children.

The Kidwais also played a heroic role in the Battle of Buxar and other encounters with the British Empire. Now that I have briefly touched upon my ancestry, I'll return to my mother and her side of the family. My mother, Zahra, was the second among eight siblings—five sisters and three brothers. The eldest among the eight was my maternal uncle, Shafiq Ur Rahman Kidwai. The younger siblings were Zahra's sisters Zubaida, Ayesha, Humaira and Maimuna, and brothers Khaliq Ur Rahman Kidwai and Atiq Ur Rahman Kidwai.

I may have been introduced to politics after marriage, but politics was in my genes, too. My uncle, Shafiq Ur Rahman Kidwai, was a full-time Congress worker and freedom fighter. Shafiq Ur Rahman, who had married his first cousin (uncle's daughter), often went into hiding but still did not escape arrest and had to spend two terms in jail on charges of agitating against the import of foreign goods. After Independence, the brothers had decided to stay in Baragaon, Barabanki, to manage the family's landed property, which included a farmland and mango groves. But life had other plans for Shafiq Ur Rahman Kidwai.

The Congress fielded him for the Delhi Assembly elections and, although reluctant to contest, Shafiq Ur Rahman Kidwai fought and won. He went on to become a cabinet minister in the first Delhi cabinet and was given charge of several ministries, including Education.

Zubaida, the second among the five sisters, got married to Jameel Ur Rahman Kidwai, and the couple's elder son, Khalil Ur Rahman, was my husband. The 'Kidwai Clan' was really an extension of each of their own families integrated with the rest of the Kidwais of Baragaon—and ever so intertwined and interrelated because of the numerous intermarriages within the extended family. My husband, for instance, was my first cousin, the son of my maternal aunt, who became my mother-in-law after I got married. I'll come back to my marriage later in this chapter.

I was born on 1 January 1932, in Banda, Uttar Pradesh, the third child of my parents who both belonged to educated, affluent and liberal zamindari families. I am tempted to mention here that I was told by the family elders that my father was undergoing many financial difficulties around the time I was born. It so happened that a rich client came to plead for his legal case in the court and gave ₹500 the day I was born. My father fought the case till the high court, where he won. My father always considered me lucky.

We were four sisters and four brothers. The eldest was our brother, Zia, who was followed by four sisters—Husna, myself, Momina and Mateena. The younger three were my brothers, Shahab, Ghayas and Salahuddin—who was better known by his nickname, Sallu. Shahab and Sallu were both good cricketers. Sallu even went on to play test cricket for Pakistan. My basic education started in Fatehgarh in 1936. Three years later, my father was transferred to Aligarh, and from there to Moradabad and then Etawah. The frequent transfers and lack of proper schools meant my education continued as a private student before I cleared my high school and intermediate examination from Aligarh.

Vacations meant an extended reunion of all the Kidwais in Baragaon at the ancestral Kidwai home, about fifteen kilometres from Barabanki. This majestic and expansive home of the Kidwai family was built in 1909 by Nisar Ur Rahman Kidwai, my parents' maternal great-grandfather. He was, as I have mentioned earlier in this chapter, one of the four sons of Nawazish Ur Rahman Kidwai. When Nawazish Ur Rahman had passed away, his family had found themselves under heavy debt. These debts were a consequence of borrowings made by Nawazish Ur Rahman, a man known to have a generous heart, who would give away money to those who asked for help, without paying attention to his own finances. This had resulted in the family's property being mortgaged.

However, Nisar Ur Rahman, the eldest among his four brothers, was financially prudent and started to pay off the debts and retrieve the mortgaged family land. After several years, when the construction of the ancestral home in Baragaon began, there was not much monetary reserve to fall back on to complete the extensive project of building the kothi. The family had to depend once again on borrowed money. This time around, the borrowings were made in anticipation of winning a court case that the family was fighting for the Mehmoodabad estate by Pandit Motilal Nehruji as the counsel and the family's advocate.

It so happened that the Raja allegedly manipulated the new son-in-law of Baragaon, whose name I do not recall, and requested him to withdraw the case. My grandfather did not want to disappoint the son-in-law and withdrew the case. This was perhaps not fully appreciated by Motilal Nehruji as the case was going in his favour and the withdrawal had disappointed him. Subsequent events showed that Raja Mahmoodabad himself softened his stand and went public to express his gratitude to Baragaon. I learnt that a treaty was signed by him, detailing that Baragaon persons, that is, my grandfather and his cousins, were like his brothers. Raja sahab also promised to treat our family enemies as his own enemies.

The Kidwais were undoubtedly expecting a favourable judgment. However, days before the judgment was to be passed, the son-in-law of Nisar Ur Rahman voiced his reservations about the family's prestige coming under the open scrutiny of public courts, even though the reasons were fair. It was then decided that they would go for an out-of-court settlement instead. Motilal Nehruji had insisted on a court settlement, which, in his opinion, would have favoured the Kidwais, but it was neither the tradition nor the etiquette of the elders of the house to disregard or disrespect in any way, the concerns expressed by a son-in-law of the family.

The family was eventually deprived of a vast property, but that did not offend the elders too much, since it had been a collective decision. There was disappointment but the task at hand was soon delegated and responsibilities were fixed. Debts were paid off collectively by all the four brothers. The construction of the Kidwai home was finally completed in December 1909—and has since remained a family haven for the descendants of Nisar Ur Rahman and his three brothers.

About forty-five kilometres from the capital city of Lucknow, this 30 feet tall magnificent structure is divided into four sections—the Kothi, the Naya Ghar, the Hata and Dera—separate quarters owned by each of the four brothers but interconnected from within.

My father finally settled down in Aligarh, and it was here that I received my formal education. A tutor would also come to the house to give all of us siblings lessons in the Quran and on the namaz, and explain the meaning of what we read. He made sure we did not miss any of the mandatory five namaz in a day. My father, an early riser, also made sure we woke up on time for our morning namaz before sunrise (Fajir), followed by the Zohar, to be offered at noon, Asar to be offered during sunset, Maghrib soon after sunset and Isha much after sunset.

Education has always enjoyed a place of pride in our family, irrespective of gender. So after I cleared high school, my father got me admitted into Muslim Women's College, which had been established by educationist Sheikh Mohammad Abdullah (not to be confused with Sheikh Abdullah of Kashmir). The college was affiliated to AMU.

Needless to say, my father, an enlightened man who had received the best education available in India during his time, never insisted that we observe purdah or wear a burqa, as was customary in traditional families—although we were expected to dress modestly. It was only when we visited our great-uncle Maulana Abdul Majid Daryabadi that we used to wrap a chadar (shawl) around ourselves out of respect for him.

While our family was liberal and considered education for women necessary, not many saw it that way. Sheikh Abdullah (1874–1965), for instance, had to face a lot of opposition from the conservative sections of society while establishing the aforementioned institution, but refused to back down, in the process playing an important role in the education of Muslim women. The curriculum at Women's College also included the study of Islam, as the founder believed that religious education was essential for the overall development of character. Sheikh Sahab's daughter, Mumtaz Jahan Begum, was the principal of the girls' college.

It was only after the advent of the British that education in India would be fully formalized, replacing the traditional guru–

shishya, ustad–shagird system. By the nineteenth century, the British government had introduced the British public school system, since education was taken up as an important responsibility by the rulers. Sir Syed Ahmad Khan would later start a movement for the education of Muslims by establishing, in 1875, the Muhammadan Anglo-Oriental College, the predecessor of AMU. He also established a public school for boys from affluent families.

Sheikh Abdullah (not to be mistaken with the Kashmiri politician sharing the same name) would take charge of the education of Muslim girls from the primary level, up to college. Muslims of Aligarh should feel indebted to him for setting up institutions of learning for both Muslim girls.

My life had settled into a rhythm of home and college when, one day, during a family visit with my parents and siblings to Baragaon, it would change unexpectedly. I was busy with household work when suddenly, I was told by our elders that my nikah was going to take place, with my cousin Khalil Ur Rahman Kidwai (my mother's sister's son), later that day. I was stunned, and soon realized that the marriage was actually going to take place. I burst into tears. It was an unusual marriage; there was no special dress for the bride and the bridegroom, no jewellery, no henna, no marriage party, no music—the members of the bride's and the groom's families were common to both, thus all were baraatis (groom's marriage party), as well as the hosts. Khalil Ur Rahman also happened to be a second cousin of my mother's.

Since Khalil Ur Rahman and I were cousins, we had spent a considerable amount of time together while both of us were growing up. That meant there was less of the unknown element in this relationship. Still, the sudden decision of marriage almost instantaneously transformed a carefree girl into a shy and demure, and somewhat nervous bride-to-be. The house, though, burst into a happy fervour of mubarakbad, as everyone congratulated everybody else. The day was 17 December 1953.

Since there wasn't much time, the bride's mehndi (henna) was plucked from the garden (in those days, most homes had henna growing in their backyard) and freshly ground by the nawans. I did not change into any elaborate traditional wedding ensemble, for none was available at such short notice. So the clothes I wore—a pink gharara, kameez and dupatta—were fancy enough for the biggest event in my life until then.

There was a chhoti khala (aunt) who gave me her silver anklet (pazeb) and the silver forehead hanging ornament (jhoomer) so that I at least looked like a bride. The nikah was performed by our uncle Mubashir Hussain Kidwai, the then Chief Justice of Lucknow High Court, who left for Lucknow soon after the ceremony got over.

At that time, after the nikah, the bride was not allowed to go on foot, but used to be carried to her in-laws' house by a family member. My first cousin, Khalida, carried me to my in-laws' house—in the same building. The nikah was followed by dance, music and dinner, and the celebrations went on for days. Frankly speaking, I hardly knew what was happening.

Marriage with a first cousin has its benefits. One knows everybody in the family as well as their habits and traditions. Moreover, since everybody knows everybody else, there is no question of dowry demands. Today, both girls and boys are averse to marrying within the family, especially for reasons related to the health of the offspring.

My mother was the first in her family to have got married to an outsider. From what I have heard from my mother, her marriage was truly an occasion to remember. She told me her father and brother had given them a horse, fully decorated with silver and loaded with shakkar (sugar), as dowry, as she was getting married outside the family setup. My father was not from our family, although he was a resident of the same area, Daryabad.

After my marriage, too, there were elaborate arrangements and many ceremonies. I gradually settled into my married life in Barabanki, where my husband ran a business. His younger brother, Jalil Ur Rahman Kidwai, was a student of AMU. He later joined the Central Drug Research Institute (CDRI). My sister-in-law, Aquila, was a student at Lucknow University. She was fun-loving and full of life, and with her, I got along very well. I remembered her from much before my marriage, when Nehruji had visited Barabanki. On way to the public meeting, Jameel sahab had left Aquila in the car and somehow, during the political discussions, he forgot her. Nehruji spotted her after Jameel sahab had left and he picked her up, calmed her nerves and brought her out, calling out for Jameel sahab, who then returned to see Aquila playing and enjoying her time with Nehruji. Earlier, when Jameel sahab had introduced Aquila to Nehruji, she commented, '*arrey yeh toh insaan hain*'. Nehruji replied, '*toh kiya tum mujhey janwar samajhti thi?*'

My eldest daughter, Seema, was born in 1954, but motherhood was hardly a strain as I had very good support in Sughra, who worked under my employment for decades in an inseparable manner. My children and the rest always addressed her as 'Apa' and her family had been associated with our family for generations. Thus, I had a lot of time to spare, but what I lacked was companionship. I realized this and established a Ladies' Club and gradually got involved in social work. The club was formed and the members decided their main concern would be problems that women faced. We started visiting neighbouring villages and met women, particularly those from the weaker sections, to try and help them.

Soon, we became members of the district Social Welfare Board and I was the choice for chairperson by consensus. We opened a school till class VIII for adults and also trained young women, particularly widows, to become teachers, midwives or nurses. This school is now a full-fledged institute with over 1,000 students. I also played an active role in establishing another centre that trained girls in sewing and embroidery. The products made here were sold in Lucknow and Delhi. The centre was later expanded and a section was set up for providing training in handicrafts to orphans.

Social work or welfare was my first passion and perhaps remains to be, even today. Early in life, I had read somewhere that social work is the art of listening and the science of hope. Somehow this remark still rings a bell. Moreover, Mahatma Gandhiji had taught us that we must not lose faith in humanity. Humanity is an ocean; if a few drops of the ocean are dirty, the ocean does not become dirty. This Gandhian motto kept me going.

Sometime reflecting on my past, I view my stint as chairperson of the district social welfare board as the most rewarding and cherished period of my public life. We ran a successful literacy house, still functioning at Barabanki. Girls used to remain busy in stitching activities and did various condensed courses. I still remember a girl, Uzma, who strived hard to get her B.Ed degree and rose to become the principal of a school. My passion with social work was so intense that when I was nominated by my party to fight the MLC polls, I secretly toyed with a wish to lose so that I remain in the world of social work activities.

My father-in-law was a visionary, particularly concerned with the upliftment of women. He wanted to see women out in the open, holding positions of responsibility. I am basically a social worker, but I am his dream-come-true, too. My husband too supported me at every step I took. Even if it inconvenienced him, he never stopped me from discharging my duties.

11
A Political Phase

I HAD BECOME DEEPLY INVOLVED WITH social work when, one day, life tossed another surprise at me. The year was 1960 and there was a vacancy in the Uttar Pradesh Legislative Council. Chaturbhuj Sharma, who headed the state Congress then, was on very good terms with Jameel sahab. One morning, residents of the area came across a puzzling news item in the local newspaper. A Mrs Kidwai, it said, would be contesting for council membership. People around me could not identify the candidate, but they knew that Jameel Ur Rahman sahab's daughter-in-law was also known as Mrs Kidwai.

When Jameel sahab went to the PCC headquarters, Sharmaji informed him that Mohsina Kidwai had been given the Congress ticket. When Jameel sahab asked him why I had been fielded, Sharmaji said he was aware that I was a social worker. 'I like the work she is doing,' he added.

The members of the electoral college were gram panchayat pradhans and the chairperson and members of the district boards. As all these bodies were then controlled by the Congress, it was not difficult to get elected, but the candidate was expected to canvass for votes. I am grateful that I was successful in getting elected—

not nominated—and became an MLC for six years, according to the rule.

Whatever I am today is because of the support of my father-in-law and husband. My husband was not interested in politics; otherwise he would have been involved in politics by my father-in-law. An active member of the Congress, Jameel sahab was a dedicated follower of Mahatma Gandhi and had worked closely with Nehruji. Unlike other young men from zamindar families, who chose the relative security of government jobs, Jameel sahab was actively involved in politics and the freedom movement, and even spent time in jail as an Independence activist. While in jail, he learnt spinning and switched to wearing khadi.

When I joined politics in 1960, I was the youngest among the women politicians. People don't realize that politics, especially for women, demands a lot of sacrifice, as involvement in public life often means neglecting one's own family. Not only that, for those who have embraced politics as an ideological commitment, it often calls for giving up simple pleasures. Let me cite an example. My move from a young homemaker to the council meant giving up wearing fashionable clothes as well as jewellery. Perhaps it was not much of a sacrifice compared to those who had given up lives of comfort for the cause of the greater good, but then one can speak only for oneself, not others.

When I attended the first meeting of the Legislative Council, it was mandatory to wear khadi. It was a must for anyone who took pride in being a Congress activist. Slowly, I took to wearing khadi even to weddings. Although I was now a politician, social work remained my priority—it helped me remain aloof to the factionalism in the state Congress. Jameel sahab, a committed Congressman, kept away from faction politics and had friends in every group, and I adopted the same approach. Such internal feuds were really a pity when one considers the rich tradition the state

Congress had inherited from its stalwart leaders, such as Pandit Motilal Nehru and Pandit Madan Mohan Malviya, and later, Jawaharlal Nehru. It continued to draw prominent leaders into its fold, among them Acharya Narendra Dev, Pandit Govind Ballabh Pant and Rafi Ahmed Kidwai. Chandra Bhanu Gupta, who thrice served as the chief minister of Uttar Pradesh, and Kamalapati Tripathi, joined the party in the 1920s. Both were members of the Congress Socialist Party, which had been formed within the Congress. They later became rivals and each had his own band of supporters.

The faction politics reached a new low in 1960, when Dr Sampurnanand resigned as chief minister, following a political crisis in Uttar Pradesh initiated by Kamalapatiji and Guptaji. Dr Sampurnanand was later appointed as the governor of Rajasthan. I must, however, put on record that Guptaji had a fondness for me, which may have been because of my age or the rapport he shared with my father-in-law.

Guptaji had been a freedom fighter and preferred to act independently as chief minister, being a firm believer in democracy and liberalism. It is said that the intellectual class was particularly critical of him. Apparently, he was not in Nehruji's good books either, although independent India's first prime minister was a true democrat himself.

Once, at a meeting of the UPCC, party leader Banarasi Das had started criticizing Nehruji, who was also present there. When the other members objected, Panditji requested them to listen to what Das was saying without interrupting him, as everyone had the right to express their opinion in a democracy.

Nehru was on a visit to Lucknow when a senior Congress member, Syed Ali Zaheer, in a meeting with him, complained about Guptaji. Nehruji got annoyed with him and asked Ali Zaheer if he wanted him to behave like a dictator. Syed Ali Zaheer had served as ambassador to Iran and Indonesia and had been a minister in the interim government at the Centre in 1946. He supported the faction led by Kamalapatiji and had even suggested to Nehruji that he remove Guptaji, but Nehruji declined the suggestion. Guptaji continued to have a hold on the state's politics, despite electoral reverses. During the splitting of the Congress in 1969, he opted for the Nijalingappa group.

When K. Kamaraj was appointed the president of the Congress, Panditji had asked him to prepare a plan for reallocation of the work of senior leaders. The programme was launched on 15 August 1963. Under this plan, top leaders and chief ministers were asked to give up their posts and take on party work—those prominent among them being Morarji Desai and Guptaji. Sucheta Kripalani, wife of former Congress president Jivatram Bhagwandas Kripalani—popularly known as Acharya Kripalani—was appointed as the chief minister of Uttar Pradesh. The Kripalanis were prominent Gandhians and had worked with Gandhiji at his ashram. Guptaji took over as the president of the state Congress.

The Kamaraj Plan would play a big role in reshaping the Congress, while politics in Uttar Pradesh were undergoing a major change with the appointment of Sucheta Kripalani. Although she did not believe in factionalism, Kripalani was dragged into it and was identified as a supporter of Guptaji, who had backed her appointment as chief minister. This period also led to the erosion of the party's strength, following defections to the Socialist Party and the Jana Sangh—the BJP's forerunner.

The first defection from the Congress took place in Haryana, followed by those in Uttar Pradesh and Madhya Pradesh, which led to the toppling of the party in several states in 1967. Guptaji stood in the elections to the Uttar Pradesh Assembly in the same year. The party returned with a marginal majority, but Kamalapatiji and Bahugunaji were defeated. Chaudhary Charan Singh, who was re-elected, was given a ministerial post, but he was unhappy as his confidant, Jairam Verma, had not found a berth. That widened the rift between the two factions. Although a ministry was eventually formed under the leadership of Guptaji, rumours would start doing the rounds soon that Charan Singh was planning to defect. The rumours would eventually prove correct.

As packed galleries watched a debate related to allocation of grants for education in the budget, Charan Singh stood up to express his disapproval of the way the ministry headed by Guptaji functioned, and requested a vote on the motion. Charan Singh, along with the majority, voted against the government. Guptaji announced his resignation on the floor of the House then and there, and said he would meet the governor to hand in his papers. Charan Singh's action was welcomed by his supporters and he was voted in as the next chief minister. He was joined by the Samyukta Vidhayak Dal, leading to the formation of a non-Congress government. The veteran leader had a large following in Western Uttar Pradesh, popularly referred to as 'Jatland'. That was the beginning of vote-bank politics among backward castes.

In my assessment, caste considerations were always dear to Chaudhary Charan Singh. He had an emotional bond with the issue. Between 1952 and 1967, he was one of three principal leaders in Congress state politics. He had cut his political teeth under noted freedom fighter and former Uttar Pradesh Chief Minister Pandit Govind Ballabh Pant, first as his political secretary and then as the state revenue minister responsible for land reforms. Driven by personal ambition and his desire to focus on caste-based politics, Charan Singh defected from the Congress on 1 April 1967.

Like Mulayam Singh Yadav, later, he was responsible for the deterioration of Uttar Pradesh politics and the weakening of the Congress in breaking the inclusive social fabric and engaging in caste-based social engineering to get votes.

12
The Congress Splits

President Zakir Husain died on 3 May 1969, the first head of the republic to expire in office. His sudden passing hastened the split in the Congress party. V.V. Giri was the vice president at the time, and a successor to the president's post. But as per the Indian Constitution, the new president had to be elected. The Congress Parliamentary Board fixed a meeting in July that year in Bangalore, and the election was scheduled for August.

Usually, the issue of nomination would first be discussed jointly by the CWC and the Congress Parliamentary Party, and not in the Congress Parliamentary Board. In 1969, the Congress Parliamentary Board raised the matter without issuing a proper notice. Even Indiraji, the prime minister, was kept in the dark.

In her initial years in politics, Indiraji was not assertive due to her own shy nature, strong sense of decency and philosophical attitude towards life, particularly with regard to the trappings of power. Some disgruntled Congress leaders, particularly the ambitious old guard, felt that her only credential was that she was Jawaharlal Nehru's daughter. Pitted against many leaders, the high and the mighty who formed the formidable 'syndicate', Indiraji checkmated them within the organization by repeatedly taking them on and representing the real Congress before them.

Although Indiraji had served as the Congress president for a year under Nehruji in 1959, the test of her leadership came shortly after Nehruji's death, in May 1964. The CWC had asked the then party chief, K. Kamaraj, to recommend Nehruji's successor. Kamaraj had picked Lal Bahadur Shastri over Morarji Desai, practically bullying Desai into accepting Shastriji who, until then, had good 'functional ties' with Indiraji. Shastriji had wanted Indiraji to take charge of the foreign ministry, but she had declined. The prime minister insisted, arguing that as Nehru's daughter, her presence in the Union cabinet would lend it prestige and help him carry out his responsibilities. Indiraji had eventually yielded, agreeing to become the minister for information and broadcasting.

The war with Pakistan broke out in 1965. Indiraji was the first cabinet minister to go to the battlefront. She visited the Indian troops in the field and in frontline hospitals. When the war was halted in January 1966, Shastriji and the Pakistani leadership were invited to Tashkent to sign a peace treaty. Hours after signing the pact, Shastriji had a heart attack and died.

The Congress, which had a majority in the Lok Sabha, was supposed to pick the leader, but the MPs sought the views of the CWC and Kamaraj instead. Indiraji made no move on her own, sensing a sharp division within the CWC. There were several claimants led by Morarji Desai, who was the defence minister, Y.B. Chavan, Jagjivan Ram and S.K. Patil—the Congress boss of Bombay, as Mumbai was known then, and a leading light of the 'syndicate' that controlled the party-led governments in nine states. The CWC was anxious about the party's future and wanted someone popular with a pan-Indian identity to lead them to victory in the elections.

Kamaraj acted as the kingmaker, sounding out Indiraji for the coveted post. Indiraji said she would do whatever her party chief directed her to do. In other words, Indiraji was ready if the majority of the party MPs were in her favour. Desai refused to accept her. A contest was announced on 19 January 1966, nine days after Shastriji expired.

That day, Indiraji got up early and visited Rajghat, Mahatma Gandhi's final resting place on the banks of the Yamuna in Delhi. She stood alone before Gandhi's samadhi. Her next destination was Shantivan, where Nehruji had been cremated. As she stood in silence, Indiraji thought of a letter Nehruji had written to her from prison on her thirteenth birthday: 'Be brave, and all the rest follows. If you are brave, you will not fear and will not do anything of which you are ashamed.'

At 3 p.m. on 19 January 1966, the presiding officer handed over the result to Kamaraj in the central hall of Parliament. Kamaraj spoke in chaste Tamil, announcing the winner. Few MPs and AICC office bearers could understand what the Congress chief had said. The suspense did not last long as someone shouted in excitement: 'Indira 355, Desai 169'. As Indiraji made her way to the dais, dressed in a plain white khadi sari, a fawn-coloured Kashmiri shawl around her shoulders and holding a single red rose, she greeted a grim and sulking Desai with the words, 'Will you bless me in the tasks that I have ahead, Morarjibhai?'

According to those who were present there, a stony-faced Desai had replied, 'I give you my blessings.'

But that was not the end of the internal problems for Indiraji. Desai and the syndicate turned their attention to the Congress organization. The year 1969 saw a group of senior partymen trying to evict her from the Congress, leading to a vertical split in the party. An emotional Indiraji had insisted that Congress membership was her 'birthright' and that she had been irrevocably born a Congress person, many years ago in Anand Bhavan.

'Nobody can throw me out of the Congress. It is not a legal question, nor one of passing a resolution to pronounce an expulsion order. It is a question of the very fibre of one's heart and being.' I vividly recall her words.

It was against this backdrop that Indiraji decided to support V.V. Giri, her nominee for president, against the old guards' choice of Neelam Sanjiva Reddy. Indiraji's party was called Requisitionist or Congress (Ruling) because this faction subsequently requisitioned a meeting of the CWC, party MPs and the AICC to challenge Congress Chief S. Nijalingappa's decision to 'expel' Indiraji from the party.

Indiraji managed to win the support of 310 of the 429 party MPs. At the subsequent AICC meet on 22 November 1969, 446 out of 705 delegates accepted her leadership. Indira Gandhi kept meeting the young members, Chandra Shekhar, Krishna Kant, Mohan Dharia and Shashi Bhushan, popularly called the Young Turks of the party. It was decided that Indiraji should announce to the party members that all were free to support the presidential candidate their conscience approved of. Giri announced his decision to run for the post and Congress members now knew whom to vote for. Indiraji decided to send senior leaders who supported her, to visit different states.

Shri Uma Shankar Dikshit was given organizational charge of Uttar Pradesh. He was not satisfied with the decision; he felt and expressed his advice that Indira Gandhi was to stay in the background. Indira Gandhi did not agree as she felt the decision was hers and she should make it known to the members. Kamalapati Tripathi was not happy with the decision either, but was a strong supporter of Indira Gandhi and thus accepted her decision. Finally, V.V. Giri won.

In 1969, the state of Uttar Pradesh went through a midterm poll, where my father-in-law Jameel Ur Rahman Kidwai contested against independent candidate Mustafa Kamil Kidwai and lost. Bahugunaji, who was elected chief minister, wanted to bring Mustafa Kamil Kidwai to join the Congress. My father-in-law told Bahuganaji and others that if Mustafa Kamil's entry was beneficial for the organization, he had no reservations. In fact, he visited Mustafa Kamil Kidwai's residence and extended all cooperation.

This was a time when there was a strong wave of opposition against the Congress. Thankfully, the party maintained its unity because of its strong sense of discipline.

Soon after the Assembly polls, UP council elections for local bodies were announced. There were thirteen seats, which were to be filled on a rotational basis. The Congress enjoyed a comfortable majority in the electoral college. The two groups within the state Congress decided to share six seats each, and leave one reserved seat for a candidate from a special category, such as women. My name was proposed and C.B. Guptaji readily agreed. Tripathiji, however, had his reservations.

In 1974, Hemwati Nandan Bahuguna was the Congress chief minister of Uttar Pradesh when I was made minister of state for food and civil supplies. In those days, ensuring availability of kerosene was the biggest challenge. Kerosene was in acute short supply in villages, where it was the main source of fuel for cooking and internal lighting in the houses. Rajendra Kumari Vajpayee was my senior minister. We handled the challenge quite effectively with mutual coordination.

Sometime later, I was given independent charge of the social welfare department. I served as cabinet minister for small-scale industries, too.

SECTION IV

DAUGHTERS AND OTHER REMINISCENCES

13
A Mother's Confession

How I ended up in politics as a young mother and homemaker, and how politics with its twists and turns and ever-present intrigue have shaped my life! It has been a long narrative, perhaps not always lucid because I have, at times, moved back and forth. But what I can say for sure is that it has been an honest account. Before I end this part of my story, however, I have a confession to make. While I enjoyed public life to the fullest, I can say that I was somewhat less than fair to my daughters, Seema, Farida and Irum, when they were children.

Seema, born in 1954, was six years old when I contested the council election. Farida, born in 1958, was a toddler then, barely a year old. Looking back, I must say that it would have been difficult to bring up the children had I not been part of a joint family. Today, the social evils being witnessed are all owed to the gradual disintegration of the joint-family system that has now been replaced by nuclear families. This is, of course, my personal view but the growing trend of both parents working means that children now grow up deprived of the nourishing touch of the family's elders and their caring, unconditional love.

But I digress. As I was saying, my plunge into politics meant that my daughters often missed their mother when they needed her the most. Although they were looked after well by their grandparents, it's the mother who plays the most important part in a child's upbringing, and I often think that I really did the greatest injustice to my youngest daughter, Irum, with politics taking up most of my time as I immersed myself full time in public service.

Irum was born in December 1969. She was around seven years old when I took over as the president of the Uttar Pradesh Congress, a post that brought with it huge responsibilities, given the state's importance to Indian politics. In 1977, Indira Gandhi was voted out of power. Not only that, the Congress was routed in Uttar Pradesh as well. It was a blow to my self-esteem and I set about reviving the party with even greater vigour—which meant having even less time for my family.

I remember Irum crying whenever I would step out of the house, especially for outstation work, and then me being miserable throughout the journey thinking of her swollen eyes. Seema and Farida—both young ladies by then—had already got used to their mother's frequent absences from home. But Irum was still a child.

Do I have any message for young women who need to step out of home? Only one. I would say that for a lady, whatever her profile of work—IAS officer, a pilot or a politician—her basic duties towards her family remain unaltered and can never be compensated for by anybody else in the family. Neglect of children can be more harmful to the society in the long-run. I have raised this issue in the Parliament, too, that parents should devote time to their children.

'Words are not enough to express the unconditional love that exists between a mother and a daughter', as Caitlin Houston said.

The person who wrote these words knew what she was talking about—the tender subtlety of a mother–daughter bond that becomes stronger as they grow more compatible over the years.

Only a woman can understand the depth of such a relationship and I consider myself more fortunate than most, because it's a bond that I share with three persons: my daughters Seema, Farida and Irum. Their laughter is the best music I have ever heard. And in Razi, Arif and Javed, my sons-in-law, I have three sons who are known for their integrity, ready wit and easy affability.

The Hadiths of the Prophet (peace and blessing be upon Him) about raising girl children are beautiful and amazing. There is a Hadith or saying of our beloved Prophet Muhammad, that says, 'Whoever has three daughters and is patient with them and gives them to eat and drink and clothes them, they will be a protection for him against the Fire.'

I firmly believe that the basic teachings of Islam do not discriminate much between men and women. It is largely due to the cultural and social ethos of Muslim societies and their human failings that such perceptions of inequalities have evolved. The rights of women granted by Islam are many. Women are, however, often denied what Allah and His Messenger have granted them. In the blessed era of Prophet Muhammad (peace be upon Him) and the rightly guided caliphs, Muslim women enjoyed an equal standing in society and were entrusted with public duties. They had their say in policymaking and governing market trends, and ensured supply of provisions to the battlefield, apart from taking care of wounded soldiers. As far as the *Holy Quran* is concerned, it describes women and men as complementary to each other and as 'soul mates'.[7]

I wish to return to the subject of my greatest accomplishment, and my greatest pride and joy. My three daughters are indeed my greatest successes. I can go on with this emotional rant but will refrain from it. Instead, I will try giving anecdotal accounts of our shared experiences as mother and daughters.

Seema and Farida gave shape to Phool Patti workmanship, a fine applique fabric craft from Western Uttar Pradesh. It was named Brēze and came into being about thirty years ago, when Seema and Farida, along with Sabiha, decided to come together to basically empower the artisans of Phool Patti work in Aligarh. It turned out to be an all-women venture. They mentored the artisans in their personal matters, worked with Contemporary Arts and Crafts (CAC), based in Mumbai. They worked in close association with Dastkar and Sanatkada, which are craft-oriented organizations, committed to artisans. For three decades now, Brēze has been improvising and innovating the designs of Phool Patti, to make it acceptable to the crafts-loving people in India and abroad. Initially, it faced a lot of resistance to change fabrics and designs, but perseverance paid off and the artisans gradually started to believe in their expertise and produced excellent results.

Gradually, artisans' standards of living and incomes rose. My daughters were not merely entrepreneurs. They focused on the artisans' health and hygiene, empowering girl children, looking after their education, mental health and family lives.

Seema is a postgraduate in English and looks after public relations of Brēze and its coordination, while Farida, a management postgraduate, looks after the overall management, design inputs, behavioural issues of Brēze artisans.

Seema, Sabiha and Farida built Brēze Collections, an Indian fashion house, which they founded in 1990 and it specialized in this unique Phool Patti applique craft mastered by women artisans in the interiors of Uttar Pradesh. As we are aware, ethnic chic is in trend, both in India and abroad. India, an ancient land, has an especially rich artistic heritage to draw upon, with myriads of mesmerizing handloom and handicraft forms, to offer to the world. Phool Patti is one such craft and Brēze was the pioneer.

Here, I must add that in Phool Patti craft, every stitch depends upon the nimble fingers of the craftswomen and hence cannot be mass produced, thereby enhancing the craft's exclusivity. Quality control is, of course, essential, along with regular innovations in colour combinations, design and style, to keep pace with changing fashion trends.

Now, in retrospect, I wonder how they must have felt when my entire 'battalion' walked past—television crews and photographers in tow—skipping their stall. Apparently, our family driver too had got annoyed, wondering why everybody's car was going inside while he had to wait outside.

As a minister, I often led delegations abroad but my family seldom travelled with me. Seema, who lived a good part of her life in the UAE, however, reminded me how during the month of Saawan (my favourite season), I would send her saris and bangles. There, too, I was perhaps found wanting. As someone steeped in Gandhian values, I not only wear cotton saris, but also prefer earth colours. While buying my daughters' clothes, I would often opt for colours like beige, brown and mustard. This seemingly 'innocent' colour choice would eventually open our eyes when teachers in Dubai would summon Seema to ask her why my grandson, Adil, drew only using shades like beige, grey, brown and rust. We then realized that it was because we, as a family, had so far exposed him to only these colours.

Not that colour had completely gone out of our lives. What I eschewed in shades, my daughters more than made up for it with their vivid celebration of events. On my seventy-fifth birthday, for instance, when they held a surprise party for me at a house that was vacant. To my delight, there were no political friends or the media; they had invited only close friends and relatives from Lucknow. The food was not only sumptuous but consisted of my favourite dishes, too. It was a memorable day.

The roles had reversed—it was the daughters who were now indulging their mother. In fact, they would do that more often as they grew older, pampering me with praise. They would often tell me that God had gifted me with a good voice. It reminded me of my younger days, as a student at Girls' College, AMU, when I would be called upon to sing at college festivals. But I was uncomfortable appearing on stage, so I worked a way out. I would agree to sing but on one condition: I wouldn't appear on stage but sing from behind the curtain. Introverted and extremely shy, my biggest fear was facing an audience.

Ironically, my plunge into politics left me with little option but to appear before hundreds of people—whether at public meetings or in the state Assembly, or in Parliament. Life, needless to say, is one long series of surprising turns, choices, joys and, of course, adversities.

14
Life Lessons

I WOULD OFTEN PUT SEEMA AND Farida to difficult tasks at short notices as part of their overall education so that they could handle any challenge life might throw at them.

One day, when Indiraji was coming over for lunch, I called home (there were no mobile phones then), asking them to prepare the food within an hour. At another time, one of the guests who was coming over was not only a vegetarian but also avoided garlic and onion. Seema learnt to prepare all such dishes. Sometimes, the number of guests coming over for lunch would go up from twenty to seventy-five. I shudder to think how Seema must have managed, but she always did.

My daughters learnt some seemingly small but significant life lessons from Indiraji. This would include sometime in 1972–73, when Indiraji, who was the prime minister then, had come to our house in Barabanki. Indiraji was speaking on the landline when, with her other hand, she pointed to the washroom. Nobody was using the washroom then but the light was on and Indiraji was trying to tell me to switch it off. Resources and energy were scarce but when your prime minister tells you to switch off a lit bulb in an empty room, it drives home the message that conservation is important, whoever you are, because nothing is guaranteed.

That nothing comes for granted is a lesson that my daughters picked up early. Their mother's proximity to the high corridors of power did not mean automatic publicity for them. That's something I stuck to through the years that I was in active politics, making it a point never to involve my children in campaigns. That did not mean I would keep them entirely away from the thrill of elections. Ahead of polls, my home would turn into an open house for everyone with unlimited supply of tea and food.

My daughters and other family members would write chits for voter lists and make flags and posters, using homemade glue.

Those were exciting times and I treasure these reminiscences as much as I regret other memories of missing parent–teacher meetings at school, for instance. At a time when everybody's parents would be present at such meetings, for my daughters, their grandparents would go. I think they missed me being there and I missed it too.

But what is heartening for me, even now after so many decades, is that my daughters have never regretted that they didn't get a chance to travel in railway saloon coaches when I was minister of railways or the Union tourism minister, or get treated to five-star lunches. They also say with a sense of pride how I never entertained any recommendations, nor encouraged them to recommend anyone.

At times, our insistence on keeping a distance between my public life and our family would lead to interesting situations as my daughters would take care not to let slip that I was their mother. At Lucknow, I would often be invited to be the chief guest at their school or college annual fests, and once it so happened that Seema was the secretary of the Social Service Club of her college and it turned out to be her duty to escort the chief guest (me) to the function. So Seema had been told that Minister Mohsina

Kidwai was coming to the event, without anyone knowing that I was her mother.

I admire my children for their deep understanding of ethics and probity in public life. Often, I feel, they suffered too while maintaining a poise and dignity about the inadvertent slight they had to face. On one occasion when I was a central minister, I decided to visit their stall at a mela at Jawaharlal Nehru Stadium, in the grounds. All the bureaucrats' cars were coming inside, all their orderlies were getting in, but my daughters later told me they had to take everything themselves due to my instructions that neither government vehicle, staff, position or resources should be used for personal advantage. I was the chief guest there but skipped their stall, they tell me now with a smile in the presence of my grandchildren. In retrospect I wonder how they must have felt that my entire 'battalion' had walked past, TV and still camera persons in tow, skipping their work! Apparently, our family driver, a simpleton, had got annoyed too, wondering why everybody's car was coming inside while he had to wait outside.

My children and I were used to living in a joint family. While my political commitments kept me away for the most part during my children's growing years, my in-laws, husband, his sisters and other close relatives maintained a vibrant and bustling household. We also had a majordomo, governess and housekeeper who was more like family and did her best to fill in for a frequently absent mother. My children called her Apa. Her name was Sughra and she had come when Seema was a toddler. She was with us for fifty-four years and passed away at our home in New Delhi on 7 April 2008.

My youngest daughter, Irum, born in 1969, perhaps missed me the most. She used to always carry a particular bedsheet with her which she thought smelled of me! I vividly recall a visit to my hometown, Barabanki, with Indiraji when Irum was young and was living with her grandparents there. From the podium, I could see her and a host of close relatives. I waved and they waved back as Indiraji allowed herself a broad grin.

Maybe, as a mother, she could sense my longing for them. When the meeting got over, we headed back to the helipad nearby and the crowd began to thin down. I suddenly saw someone rushing towards us with a young girl in his arms. Then both of us, Indiraji and I, spotted my brother-in-law carrying Irum, who was crying. I could hear him calling out to us. We panicked and got off the helicopter.

'What happened?' Indiraji and I asked at the same time.

'Nothing, Irum wanted to say goodbye to you and meet you before you left,' Imran Kidwai said, when he had finally caught his breath.

Indiraji was somewhat relieved to note that the 'security breach', as per the prime minister's protocol, was nothing serious. She patted Irum's tear-stained cheek while I too gave her a comforting hug before heading back and climbing up the steps to the helicopter. We kept quiet for a good part of the journey.

Because of my in-laws, my children have imbibed a strong sense of values. While my daughters were growing up, my father-in-law taught them to consider boys as their friends and interact with them in a decent, civil manner without inhibitions. Those days, bell-bottoms were in fashion and my daughters were told they could wear them if they felt like it. It was the same with dupattas, which they were asked to wear if they chose to and according to their own consciences. Ditto about kitchen work. They were never forced or compelled to learn cooking.

The late Sheila Dikshit was very much a part of our household. My daughters' early memories of Sheilaji are of a train journey. Irum was very young then and our overnight train had got delayed. When she started crying, Sheilaji came up and said she had some biscuits and asked me not to worry. She gently asked me to always carry something to eat, especially when traveling with children.

As my children grew older, I could sense their concern for my health and whether I had my meals at the right time. I loved meeting people and a crowd of visitors would come to my Delhi residence on Bishambhar Das Marg each morning, even when I had ceased to be a Union minister.

When Irum was still a kid, she would resent my absence from the breakfast table when I met party workers and visitors. I could sense her resentment, but what could I do? Some of these visitors would come from far-flung areas of the country, at their own expense, just to discuss party matters which they felt was important for the country. Irum, otherwise polite to a fault, would often come into the room when I was meeting these political activists, and give them a time limit. Whenever the allotted time was over, she would intervene. This was terribly awkward, to say the least.

In Delhi, I enjoyed hosting iftar parties. Iftars, which have faded away from the political turf now, mark the customary breaking of the day-long fast at sunset during Ramadan. The legacy of hosting political iftars is attributed to Indiraji, who began the tradition in 1980. In Uttar Pradesh, the move to play host to 'rozedars' was first set in motion by Uttar Pradesh Congress Chief Minister Hemwati Nandan Bahuguna, sometime between 1973 and 1975.

Slowly, Rashtrapati Bhavan too started hosting iftars. As such, there's nothing official about the practice but iftars were held as a sign of goodwill for the Muslim community. The guest list would include leading clerics, eminent Muslims, ambassadors of Islamic nations and assorted political personalities. Modesty prevents me from saying more, but everyone invited would come to the iftar I hosted.

According to protocol, the president and the prime minister couldn't be at the same place at the same time, and were seldom seen together, except at the Rashtrapati Bhavan or in Parliament. But, at my 12, Janpath residence, President Zail Singh and Prime Minister Rajiv Gandhi would both be seen together.

The last time I hosted an iftar was at 80, Lodhi Estate, when the United Progressive Alliance was in power, and Sonia Gandhiji, Dr Manmohan Singh, Sheila Dikshit and Hamid Ansari sahab were gracious enough to visit. There were numerous other guests, too. Keeping in mind the sensitivity of the occasion, both Soniaji and Manmohan Singhji had told me they would prefer to come after the breaking of the fast so that the other guests could perform their religious duties without any hindrance. They arrived immediately after the roza was over and sat with the people.

According to another protocol, the prime minister can leave a place only after the vice president has left. But Ansari sahab said he would stay back for a while as he had met many of his former acquaintances and friends. Nobody noticed that the protocol had been broken.

I am reminded of some of my close associates and fondly recall services of Manorma Bhatnagar, S.S. Kapoor, K.C. Kapoor, Som Sharma, M.S. Rawat, Dr Dataram Juyal and Jayant Mukherjee were also part of my staff. Another key member of my staff was Anwar Hussain, my private secretary. He belonged to Barabanki and had worked closely with my father-in-law, too. He was more like a family member to me. My house was effectively and efficiently run by Ismail. My driver Ram Sundar has been with me for over three decades and still active.

On 16 February 2013, I faced the biggest tragedy in my life when my husband, Khalil Ur Rahman Kidwai, died. My world changed. The pangs of sorrow and grief became an inseparable part of my life. It was both physical and emotional pain. He was the light of my life and his memories still bring me comfort. Khalil may have left this world, but not my heart. As Terri Irwin has remarked—I draw some strength from this,

> Grief is never something you get over. You don't wake up one morning and say, I've conquered that; now I'm moving on. It's something that walks beside you every day. And if you can learn how to manage it and honour the person that you miss, you can take something that is incredibly sad and have some form of positivity.

15
The Premonition That Proved Right

An incident that my family and relatives remember vividly is from September 1982, when I was inducted as a Union minister of state in Indiraji's cabinet. I was going to Delhi by train and we were running late. When the train reached New Delhi station, someone from the Prime Minister's Office was there to pick us up. My daughters were travelling with me and so were some relatives who, because of their memories of the Emergency, were dead against the Congress.

When all of us reached the prime minister's 1, Safdarjung Road residence, my daughter Seema and the others were surprised to see Indiraji waiting for me on the veranda with laddoos. She applied a tilak on my forehead and asked me to go to the Rashtrapati Bhavan and take oath as a Union minister of state. My relatives who had harboured ill-conceived notions about Indiraji were humbled by the sight of her simplicity and her affection for me.

I can say with pride that our family and children followed the best traditions of our country's syncretic culture, epitomized by what is known as the 'Ganga-Jamuni tahzeeb'. Perhaps it was because of my father-in-law Jameel Ur Rahman Kidwai's sense of nationalism and a liberal and secular outlook or the Congress culture directly imbibed from Mahatma Gandhi, Jawaharlal Nehru and Maulana Abul Kalam Azad that we celebrated Holi, Diwali and Christmas with the same fervour as we observed Eid and Eid-uz-Zuha.

Before I move ahead in this chapter on reminiscences, I would like to mention an incident my father-in-law once narrated to me. It happened in 1942, when the struggle for freedom had reached its final phase. One evening, a freedom fighter named Chandra Bhushan Shukla, an acquaintance of Jameel sahab's, came to my father-in-law, pleading for shelter. Shukla said he had been involved in an arson attack on a station and dacoity, and the police were after him.

After hearing about his daredevilry, my father-in-law had told him, 'Shukla, what you have done will take you to the gallows and, if I help, I too will be hanged.'

After a pause, my father-in-law said, 'But now that you have come to us, it is our responsibility to save you. You can stay with us.'

Our village house—an old mansion—was quite big with many passages to slip from one room to another without being noticed. Shukla was sheltered in the house. A police team came to the village to look for Shukla but could not find him. For eight days, Shukla stayed in our house.

After the police vigil slackened, my father-in-law asked Shukla to leave quietly.

These instances once again showed how the national spirit and the nationalism movement had engendered brotherhood to such an extent that freedom fighters would be ready to help each other without any consideration for religion. This tendency continued to nurture among us in independent India, too.

In December 1977, my father-in-law suffered a heart attack and was admitted to a hospital in Balrampur, Lucknow. This was the time the Congress had been routed in the general elections for the first time in independent India. My children would visit him every day, narrate the day's happenings and he would be thrilled.

I was then chief of the Uttar Pradesh Congress but had cut down on my travel and other engagements. Jameel sahab must have sensed something because he would ask me repeatedly when I was planning to get my ticket reserved to travel to Delhi. I would avoid a direct answer and delay reserving a berth. He figured out my reluctance to leave Lucknow. He insisted that I go to Delhi and explained to me how important it was to be with Indiraji at this crucial time.

This was the time a number of senior party leaders had formed their own group, claiming to be the real Congress. My father-in-law, in spite of frail health, told me in a slow but measured voice how Indiraji needed maximum support from her home state and that I was UPCC chief and had a bigger responsibility to ensure that every PCC and AICC delegate stayed with Indiraji. He also told me that in the political arena, many would not believe that I stayed away from Delhi during these testing times for Indiraji because my father-in-law was indisposed.

Finally, I had to relent.

The day Indiraji formed the 'real Congress' faction and we were to move into the new party headquarters at 24, Akbar Road, I received a call from home—Jameel sahab had passed away. It was 3 January 1978. A few months later, I was elected to the Lok Sabha from Azamgarh but my mentor was not there to witness it. Or maybe, he witnessed my triumph from the gates of Heaven, the noble soul that he was.

My election as a MP meant I had to make frequent trips to Delhi. On one such trip, I had gone to attend a public meeting for a municipal by-election, accompanied by party leaders Balram Jakhar and Buta Singh. I had just begun speaking when someone hurled a stone, hitting me on the forehead, splitting the skin open. I was rushed to Wellington hospital by my colleagues and party workers. Five stitches were needed to sew up the wound.

Indiraji left work to visit me in the hospital. She told me this was just the beginning and that there would be more challenges ahead as the Congress proceeded on its comeback trail. Indiraji dialed my Lucknow number and spoke to my eldest daughter Seema, explaining patiently to her what had happened. She said she had visited me at the hospital, and that I had needed a few stitches, but was doing well otherwise. She also specifically told Seema not to panic seeing my blood-smeared picture in the next morning's newspapers, explaining how the media sometimes dramatizes such incidents. Indiraji often came across as an imperious public figure but she never lost this ability to be in touch with her humane side.

In the summer of 1983, my family finally moved from Lucknow to New Delhi. By this time, Seema was married to Razi and Farida had got engaged to Arif.

On 25 October 1984, I met Indiraji for the last time before her assassination. I had gone to discuss some political issues with her about Meerut (my parliamentary constituency in 1980) and remember that something occurred to me just as I was about to leave the room.

'Indiraji, I am not sure if I should tell you this,' I told her, 'but on your recent visit to Lucknow, I noticed you have a lot of new faces in your security. Please be careful, Indiraji.'

Indiraji had smiled. 'Mohsina, I have immense faith in my country and its people and I am absolutely sure from the bottom of my heart that they will never let me down,' she said.

Despite intelligence inputs regarding her safety in the aftermath of Operation Blue Star, a few months earlier, she had not changed her bodyguards, thinking that might send out the wrong signal.

From what I have heard, on the morning of 31 October 1984, Indiraji had kissed her grandchildren goodbye before they left for school. Priyanka, her granddaughter, would later recall that Indiraji had held her longer than usual. Maybe, Indiraji had sensed that death was near. Earlier that month, she had written that if she died a violent death, the violence would be in the thought of the assassin, not in her death, 'for no hate is dark enough to overshadow the extent of my love for the people and my country, no force is strong enough to divert me from that purpose and my endeavour to take this country forward.'[8]

On 31 October 1984, Indiraji began her official engagements with an interview with Peter Ustinov. The cameras were in place when she had begun walking. As she crossed the wicket gate between 1, Safdarjung Road, her residence, to the Congress's 1, Akbar Road office, she acknowledged the greetings of a turbaned security guard. As she smiled back, she saw him pointing a gun at her. Before other guards of the Indo-Tibetan Border Force could reach the spot, the two assassins, Beant Singh and Satwant Singh, had pumped thirty-six bullets into her body.

Indiraji had been advised to wear a bulletproof vest and remove her Sikh security guards, but she had refused to do either. She felt it was unnecessary to wear a heavy bulletproof jacket at home and hated the idea of 'discriminating' among her security guards. In fact, a few weeks earlier, Indiraji had rather proudly pointed at Beant and said, 'When I have Sikhs like him around me, I do not have to fear anything.'

On the morning of 31 October 1984, I had gone to attend an outdoor event organized by St. Stephens Hospital, Delhi. While the event was on, I saw a taxi drive up to where the function was being held. Both my private secretaries were in the taxi. One of them broke the news of Indiraji being shot by her personal security guards. I immediately left for the All India Institute of Medical Sciences (AIIMS), where Indiraji was being operated upon.

Indiraji's death marked the end of a long and eventful chapter in India's history. If the Emergency was a controversial decision, few would deny that Indiraji had made Indians believe in themselves. The India she left behind had progressed in education, science and technology, and power. She had also ensured that the country retained its legacy of culture and diversity, and stayed on the path envisioned by Mahatma Gandhi, Jawaharlal Nehru, Maulana Azad and Sardar Vallabhbhai Patel. The challenges that lay before Indiraji and the Congress were different from what the party had faced before her. But the ideology had remained constant—secularism, respect for diversity, inclusiveness and justice for all, irrespective of caste, creed or religion.

Rajiv Gandhi took oath as India's sixth prime minister, taking up the responsibility his mother and maternal grandfather had both shouldered. While appointing his cabinet, he asked me to join as a cabinet minister. I was overwhelmed with emotion. With Indiraji gone, I told him, it was impossible for me to continue as a minister.

'*Mohsinaji, aap mera saath nahin dengi?*' Rajivji's words still ring in my ears.

16

As Union Minister in Rajiv Gandhi's Cabinet

I WAS RELUCTANT TO JOIN THE Union council of ministers after Indiraji's assassination, but Rajivji sought my cooperation to fulfil his mother's dreams and take up the causes that were dear to her heart. I had the satisfaction of serving my full term, often as the lone cabinet-rank woman minister, and held departments like transport, health and urban development.

I had first served in the Union council of ministers in September 1982, when Prime Minister Indiraji had inducted me nine days after a major cabinet reshuffle. My appointment as minister of state for labour was hailed in the media. I subsequently represented India at the International Labour Organization (ILO) meet at Geneva.

The transport portfolio was particularly weighty as I had three ministers of state under me—Madhavrao Scindia, Rajesh Pilot and Jagdish Tytler. While Scindia was given railways, Pilot looked after surface transport and Tytler, civil aviation. I was supposed to macromanage and accelerate infrastructure development in the crucial transport sector.

On my first day at Transport Bhavan, I was told by officials that the department had been created in July 1942, while World

War II was still on. The work allocated to the department included handling of ports, railway priorities and road and water transport, apart from rationing petrol and producer gas. Later, planning of exports was undertaken as a corollary to the department's transport priorities, too. In 1967, during Indiraji's time, the ministry had been bifurcated into the Ministry of Shipping and Transport and the Ministry of Tourism and Civil Aviation.

Rajivji was a visionary. When he took over as the prime minister after winning a massive mandate in the 1984 Lok Sabha elections, he had got as many as sixty-three departments of the Union government redrawn first, and forged new departments that attended to as many as 1,500 subjects. Accountability was the buzzword. As a magazine in that era had reported, the transport ministry had taken charge of everything that moved—via rail, roads, sea and air.

Rajivji had also decided to rename the Ministry of Education as the Ministry of Human Resource Development, and P.V. Narasimha Rao was appointed as its minister. Many other ministries and departments, such as Culture and Youth and Sports, were brought under the HRD ministry and ministers of state were appointed. Even the Department of Women and Child Development—which became a separate ministry with effect from 30 January 2006—was a department under the Union HRD ministry then.

I was the head of the omnibus transport ministry, but shared the cake with the three young ministers, all of them favourites of Rajivji. I had become extremely fond of Tytler, Pilot and, of course, Scindia. Meetings used to be great fun with either Scindia or Pilot cracking jokes and Tytler often quoting from scriptures to drive home a point. It is unfortunate that both Scindia and Pilot died young, one in an air crash and the other in a road accident. They had great potential and could have taken the nation to greater heights had they been around for longer.

In 1986, as head of the transport department, I had made a modest contribution towards preserving the environment, long before climate change and conserving nature had become part of mainstream discussions. I had then shelved a proposal that railway kulhars and leaf plates be replaced by their plastic versions. Nisheeth M. Katara, my efficient and far-sighted officer on special duty, backed me and together, we filed an objection to the proposal. The matter ended then and there. Had I continued for longer, India's railway tracks, now littered with plastic, may have looked better today.

Before moving to the transport ministry in September 1985, I had handled the Union health ministry, a responsibility I greatly enjoyed. It must be mentioned here that following the experience of family planning during the Emergency, sterilization and population control had become dirty words. So Rajivji had aptly dropped the name family planning, but it remained a priority area for both of us and was renamed as health and family welfare.

'The [family planning] programme has had a bad history and it is imperative that we now create a positive climate, involve every body and dispense adequate supervision,' an issue of the *India Today* magazine had quoted me as saying at that time.[9]

At meetings with experts, among them demographers, social scientists and members of voluntary agencies, Rajivji would emphasize the magnitude of India's population. We would remain closeted for hours as Rajivji sought to understand the complex issues at stake. He had even set up an autonomous non-profit society, known as the Contraceptive Marketing Organization (CMO), which had a governing board, made up of secretaries to the government, its own directors and representatives of manufacturers, as well as of two advisory councils.

I had a holistic approach towards family welfare and, along with my ministry officials, tried to motivate the masses through the media. At that time, Doordarshan ran a popular soap opera, *Hum Log*. The original plan was that my ministry, in conjunction with the Ministry of Information and Broadcasting, would fund the serial, aimed at tackling a host of social issues, including family planning. But as the programme gained mass appeal as a family serial, the focus on promoting family planning was inevitably dropped.

We helped many private players produce family planning-oriented programmes for television and held consultations with the advertising industry for better, forceful campaigns. For instance, as *India Today* in July 1985 had reported, the Do Ya Teen Bas campaign of the 1970s evolved into the 1980s. The Ministry of Health and Family Welfare had consciously recommended that the first child is delayed, the second is conceived with at least three years' space from the first and plans for a third are abandoned altogether.

I have had the satisfaction of initiating schemes for medicine distribution and pricing, among others, which brought relief to many. As a minister, I was also instrumental in supporting the nursing staff at the institutional level. I do not want to go on enlisting my achievements but wish to add here that I laid focus on major reforms and out-of-the-box thinking so that old restrictive, bureaucratic obstacles could be removed.

Rajivji's government handled a big drought in 1987 with exemplary zeal and discipline. The economy soon bounced back, with a real annual growth rate of around 5.4 per cent compared with the 3.5 per cent 'Hindu rate of growth' over the past twenty-five years. The industrial growth rate, at over 9 per cent, was another indicator of better economic management.

When I was appointed as the urban development minister, we worked hard to present the Nagarpalikas Bill 1989, on the lines of the Panchayati Raj system, ensuring genuine decentralization of power.

Let me state this before I move further. In keeping with Gandhiji's vision, we had committed ourselves to political decentralization soon after Independence and set up a system for elected panchayats to manage rural problems. But Rajivji realized that after four decades, this system had been steadily emasculated. Moreover, the jurisdiction of panchayats and nagarpalikas (municipalities) were not carefully defined and their financial resources, too, were restricted.

So, in 1989, Rajivji moved two historic amendment bills in an attempt to rectify some of these deficiencies. In the first place, they would make panchayat elections mandatory. The bills also fixed the tenure of local bodies at five years and mandated that elections must be held within six months of supersession. These provisions, it was argued by those who framed the bills, would act as adequate safeguards against the political whims of ruling parties. Furthermore, the bills provided new schedules to define the broad spheres of activity of panchayats and nagarpalikas and authorized state legislatures to define their financial powers and set up state finance commissions to review their financial position once every five years.

Seemingly, all political parties in the Parliament wanted these bills passed but the Opposition got it dropped in the Rajya Sabha by five votes. L.C. Jain, an avowed Janata Dal supporter, was also in favour of the bills. 'It [the bills] may have been brought in by one party, but all stand to gain,' he kept saying, but the Opposition ranks did not hear him.

Indeed, a week later, when I returned, I was the country's new transport minister. Rajivji had so much faith in me that he had informed me in advance what responsibility I was going to be entrusted with. In 1988, Rajivji carried out another shuffle, giving me additional charge of the ministry of tourism.

I also had the distinction of serving as union rural development minister under both Indiraji and Rajivji between August to December 1984. Since the inception of planning, three basic goals for rural development have been faster growth, equity and self-reliance. At the same time, our Five Year Plans had the objectives of eliminating poverty and ensuring equitable distribution of gains of development. Development of rural areas has been one of the abiding concerns of successive Five Year Plans and has remained a priority item.

For Indiraji, the concept of Integrated Rural Development Programme (IRDP) emerged from the realization that the rural poor enjoy benefits on a lasting basis when there is simultaneous development of agriculture, industry and tertiary sectors. Various programmes meant for the poor had to be coordinated at the micro-level and the weaker sections were aimed to be provided with appropriate assets and services in the right sequence and at the right time. I was happy when Indiraji often allowed my arguments to prevail in official meetings, pointing that I had ears on the ground.

My understanding of the Sixth Plan (1980–85) was that it was essentially an anti-poverty programme. IRDP was extended to all the 5,011 development blocks in the country. It had also become part of the Indira government's 20-Point Programme. Sixth Plan had accepted poverty alleviation in the rural sector as its prime objective and had optimistically proposed to increase the productive potential of the rural economy as an effective solution to the problem of rural poverty. IRDP had offered employment opportunities for people in the rural area during off-seasons and thus increasing their productive capacity.

The first step of the procedure was to conduct a household survey for identification of targeted families. Second was limiting the preliminary survey families' owning or operating to less than 5 acres of land and other families, whose income, prime facie, was less than ₹3,500 per annum, and classification of the families according to various income ranges. Third involved the selection of the poorest among the poor for assistance under the programme.

We had given high priority to the coverage of Scheduled Castes and Scheduled Tribes.

Subsequent studies showed that financial, physical and qualitative aspects of these achievements exceeded the targets decided by us. The total number of SC/ST beneficiaries exceeded the target and the achievements in this respect were at 110 per cent. This spoke very well of the social justice credential of the programme, even as the per household investment had gone up from ₹1,642 in 1980–81 to ₹3,339 in 1984–85. There was also a definite shift in the sectoral coverage pattern with the secondary and tertiary sectors activities together having increased from about 6.44 per cent in 1980–81 to about 45.5 per cent in 1984–85.

17
My Foreign Visits

As a minister, I had the good fortune to travel to several countries as India's representative. One of the countries I visited was the German Democratic Republic (what was then East Germany) where I had gone as a delegate to attend a women's conference. I also attended a World Peace Conference in the then USSR and inaugurated a restaurant in Moscow during the visit. Among other global meets where I was present was one organized by the United Nations Centre for Human Settlements. Another time I represented India was at a SAARC summit. I was also part of the delegation that attended Algeria's twenty-fifth Independence Day in July 1987, when I was urban development minister at the Centre.

Another country I visited was Vietnam. That was after Aruna Asaf Ali, the independence activist hailed for her bravery during the Quit India Movement, had called up the prime minister with a request to send me to Vietnam. When I met the prime minister before leaving for Vietnam, he said I was going as health minister but would return as the transport minister.

Once, I was the guest of honour on the national day of Brunei that falls on 23 February. The day marks the nation's Proclamation of Independence from British control on 23 February 1984. I was asked to carry the President of India's message and represent my country on the occasion. It was a matter of great pride. Always particular about protocol, I reached the parade ground much before 9 a.m. but the chief guest, the Sultan of Brunei himself arrived half an hour late. It was amusing as many dignitaries had been kept waiting.

The main elements binding India and Brunei are: (i) Brunei is an important source of crude oil for India and its contribution to our energy security is significant; (ii) Brunei's role as an important ASEAN country gained prominence with the hosting of Eleventh ASEAN–India Summit. (iii) Brunei has an 11,500-strong Indian community. I was pleasantly surprised to meet many Indian expatriates who hailed from Azamgarh. They came to see me after hearing that I was representing India.

The high point for me on foreign visits was the opportunity to address the United Nations General Assembly as India's urban development minister in April 1988. The focus was on human settlement. I spoke telling the world how we needed to ponder over the growth of urbanization and population. I drew the world's attention to the quality of water and air. I also got an opportunity to highlight the Indian experience of developing the village economy, providing shelter to the urban poor, the national urban housing policy and preparing the legal and institutional framework for the housing for all objectives.

I greatly cherish my visit to the USSR, while Inder Kumar Gujralji was the Indian ambassador in Moscow. Gujralji introduced me to the various facets of Russian society, theatre, literature and lives of industrial workers and working women. It was a great learning experience. At official banquets, each time I was asked to raise a toast, I would deftly throw it away because drinking or participating in the ritual was against the tenants of my faith. My memories of visiting Hungary, Germany, Switzerland, Saudi Arabia,

UAE, Pakistan and a number of other countries are extremely fond and full of meeting some of the most remarkable personalities, politicians, public servants, chefs, intellectuals and others from diverse walks of life.

I was going to Maldives in December 1988, when I suddenly received a communication that Prime Minister Rajiv Gandhi wanted me and my ministerial colleague, H.K.L. Bhagat to go to Islamabad. A special aircraft took us to the Pakistani capital. Rajivji, a peacenik, was attempting to usher in a new, more peaceful era of Indo-Pak relations. He was in Islamabad to attend the fourth summit meeting of the SAARC, which was held between 29 and 31 December 1988. Behind the scenes, both the Indian and Pakistani governments had been working overtime to ensure that the visit did indeed take place.

Benazir Bhutto had assumed the office of prime minister only four weeks ago. For her, this was the first opportunity to host leaders from across the region and liaise with them. After she had been sworn in, Rajivji had sent her a message of felicitation and expressed hopes that their mutual efforts could bring about peace and prosperity to both countries and the region at large. When Rajivji met Benazir Bhutto, he made me sit on his right, while K. Natwar Singh, a career diplomat turned politician and now a minister, sat on his left.

There was a hilarious episode that I remember even now. We were chatting with Begum Nusrat Bhutto, mother of the PM, who was heading the Pakistan Peoples' Party (PPP) then. Somehow, Bhagatji mistook her to be Benazir and kept complimenting her on her 'youthful' looks diplomatically. It was turning awkward until Natwar Singhji sensed Begum Nusrat's discomfort and gently told Bhagat about Begum Nusrat's background and status in the Bhutto family. On our way back, when Natwar Singh told Rajivji about the episode, everyone had a good laugh.

18
The Breakaway Congress Experience

AFTER INDIRAJI'S DEATH, WHEN THERE was gloom and darkness all around, Rajivji had approached me and P.V. Narasimha Raoji to lead the ashes procession along with members of the Nehru-Gandhi family. Even thinking about it now, tears roll down my cheeks—so painful, it was. Yet, looking back, I feel privileged that he and his family had so much faith in me. It also made me feel a sense of belonging, which is difficult to express, but then close bonding is something that words have seldom been able to define. Rajivji had said that he chose me and Rao sahab keeping in mind his mother's proximity to us.

After Rajivji's assassination, Rao sahab took over as Congress president under difficult circumstances. It's possible that when Soniaji learnt that Rao sahab had been chosen to lead the party, she did not oppose his candidature—which was seen as her endorsement of the appointment. She was, in any case, hardly in the frame of mind to think about such issues.

Within the Congress, Rao sahab was considered a recluse. Even at the age of seventy-one, and after spending decades in the party, there were many who knew little about him. He had been the chief minister of Andhra Pradesh and a Union minister for external affairs, human resource development, home and finance, among other portfolios. His long stint in Delhi had made him somewhat of an outsider in his native state of Andhra. But in Delhi, he had many friends and admirers. Indiraji, for instance, had been extremely fond of Rao sahab and had even given him key assignments in spite of stiff opposition from some towering leaders of Andhra. Rao sahab was among the few who had access to Indiraji's residence.

Rajivji, too, had found much to admire in Rao sahab, including his low-key style of functioning, interest in technology and his ability to defuse even the most volatile of situations.

Running a government with the help of outside support was not easy. I vividly recall how after the Babri demolition when P.V. Narasimha Rao sahab was the prime minister, and how the Sangh parivar and the BJP blatantly mixed religion with politics. About Rao sahab, I feel, there were many issues where his handling of situations was, at best, a mixed fare. He excelled at handling the economy with the help of his finance minister, Dr Manmohan Singh, but in the political arena, he would often be surrounded by advisers who were not too sincere either towards him or the party.

That was also a time when, on the personal front, I was in turmoil as my younger brother, Ghayas, was not well. Doctors in both Saudi Arabia and in Canada—otherwise known to have excellent medical services—were not too optimistic about his condition. I had brought him to Delhi and, after a long period of treatment, his health had started improving. As I was both mentally and physically occupied with Ghayas and his family, I could not devote much time to politics and, perhaps, met Soniaji far less than usual.

Many of my party colleagues—N.D. Tiwari, Arjun Singh, M.L. Fotedar, K. Natwar Singh, K.N. Singh and Sheila Dikshit—felt that all was not well in the Rao government, whether it was with regard to issues related to the Ayodhya dispute, the economic reforms which were seen in many quarters as being anti-poor, the tardy probe into Rajiv Gandhi's assassination, or the alleged cases of corruption. They felt, not without reason, that some Nehruvian principles of secularism, plurality, non-alignment and left-of-centre economics were being tinkered with.

This group also raised the 'one-man, one-post' norm, a Congress tradition from the time of Nehruji that ensured that the leader of the party and the prime minister were not the same person. Rao sahab and his supporters had refused to oblige. In 1994, Arjun Singh and some others tried to force a vote at an AICC session at Surajkund, but the Rao camp carried the day with a resolution that in the case of the prime minister, an exception to the one-man, one-post principle should be made.

By early 1995, Rao sahab had succeeded in securing a majority in the Parliament, following defections from the Janata Dal. Congress dissidents came out in the open for a final showdown on 19 May 1995, at Talkatora Stadium, New Delhi.

Fotedarji had come to meet me before the Talkatora session, claiming that Soniaji was unhappy with Rao sahab and wanted me to join Arjun Singh, N.D. Tiwari and others who had challenged Rao sahab. As I have stated earlier, my mind was then preoccupied with my brother's illness and other domestic issues. I believed Fotedarji's words and regret not having checked with Soniaji personally. In retrospect, I feel I should not have become part of the breakaway group that was called Congress (Tiwari). With many senior leaders around, had we fought internally about issues that were dear to us, perhaps the course of the future polity would have been better and brighter for the Congress.

As far as I know, Soniaji has never publicly commented on what actually happened in May 1995. However, before she took over as the Congress chief in 1998, she ensured that all factions who had left the parent organization were taken back in the fold with respect and dignity. Other than the Congress (Tiwari), the groups

Indira Gandhi visited my Lucknow residence at 6-Darul Shifa. Seen with her is my mother-in law Zubeda, my daughters Seema and Irum, sister-in-law Aquila, nephew Fuad, sister-in-law Sultana and aunt Habiba.

Prime minister Rajiv Gandhi walking in with former Lok Sabha speaker Dr Balram Jhakhar at my 12, Janpath residence. My husband, Khalil, can be seen just behind me.

Travelling by train for a poll campaign with Sonia Gandhi

At a public meeting

President Dr Shankar Dayal Sharma gracing my 12, Janpath residence

At Congress president Sonia Gandhi's residence with my youngest daughter Irum, son-in-law Javed Matin and grandchildren Omar and Zehra

Rajiv Gandhi at my 12, Janpath residence

With Sonia Gandhi in Himachal Pradesh. Also in picture is party colleague Vidya Stokes

Happy times of the UPA: R.K. Dhawan on my left; on the right: Dr Karan Singh, Arjun Singh, Pranab Mukherjee, A.K. Antony, Shivraj Patil, Dr Manmohan Singh, Sonia Gandhi, Motilal Vora. Also, in the picture (standing) are my young colleagues Digvijaya Singh, Ambika Soni, Saifuddin Soz, Mukul Wasnik, Rahul Gandhi and others.

At the United Nations

Me and Rahul Gandhi

At the Congress party conclave in Mount Abu. Sonia Gandhi facing us: me with Ambika Soni, Archana Dalmia and Margret Alva

My brothers and sisters (L-R): Salahuddin, Ziauddin, Ghayasuddin, Shahabuddin, Momina, Husna, me and Mateena

Newly wed me with husband Khalil Ur Rahman Kidwai

Me at a younger age

Standing (L-R): Brother Ghayasuddin, brother Ziauddin, brother-in-law Kazi Moinuddin, brother Salahuddin, brother Shahabuddin; sitting: sister Mateena, me, sister-in-law Haseena, mother Zehra, father Qutubuddin Ahmed, sister Husna, sister Momina, nephew Fahim; front row: niece Samina, niece Jabeen, nephew Javed, nephew Shiraz, niece Tehmina

Standing (L-R): Me, eldest brother Ziauddin, elder sister Husna; sitting (L-R): younger sister Momina, father Qutubuddin, mother Zehra, sister Mateena, Shahabuddin (with father)

Daughter Irum showering affection

My three daughters (L-R) Irum, Farida and Seema, who mean a world to me

Standing (L-R): Son-in-law Arif, grandson Faraz, granddaughter Kulsum, daughter Farida, daughter Seema, son-in-law Razi; sitting (L-R): grandson Adil, daughter Irum, me, granddaughter Zehra, husband Khalil, grandson Omar

With my entire clan, almost, at my ancestral home in Badagaon in Barabanki, Uttar Pradesh
Photo credit: Fuad Kidwai

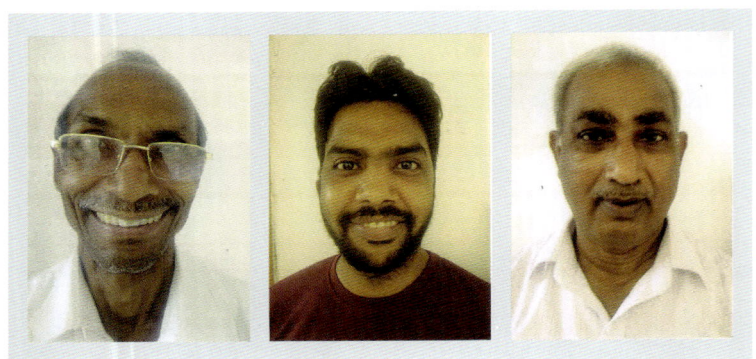

Left to right: Ram Sunder, driver for over three decades;
Anis, household help; Ismail, housekeeper

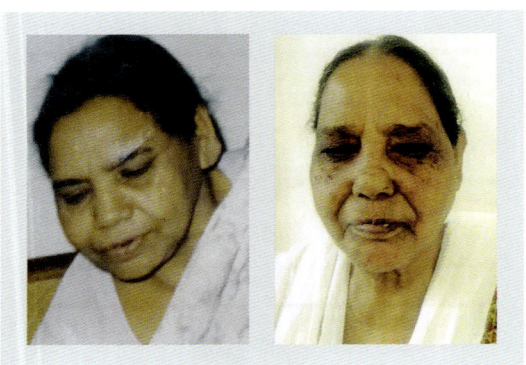

Left to right: Sughra, apa to my children, second-generation housekeeper-cum-chef, life-long association; Kaneez Fatima (Chhammi), housekeeper for over seven decades

led by Madhavrao Scindia and former Karnataka chief minister S. Bangarappa were also brought back. As AICC chief, Soniaji accorded importance and respect to those who had left the party during the Narasimha Rao regime. At the same time, those who had actively sided with Rao sahab were not ignored or sidelined either. She was the head of the Congress and treated everyone equally—never an easy task to practise.

I must also mention here that during the Rao era, specifically on 24 August 1995, Soniaji had gone public to express her deep sense of anguish over the delay in the trial for the Rajiv Gandhi assassination case, while addressing a large gathering at Amethi, the Uttar Pradesh constituency she would represent in Parliament from 1999 to 2004. In her seven-minute speech, she asked Amethi's citizens to share her vedna (pain) at the delay. She said if a probe into the assassination of a former prime minister could take so much time without making much headway, what might be the plight of ordinary citizens seeking justice? 'You people can understand my feelings,' she said in fluent Hindi, thumping the lectern as she complained about the slow progress of the investigation and the pace of the judicial system in the country. 'There is divisiveness all around,' she had added. 'This is the time when we should follow the example set by those leaders for whom the nation stands above everything else.'

Her words still echo in my ears.

SECTION V

INDIAN POLITICS (1947–2022)

19

Hope, Turbulence and Tragedies

Long years ago we made a tryst with destiny, and now the time comes when we shall redeem our pledge, not wholly or in full measure, but very substantially. At the stroke of the midnight hour, when the world sleeps, India will awake to life and freedom. A moment comes, which comes but rarely in history, when we step out from the old to new, when an age ends, and when the soul of a nation, long suppressed, finds utterance. The ambition of the greatest man of our generation has been to wipe every tear from every eye. That may be beyond us, but so long as there are tears and suffering, so long our work will not be over. And so we have to labour and to work, and work hard, to give reality to our dreams. Those dreams are for India, but they are also for the world.

—An excerpt from Jawaharlal Nehru's 'Tryst with Destiny' speech, 15 August 1947

I HAVE BEGUN THIS CHAPTER WITH one of the greatest speeches ever made by a leader and one that has been quoted or excerpted millions of times since that triumphant midnight of newly wrested liberty. Apart from being a soul-stirring peroration, the speech also aimed at putting into context the tasks that lay ahead. My purpose in beginning with this excerpt is to use it as a touchstone to gauge whether those who came after Nehruji have been able to live up to the transcendental essence of what independent India's first prime minister had envisioned for us.

Seventy-four years have passed since and this section is an attempt to trace that journey from 1947 to 2022. Some of my readers might not agree with my views, but I am perfectly comfortable with that. This is a memoir and I am not a historian, so personal biases are bound to intrude. Also, often I might digress in my narrative as I travel back and forth, since politics, unlike projectiles, rarely travels in a straight line. So my readers will have to bear with me just a little more.

Among the early influencers of Indian politics, Nehruji would always be remembered as the man who helmed a newly independent nation ravaged by serious socio-economic problems, a legacy handed down by the British who plundered our economy and played on deep-rooted communal antagonisms in their bid to further their own objective of 'divide and rule'. At that crucial point in India's history, Nehruji and his fellow Congress leaders had carried forward Mahatma Gandhi's compassionate vision of governance, combining it with a modern scientific approach to policymaking.

Nehruji's deep belief in scientific socialism and the stress he laid on cultural harmony helped create a polity that had no religious preference. So India's journey, that started on 15 August 1947, became a role model for progressive and inclusive development, besides strengthening its position in the world. Nehruji was a true statesman and we, the people of India, should be grateful to him forever.

Lal Bahadur Shastriji, who assumed charge as prime minister in June 1964, should be remembered for upholding the ideals of the freedom struggle and also for guiding the country through experiments in the early years after Independence, as it navigated the uncharted territory of inclusive growth.

Shastriji was an ideal successor to Pandit Jawaharlal Nehru. Son of a humble schoolmaster and orphaned at a tender age, he knew what poverty meant. A diligent freedom fighter, who had spent nine years in prison during British rule, Shastriji had numerous qualities—a strong sense of purpose, zeal, gentleness and humility, moderation in speech and decisiveness in action, all backed by his homespun wisdom, humour and unwavering common sense.

I had been hearing about political activities at home because my maternal uncle, Shafiq Ur Rahman Kidwai, had begun taking part in the Khilafat movement. My first memories of Shastriji date back to sometime in the early 1950s—a few years after marriage. Before marriage, I hardly took any interest in politics, although I would get to hear about political developments from time to time because of my uncle. After marriage, I found that politics was a part of life in my marital home. That was how I saw Shastriji, who had come to meet my father-in-law. Jameel sahab had stood for the elections and Shastriji was canvassing for him.

Shastriji was a simple man. Our domestic help, who did not recognize him, asked him where he had come from. Shastriji, by then already a Union minister, replied that he had come in connection with the election and wished to meet Jameel sahab.

'He will return home in the evening,' the domestic help told Shastriji and asked him to wait. Shastriji waited. The servant served him tea. In the evening, when my father-in-law returned, he saw Shastriji waiting. A little embarrassed, my father-in-law scolded the servant for not informing him about the guest. After that, Shastriji went on to become a member of our extended family.

On 2 June 1964, six days after Nehruji's death, this remarkable person who had risen gently to the top of Indian politics without making a single enemy, was unanimously chosen by the Congress to be its parliamentary leader and, in that capacity, to serve as Prime Minister of India.

In his first address to the nation as prime minister, Shastri had said,

> There comes a time in the life of every nation when it stands at the cross-roads of history and must choose which way to go. But for us there need be no difficulty or hesitation, no looking to right or left. Our way is straight and clear—the building up of a socialist democracy at home with freedom and prosperity for all, and the maintenance of world peace and friendship with all nations.

Needless to say, India–Pakistan relations occupied most of his time and energy during the nineteen months he ruled. 'India and Pakistan are two great countries linked together by common history and tradition,' he had declared, at the very outset of his onerous stewardship.

> It is their natural destiny to be friends with each other and ... close co-operation between these two countries will not only be of immense benefit to them but will [also] make a great contribution to peace and prosperity in Asia. For too long have India and Pakistan been at odds with each other ... We must reverse the tide. This will require determination and good sense on the part of the governments and people of both India and Pakistan.

But peace is a two-way street. Early in 1965, Pakistan sent troops across the border in Kutch to enforce its claim to territory in that region. Shastriji acted with decision and courage. 'We would prefer to live in poverty for as long as necessary but we shall not allow our freedom to be subverted,' he declared.

War led to a shortage of foodgrains. The United States also threatened to stop export of foodgrains to India. Shastriji, who was aware that the country was dependent on food imports from America, didn't nod his head and said that the war by America in Vietnam was an act of aggression too. His statement wasn't received well by America, and they stopped food exports to India under a Stop-go policy. India was then in such dire straits that the Food and Agriculture Organization of the United Nations had to appeal to the US to resume food exports.

Shastriji urged the people of the country to fast once a week. Not only that, he set an example himself. In his family, he said, the 'stove will not burn in the evening for one week from tomorrow'. The announcement had such an effect that it was followed even by restaurants and hotels for a few days. Shastriji also appealed to his countrymen to donate funds to combat external threats and set up the National Defence Fund for that purpose.

The Government of India appealed to former rulers, too, for their help. As prime minister, Shastriji approached the Nizam of Hyderabad, Mir Osman Ali Khan, who contributed five tonnes of gold for the National Defence Fund. At today's gold price, the Nizam's contribution would have translated to a whopping ₹2,000 crore.

Shastriji knew and understood the significance of soldiers and farmers, and came up with the slogan '*Jai Jawan, Jai Kisan*' (Hail the Soldier, Hail the Farmer), which continues to be one of the most popular slogans in the country to date. The war with Pakistan came to a halt on 23 September 1965, under the terms of a UN Security Council resolution.

Shastriji, who had earlier underscored that peace was more important than living from ceasefire to ceasefire, outlined how such viable peace could be brought about, in a broadcast to the nation on the day the ceasefire came into force. 'While the conflict between the armed forces of the two countries has come to an end, the more important thing for the United Nations and all those who stand for peace is to bring to an end the deeper conflict,' he said. 'How can this be brought about? In our view, the only answer lies in peaceful coexistence.'

The USSR invited the Prime Minister of India and the President of Pakistan to meet in Tashkent to discuss peace. After six days of discussions, the President of Pakistan came to appreciate the Indian viewpoint that a firm declaration ruling out recourse to force would create the right climate for settling the differences between the neighbours. So an agreement was reached at Tashkent; an agreement that was rightly hailed as a victory for peace.

Shastriji had caught the nation's imagination for probity in public life much before he took over as the prime minister. As the minister for railways in 1956, Shastriji had resigned his post, owning responsibility for the death of 144 passengers in an accident that took place near Ariyalur in Tamil Nadu. 'I must do penance for this. Let me go,' he had told Prime Minister Nehru.

The unprecedented gesture had been greatly appreciated by Parliament and the country. Nehruji had extolled Shastriji's integrity and high ideals, saying he was accepting the resignation because it would set an example in Constitutional propriety and not because Shastriji was in any way responsible for what had happened. Replying to a long debate on the accident, Shastriji had said, 'Perhaps due to my being small in size and soft of tongue, people are apt to believe that I am not able to be very firm. Though not physically strong, I think I am internally not so weak.'[10]

Shastriji was deeply influenced by the political teachings of Mahatma Gandhi. 'Hard work is equal to prayer,' he once said. His daughter's death, his son's illness, poverty—none of them distracted him from his devotion and service to the nation, the path he had chosen. Even when he became a Central minister and later, the prime minister, he was never attracted to a life of luxury and comfort.

As the Union transport minister, Shastriji was the first in India to make it possible for women to be appointed as conductors. It was also Shastriji's idea that instead of batons, water jets should be used as a crowd-control tactic to disperse protest demonstrations.

Indira Gandhi would give the country some of its proudest moments, not only by ensuring fairness and justice within, but also in the immediate neighbourhood. Who can forget her ethical intervention in the Bangladesh Liberation War? She epitomized ethics, courage, patriotism and progressivism and—away from the public eye—a tenderness only some, like me, got to see.

That's a chapter in my life that makes me emotional even now, fifty years later. The 1971 war had ended in India's victory over Pakistan and the formation of East Pakistan as the new nation of Bangladesh, a huge military and political triumph for Indiraji, but the conflict would leave me suffering over a deep personal loss.

My elder brother, Ziauddin Ahmed, had been a general manager in a tea estate in East Pakistan when the war broke out. His company, Duncan Brothers, was headquartered in London. During the war in 1971, my brother had sent his family to Karachi, but had stayed back himself, despite their repeated pleas to join them. After some time, we lost contact with him. I asked Indiraji if it was possible to trace my brother's whereabouts. Indiraji would call me every day but the news would be the same: my brother had still not been traced. Then, one day, Home Secretary Govind Narayan told me to stop searching for my brother. 'Your brother is no more,' Govind Narayan said. His words still haunt me in my unguarded moments. I later learnt that a fanatic, who worked as his assistant, had killed my brother. That incident had made me emotionally vulnerable and I had turned to Indiraji for solace. What I want to say is that Indiraji may have been a tough political opponent, but she took great care, personally, of those associated with her.

A few years after the 1971 war, Indiraji's reign would run into its biggest internal challenge yet, as the country went into a churn with socialist veteran Jayaprakash Narayan's call for 'Sampoorna Kranti', or Total Revolution.

Jayaprakash Narayan, a seasoned former Congressman famed for his fearlessness during the Quit India Movement, may have had good intentions when he came up with his call, but it did not work out. JP, as he was popularly called, was a young man, when Nehruji and Abul Kalam Azad spotted him, in 1921. To keep him away from the freedom struggle, JP's family had packed him off to the US, where he spent seven years in various colleges. But JP could not resist joining the Congress and the freedom movement. In 1930, he met Nehruji and joined the party.

After spending considerable time in various prisons, JP was finally released in 1946. Soon after Independence, he developed differences with Nehruji and joined the Congress Socialist Party, which was also known as the Socialist Party (India) or Praja Socialist Party.

Many people say the 1975 Emergency—that led to a prolonged suspension of civil rights—was an atrocious move, but I think that's a one-sided view. I think Indiraji was right in declaring the Emergency. It was not an unconstitutional move, as Emergency provisions are duly mentioned in the Indian Constitution. It so happened that the declaration of Emergency and subsequent events did not go down well with a democratic country like India.

The country had become vulnerable, too, with international intelligence networks fishing in its troubled waters. Where the government failed, was in its inability to effectively communicate the reasons for such a move, perhaps because back then, conventional media didn't have as wide a reach as it has now. In fact, the media had itself turned hostile to the very logic of imposing the Emergency to stop the further deterioration of the political culture in the country.

Before judging Indiraji's government for this move, it is important to know how self-serving JP's Sampoorna Kranti was. On 25 June 1975, the entire Opposition showed its strength when JP appealed to the police and the armed forces to 'disobey' any illegal orders of which their conscience did not approve. In effect, it amounted to waging a war against the State as the movement made it a point to defy existing political practices and tradition, institutionalizing identity-based politics in a manner that was highly aggressive.

The deep-rooted politics of caste in Uttar Pradesh—and the Hindi heartland at large—would eventually change the natural course of Indian politics from the path of idealism our freedom fighters had followed.

The Emergency, as I see it, was not a luxury for the Congress government headed by Indiraji. Nor was it optional—the rabble-rousers from the JP camp did everything possible to end civility in India's public life. Indiraji had to declare the Emergency to combat this political situation and not let it become a country-wide revolt; hence the widespread crackdown on the opposition, without any cogent reason, which resulted in most top leaders landing in jail. It was the suspension of fundamental rights that diluted the effect of the Emergency.

It was, however, not the first time that an Emergency had been declared in the country. Earlier, a state of 'external' emergency had been declared during the 1962 war with China and later, during the 1971 Bangladesh war. Even in the UK, the Edward Heath government had called for it five times in the four years of its existence (from June 1970 to March 1974). In Australia, the governor-general had dismissed the prime minister in 1975 and called for fresh polls.

Not many people know—and are thus unable to appreciate—that the 20-Point Programme Indiraji had started in July 1975, not long after the Emergency came into force, was essentially inclusive in its approach. The programme included the restoration of alienated tribal land to people who belonged to the Scheduled Tribes—we would accompany her in handing out free land certificates. The Scheduled Tribes had, by and large, enjoyed traditional and customary rights to vast swathes of land. But loss of land was the single biggest cause of deprivation of their livelihoods, a problem that persists even today. Although there are Constitutional provisions specifically aimed at protecting tribal homelands from such loss, expropriation continues unabated. The move to distribute free land certificates among tribal people was aimed at addressing this problem and fulfilling the constitutional objective of ensuring that tribals retained control over their homelands. This is just one example. In general, Indiraji came up with the best possible response under the circumstances in a bid to ensure good governance and defeat the forces of anarchy.

I, however, wish to make it clear that while I supported the Emergency, I was uncomfortable over media curbs and curtailment of the freedom of expression. I always believed that vigorous independent and critical media are indispensable in a democracy. In a participatory democracy like ours, an informed citizenry is the very basis for a healthy democracy where an independent, non-corporate media is more crucial and critical today than ever before.

Sanjay Gandhi was young and well-meaning, and wanted India to break free from the shackles of corruption and political wrongdoing. He was fearless, full of enthusiasm and had the courage to take bold decisions, but was impatient and wanted everything done fast, every decision implemented immediately. His aims were not wrong, but the hasty path he chose to achieve those aims was undesirable. I admit that a big shortcoming of his was to adopt any means, fair or foul, to implement his ideas.

A few isolated incidents during the Emergency, including those related to the family planning programme and city redevelopment, were seized upon by the opposition parties and followers of the JP camp to target Sanjay. When we visited villages, we even heard about deaths of teachers and many others because of the family planning programme; but there was no way of telling the public not to pay heed to rumours. Some ultra-Right organizations have been masters in the past at distorting facts, and continue doing that even now. To know their character, one must first understand their core beliefs and their ideological fulcrum. For them, what matters most is to keep politics aligned to identity and sectarianism, and to belittle India's socio-religious diversity.

I accept the argument that the real downslide of the Congress began from 1977, largely because of the faulty implementation of the family planning programme. As I have stated consistently in my public life as well as in this memoir, I was not personally against the Emergency because the circumstances then had left Mrs Gandhi with no other option. If you provoke the police and even call upon the army to revolt, what can any leader do but resort to such a step, as Indiraji did?

I was then president of the Uttar Pradesh Congress. In the initial days of the Emergency, the situation in the country was alright. Because of accountability and penal actions, trains ran on time and things were available in markets at proper prices. It was because of the faulty implementation of the family planning programme and Opposition propaganda that the Emergency got its bad name even though the move to stabilize the population itself was relevant to a country like India.

I had myself received a host of complaints about excesses of the family planning programme in Uttar Pradesh. This led me to suspect that the abuse of the programme was well-planned. I met Indiraji and told her about my misgivings; that I was worried about whatever was happening in the name of family planning. She asked me to explain. When I did, she pleaded ignorance.

Indiraji often toyed with the idea of opting for early Lok Sabha polls but I told Indiraji that if she had elections in mind, this was just not the right time. She asked me why.

'Look, we can face the leaders, but we cannot face the wrath and anguish of the people. I am saying this after gauging the mood of the people. Let things settle,' I told her.

I also apprised Indiraji about reports in the international media. I had gone to Canada to meet my sister and, after I returned, I showed Indiraji foreign newspapers with screeching headlines on the excesses of the family planning programme in India.

Since newspapers in India were being censored, I said, people were relying on reports about India published and broadcast in the foreign media.

'For God's sake, don't hold elections right now,' I told Indiraji.

'But intelligence reports say this is the right time to hold elections,' she countered.

I asked her if she trusted intelligence reports. 'We have to rely on intelligence, at least up to 60 per cent,' she replied.

Eventually, Indiraji went by what intelligence officials had recommended and, in January 1977, called for fresh elections in March. The Congress would be routed. In Uttar Pradesh, it lost in all the eighty-five parliamentary seats. Among those who lost was Indiraji herself.

The Emergency and the resultant curtailment of civil rights did affect Indiraji's political legacy, but the BJP too has not acquitted itself entirely in this aspect. The party's disregard for Constitutional values has been glaring. And since it can in no way stake claim to the legacy of the independence struggle, it has been tampering with history, presenting, for instance, Mahatma Gandhi and Sardar Vallabhbhai Patel as rivals of Jawaharlal Nehru. What can be further from the truth? The fact remains that Patel had banned the RSS after Nathuram Godse assassinated Gandhiji. I hope today's young generation will interpret history with their own wisdom instead of falling into the vicious trap of hatred, lies and distortions that drive the narrative of the RSS-BJP and their allied organizations.

The question that we need to ask and debate is this: why has the RSS succeeded? If anyone looks into its history, they will find no bigger whisper campaigner than the RSS. The Sangh is a past master at peddling half truths and disinformation, and often dubbing truth as lies. Let me cite an example.

Indiraji's government had distributed land pattas (documents) among the landless poor under the 20-Point Programme that was launched in 1975. I was in Patna when the empowerment programme was launched. I later learnt that a group of five or six persons held a secret meeting to hatch a conspiracy against the programme. George Fernandes' supporters were reportedly at the forefront of this conspiracy. In my assessment, George Fernandes was a man of many flavours. He would often turn anti-establishment and confrontationist. He had a sharp mind and good sense of timing, but he could often act in an unconventional manner.

Indiraji's political opponents, including Fernandes, reportedly discussed the 20-Point Programme and concluded that if the Congress succeeded in implementing it, the party would remain in power for another twenty years. So what they did was club Sanjay Gandhi's 5-point programme with the 20-Point Programme. They then started a propaganda against one of the programmes, which was about family planning, basically picking on one point because of its potential for controversy and exploiting it, while ignoring the others that might have benefitted the country.

Coming back to the Emergency, I admit, no matter how adverse the situation was and difficult for the government to serve the masses in the face of a planned campaign to topple it, the media should have been allowed to function freely without any bans or restrictions. The censorship of the Press meant people were in the dark about what was going on. To make matters worse, this was blown out of proportion, and the misinterpretation of the Emergency dented the party's and Indiraji's fortunes and the Congress was voted out in the 1977 elections.

Indiraji was extremely caring and attentive. I can go on talking about many instances. Sometime after 1977 Lok Sabha polls, when Indiraji was in Opposition, she planned to visit Badrinath for puja. Narayan Dutt Tiwari and I accompanied her. It was October. We were told that puja starts from 4 a.m. Asking us to wait, she went to the temple for the puja. We were to start at 6 a.m. on return journey to New Delhi. At 5 a.m., Indiraji returned from the temple and checked whether all the vehicles of our convoy were ready. The pundit of the temple offered us breakfast. When we were having breakfast, the drivers were heating the engines of their respective vehicles. I told Indiraji that while we had had breakfast, the poor drivers must be hungry. They had not had even tea as they were busy heating the vehicles' engines. I suggested we stop at the first tea shop on our return for the drivers to have tea. She agreed.

Indiraji had the habit of carrying some snacks with her during travel, in a basket. After a while, I saw her taking out some biscuits from the basket kept beneath her seat. She broke the biscuits into four pieces and asked the driver to pick the pieces one by one from her hand while driving. She extended her hand carrying biscuit pieces and the driver did what he was told to do.

Indiraji used to enjoy such affection and the spontaneous display of it so much that it often stunned me and used to fill my heart with admiration and pride for my leader. Once, we were travelling to a famous Gurudwara in Haridwar, when her convoy was suddenly stopped by a group of Sikh devotees. She was in Opposition then and without much security arrangements. Indiraji got off to greet them. In a flash, a Sikh woman flashed her kripan and slit a part of her hand and quickly put a tilak of blood on Indiraji's forehead saying, '*Indiraji, aap ki haar ka badla hum lenge*' (We shall seek revenge for your electoral defeat). This quick display of affection and respect mesmerized me and all those who were accompanying Indiraji then.

Indiraji could also sense what the people around her were feeling. Once, when we were travelling by an overnight train to Gorakhpur, I suddenly realized I was alone with the prime minister in the first-class coupe. She sensed that I was a little uncomfortable and directed me to turn my face towards the wall and go off to sleep.

I vividly recall another occasion when Indiraji visited Anandamayi Ma, the smiling saint, at her ashram in Kankhal (Haridwar). That was after Sanjayji had died and Indiraji was in emotional turmoil. From a distance, I could see Indiraji had placed her head on Anandamayi Ma's lap and the saint was gently stroking her hair, trying to comfort a grieving mother.

Anandamayi Ma was a deeply spiritual soul who perhaps never advised anyone to become a renunciate. She would dismiss spiritual arguments and controversies by stating, 'Everyone is right from his own standpoint.' She also did not issue formal initiations and refused to be called a guru, as she maintained that 'all paths are my paths' and 'I have no particular path'. She welcomed and conversed with devotees from different paths and religions—Shaivite, Vaishnavite, Tantric, Islam, Christianity, Judaism, Sikhism, Buddhism or Zoroastrianism. Every faith was welcome. Even now, Muslims of

Kheora, Brahmanbaria District in present-day Bangladesh, refer to her as 'our own Ma'.

However, by the time the Morarji Desai government had completed a year in office, the Janata Party's spiritual eminence grise, Jayaprakash Narayan, had turned a very angry man. 'I am completely disappointed with the Janata Party's performance,' *India Today* magazine had quoted JP as saying.[11]

Indiraji eventually returned, her work and efforts bringing the Congress back to power at the Centre in early 1980, less than three years after being voted out. Sadly, despite believing in the idea of one India and communal harmony, she was assassinated by her own Sikh guards on 31 October 1984.

Rajiv Gandhi, who had entered politics following the death of his younger brother Sanjay in 1980, assumed charge under unfortunate circumstances. In the elections that followed soon after Indiraji's assassination, the grieving country reposed its faith in the Congress, which secured 404 out of 541 parliamentary seats. The mandate was for continuity as well as change—Indiraji's ideals and unfinished tasks and Rajivji's promises for revolutionizing India's growth potential. As the face of modern India, Rajivji started the much-needed communications revolution in the country and lent support to its transition towards a programme of economic liberalization that was finally implemented in 1991.

One of the world's fastest-growing economies and a power in the information and communications technology (ICT) sector, the Indian economy was given the Midas touch by Rajivji and effectively shaped by successive governments he headed as prime minister.

I feel that in some ways, Rajivji was the true architect of economic reforms. Between 1984, when he became prime minister after his mother's assassination, and 1989, the young leader made sincere efforts to take the country into the twenty-first century. Rajivji laid the foundation for a modern India and, as a former cabinet colleague, I can vouch for his passion and drive for economic reforms. Rajivji is rightly hailed as the 'Father of Information Technology and Telecom Revolution of India' and a founder of Digital India.

His vision for the Centre for Development of Telematics (C-DOT) and advancement of state-of-the-art telecommunication technology not only met the needs of the Indian telecommunication network, but also established a robust network in towns and even villages. It was because of Rajivji that the 'PCO revolution' took place, with public calling booths being set up to connect rural areas to the world outside.

Rajivji promoted science and technology and associated industries in a big way, and was instrumental in the reduction of import quotas, taxes and tariffs on such industries, especially on computers, airlines, defence and telecommunications. The Indian Railways was modernized after the introduction of computerized railway tickets.

As a young leader himself, Rajivji sought to empower the vast majority of the country's youth. Towards that end, the Sixty-second Amendment Act of the Constitution was passed in 1989, lowering the voting age from twenty-one years to eighteen years. The move allowed more youths to have a say in choosing Lok Sabha MPs and MLAs in the states. I still remember his words as spoken in the Parliament on 15 December 1988:

> We have full faith in the youth of India. The youth of India have demonstrated their wisdom, their maturity in panchayat elections, local body elections and we feel that they are now ready to participate fully in the democratic process. This amendment will bring in almost 50 million people into the electoral system.

Rajivji is rightly credited with laying the foundation of Panchayati Raj institutions as part of efforts to take democracy to the grassroots. Although the related amendments to the Constitution (Seventy-third and Seventy-fourth)—to provide statutory sanction to local government—were passed in 1992, a year after Rajivji's assassination, it was his government that had prepared the background. Rajivji's words spoken in the Parliament still ring in my ears, 'We are on the threshold of a mighty revolution ... It is a revolution that will bring democracy to the doorsteps of crores of Indians.' And this 'mighty revolution' was indeed the Panchayati Raj system. The Constitutional amendment had sought to confer certain powers on the Panchayati Raj institutions, including the power to raise finances and spend them on specific activities, without the prior approval of state governments. It had also given the Centre complete control over disbursement of the ₹2,100 crore which had been earmarked for rural development that year, i.e., 1989.

As prime minister, Rajivji announced the National Policy on Education (NPE) in 1986 to modernize and expand higher education programmes across the country. With the NPE in place, residential schools called Jawahar Navodaya Vidyalayas were set up under the Central government to bring out the best of rural talent. These schools provide village students free residential education from Class VI to Class XII.

Rajivji would, however, lose power in 1989, as controversies and a debilitating combination of other problems took their toll on the Congress, which emerged as the single largest party, but ended up well short of the majority. The Janata Dal, led by V.P. Singh, Rajivji's one-time cabinet colleague, formed the government with outside support from the BJP.

The Janata Dal government was a disaster. On 7 August 1990, about eight months into its reign, the government implemented the recommendations of the Mandal Commission, or the Socially and Educationally Backward Classes Commission (SEBC), which had suggested that 27 per cent of public sector jobs and seats in Central educational institutions be reserved for the historically disadvantaged Other Backward Classes (OBCs).

The decision to implement the recommendations was an act of injustice against the people of India and the vision of socialist leader Karpoori Thakur, who had advocated reservation based on socio-economic backwardness. In fact, the father of the Indian Constitution, Dr Bhimrao Ambedkar, had never supported such an idea and his suggestions were clearly in favour of a timebound system of reservation, keeping historical backwardness in the frame. Rajivji was in favour of reservation based on socio-economic considerations rather than caste.

The backlash was swift. Protests spread like wildfire, especially among youths and on university campuses, even as pro-reservation activists took to the streets. This was a time when the Ram Mandir issue was simmering, too—a polarizing cocktail that sent the political mercury soaring. Such was the atmosphere that it almost crackled with conflict and acrimony.

20
Rise of Divisive Politics

THE POLITICS OF 'MANDAL AND Kamandal' started in the late 1980s, while insurgency in the Northeast, Punjab and Kashmir left deep scars on our public memories. In Kashmir, rising militancy would finally lead to the unfortunate exit of Kashmiri Pandits from the Valley. Lal Krishna Advani's Ram Rath Yatra in 1990, the demolition of the Babri Masjid on 6 December 1992, and the Bombay riots (1992–93) dented the country's secular credentials and exposed India's vulnerability to the religiously polarized politics of the RSS, Vishwa Hindu Parishad (VHP) and the BJP. Such high-order, institutionalized fundamentalism, detrimental to India's natural progression as a modern, secular country, had created a breeding ground for extremism and militancy, and polarized our socio-political life in unprecedented ways. The Congress and United Front governments did try to arrest these tendencies but the virus of communal violence has seeped deeply in society.

To my mind, RSS is the real BJP. The RSS calls itself a cultural organization and prepares cadres for political ideology to be sent to the BJP, which is only a label. There is no difference between the two. The Congress has always fought against communal ideology. The RSS ideology is based on the two-nation theory. Those organizations which believe in the two-nation theory cannot run this country. Our basic character is of peace and brotherhood. Look at our neighbouring countries which are bereft of ideology—how badly they have messed up democracy.

India is fortunate to have had Gandhiji as its leader. His ideology and teachings are suited perfectly well to India's basic character. This ideology truly reflects in the Constitution that we have adopted as well. If you read the Preamble, you will find similarities between the Gandhian ideology and the Constitution of India should be credited with not giving such 'polarization politics'—as in the 1990s—any place in the electoral framework. In fact, even the two BJP governments that Atal Bihari Vajpayee headed between 1998 and 2004 were not communally inclined.

Unfortunately, the Gujarat riots had still taken place in 2002 and the state's then chief minister, Narendra Modi, not only survived but also thrived. But I'll come back to that later.

The V.P. Singh government fell in November 1990 after the BJP withdrew its outside support. The prime minister lost a vote of confidence 142 to 346 after a ten-hour marathon special session of Parliament. Chandra Shekhar, who succeeded V.P. Singh, was much more accommodative and liberal than his predecessor. His tenure was, however, shortlived and President R. Venkataraman called for fresh elections, to be held in May 1991.

The Congress, by then, had rediscovered its spirit under the leadership of Rajiv Gandhi. The cadres appeared determined and ready to take their opponents head-on. Rajivji campaigned hard, travelling from state to state and holding meetings everywhere he went. Thousands would come to hear him, see him and, if lucky enough, to shake his hand or garland him. The crowds were getting larger with each day and it seemed Rajivji was on his way back to power.

But it was not to be.

On 21 May 1991, an LTTE suicide bomber detonated the explosives strapped to her body as an unsuspecting Rajivji allowed the assassin to come near and greet him, moments before he was to address a public gathering in Sriperumbudur in Tamil Nadu.

Rajivji had, on that day, boarded a helicopter for a whirlwind tour of the coastal areas of Bhadrak, Angul, Gunupur and Paralakhemundi in Odisha before crossing over to Visakhapatnam in Andhra Pradesh. Uma Gajapathi Raju was the Congress nominee there.

Rajivji reached Chennai at 8.30 p.m., met the press for ten minutes, had a soft drink and then hurriedly left by road for Porur to address a public meeting. At 9.30 p.m., he held another meeting before heading for Poonamallee. In between these engagements, Rajiv had been giving interviews to Neena Gopal of *Gulf News* and Barbara Crossette of *The New York Times*.

When he reached Sriperumbudur, there was little of what could be described as 'security arrangements'. Constables from the Tamil Nadu police watched curiously as Rajivji mingled freely with the crowd. His personal security attendant, Pradeep Gupta, made a feeble bid to keep the mob from touching him. Senior state Congress leaders, such as G.K. Moopanar and Maragatham Chandrashekhar, sat on the dais about 100 yards away.

As he walked on the red carpet, accepting garlands from one and all, Rajivji had suddenly stopped when he heard a poem being recited by a young girl, Kokila, who was part of the suicide squad. His assassin, Dhanu, moved closer to him, carrying a garland made of sandalwood. Rajivji must have sensed something unusual because he signalled to a constable, Anusuya, to regulate the crowd. But by then, Dhanu had bent, pretending to touch Rajivji's feet, and triggered the RDX strapped around her.

At the time of the blast, a chorus at the public meeting was in full flow. 'Rajiv Gandhi's life is our life,' they sang, 'if not for Indira Gandhi's son, there is no life for anyone.'

Looking back at that glorious period when the Congress was in power in most states and at the Centre, too, sometimes I wonder why the Grand Old Party is in such a sorry state now. I can say with full honesty that the Congress adopted an ideology and stood by it, but certain newcomers in the party have not been as committed to it.

There was a time, before Independence, when many in the Congress came from zamindari, or landowning families. Our family, too, had zamindars. But it didn't take a minute for the landowning members in the party to put their signature on an Assembly resolution that was passed to abolish the zamindari system—so strong was their commitment to the party's ideology. But of late, an element of selfishness has crept into the Congress. We have for long been hearing about the introduction of an urban land ceiling law, but its implementation appears impossible.

The kind of serious challenges we are confronting today were not there before. The challenges before Nehru were not there during Indira Gandhi's time. The challenges of Indira era were not there during Rajiv Gandhi's time. Before Independence, our sole goal was to attain independence. When there is a definite goal, the nation aspires to achieve it. After Independence, there have been no definite goals for us to achieve.

I firmly believe that Nehruvian thoughts and ideology should form the core of the party's belief system. I wish to quote here how Rajivji had passionately spoken about his grandfather at Bombay during the Congress centenary celebrations, echoing our collective sentiments. Rajivji had said, 'Jawaharlal Nehru destroyed the edifice of imperialism. For he knew he had the greater task of building a new society. He was a great builder. He gave India the enduring structure of the democratic parliamentary institutions buttressed by the rule of law. Fundamental rights, directive principles of State policy, and safeguards for the Scheduled Castes and Scheduled Tribes together make our Constitution one of humanity's great charters of freedom and equality. We have passed through many a crisis, but democracy has continued to flourish—to the consternation of those who believed that democracy was for the rich, not for the poor. In India, democracy, with all its claimant contention, is alive and vibrant.

Jawaharlal Nehru fashioned the planning process to reach the ultimate objective of a socialist democracy. Planning is now a part of the national consensus. It was not always so. It used to be described as the road to serfdom. Those who scoffed have stayed to praise. We have a strong economy. We are firmly set on the path of self-reliance, which means more freedom, not less. Our planning process has succeeded. Panditji built the infrastructure of science and technology with loving care. Atomic energy and space stand out as symbols of this achievement, although no field was left untouched. Let us not forget that it was Panditji who established the great laboratories, the giant irrigation dams, the fertilizer plants and the agricultural universities. This was the foundation of our self-sufficiency.

Nehruji was a staunch believer in the public sector and considered new projects as lifelines of nation-making. He had seen in power and steel, the key steering forces of the Indian economy. He described the 680-ft Bhakra multipurpose project on the Sutlej River in Himachal Pradesh as the new temple of a modern India. Beyond the politics of big dams, the Bhakra-Nangal dams are among several hydroelectricity projects India built to tread in a respectable growth territory.

The second plan set a target to produce 6 million tonnes of steel. Germany was contracted to build a steel plant in Rourkela, while Russia and Britain would build one each in Bhilai and Durgapur, respectively. The Indian Institutes of Technology, Indian Institutes of Management and the Atomic Energy Commission were the other 'modern temples' for him and the India of his dreams. Immersed as he was in the thick of our freedom struggle, Pandit Nehru foresaw that, in the ultimate analysis, the linkages between modern agriculture and industrialization offered the only lasting solution to the poverty of India's masses.

With Independence, the time came to translate into reality the dream of a vigorous, industrialized India. Panditji created the imposing structure of our industry. Leading this mighty effort was the public sector, a strong and dependable lever for development. He envisioned for it the commanding heights of the economy. Under his leadership, basic industries, infrastructure, machine-building, oil exploration, metals and minerals and defence industries were established. In the public sector, new technology was absorbed and nurtured. New skills came to those who had never turned a simple lathe. Centres of modern industry blossomed in backward and remote areas. With confidence, the Indian people wrote a new chapter in their long and tumultuous history. Through the instrument of the public sector, Jawaharlal Nehru made the decisive break with India's colonial, deindustrialized stagnation.

Panditji was the great unifier of the Indian people. India is home to many great religions. Her many-splendoured mansion of unity rests on the bedrock of secularism. Like a great teacher, Nehru expounded in simple language, the philosophy of secularism. He repeatedly warned the nation against communalism. To him, secularism was the beacon light when waves of passion threatened to submerge us.

Panditji looked at the world with the eyes of a humanist, in love with nature and with the works of man. He perceived before many others, that the splitting of the atom had changed for all time to come the universe of discourse among nations. War in the nuclear age was no longer policy by other means—it was mass suicide. He saw no meaning in military blocs. They did not guarantee security.

They only guaranteed fear. He wanted nations to cooperate, not dominate. He evolved the philosophy of non-alignment. Non-align is the international expression of national resurgence. It is the extension of democracy to international relations. It means independence of thought and action.

Panditji abjured entanglement with power blocs, because power blocs are based on conflict, and erode the independence of countries which join them. He put forward the positive concept of peaceful coexistence and cooperation to build a better, saner world, free from anxiety, suspicion and fear. This vision of a cooperative world order, even today, guides the Non-aligned Movement, representing the vast majority of the family of nations. It is a powerful force for freedom, peace and justice in the world. In its centenary year, the Indian National Congress is proud that India has the honour of leading the Non-aligned Movement. As Rajivji had said, all this and more is the legacy of Jawaharlal Nehru, his imperishable bequest to us in the Indian National Congress. I hope we continue to follow his footsteps and realize his vision.

I think the immediate task ahead, the gravity of the task, matters a lot because the challenges we face today shape our responses in the future. The challenges we are confronting today were not there earlier. Just as the challenges have changed over the terms of the past Congress prime ministers, the challenges before Soniaji, Rahul and Priyanka today are drastically different from those in the past. Before Independence, our only goal was independence but now, definite goals will need to be set once again.

21
Political Economy: Continuity with Change

I AM NEITHER A TRAINED ECONOMIST nor an expert in the field of finance, but after nearly a lifetime in politics and association with the Congress, I can say that as an ideology, our economic thinking has followed the course of change with continuity. From Jawaharlal Nehru to Sonia Gandhi and Rahul Gandhi, the party leadership understood that a dogmatic approach would not yield the party any long-term benefits in a multicultural and pluralistic society like India. The Congress, therefore, kept reinventing itself, avoiding confrontations and sharp divisions in society.

Nehruji, who ruled from 15 August 1947, till his death on 27 May 1964, was deeply influenced by the Fabian or socialist movement in the United Kingdom. The Fabian Society was formed in London in 1884 and its members were opposed to the Marxist doctrine of revolution. Rather, they believed in a gradual transition to equality and the establishment of a socialist society. The word Fabian was derived from Quintus Fabius Maximus Verrucosus, the legendary Roman general famous for his delaying tactics against Hannibal during the Second Punic War.

Independent India's first prime minister was also deeply affected by the coal strike in England in 1926. For him, it was an oppressive face of capitalism that he abhorred. As a freedom fighter, he was also alive to show the British had systematically exploited the Indian economy and looted farmers, artisans and the nation. For him, capitalism was not a necessary tool for economic development. In fact, for most Congress activists born before 1947, including me, the belief in socialism was unwavering.

Nehruji's Industrial Policy Resolution of 1948 was the most concrete expression of his means for achieving socialism in India. At the same time, he was open to the idea of foreign investment. In a statement issued on 6 April 1949, Nehruji had clearly articulated his policy on foreign investments, noting that his government would encourage new foreign capital on mutually advantageous terms. His finance minister, John Mathai, would reiterate that policy in his 1950–51 budget speech, when he said 'foreign capital is necessary in this country, not merely for the purpose of supplementing our own resources, but for the purpose of instilling a spirit of confidence among our own investors'.[12]

Earlier, in 1948, Nehruji had told the Constituent Assembly, 'if we squander our resources in merely acquiring for the state, existing industries … for the moment we may have no other resources left, and we would have spoiled the field for private enterprise too. So, it is far better for the state to concentrate on certain specific, vital, new industries, than to go about nationalizing many of the old ones.'

This was reiterated in a letter he wrote to chief ministers on 3 March 1953, when he had sought to assure foreign investors that if their investments were nationalized, fair and equitable compensation would be given. Let us also not forget that the Indian Constitution, adopted in 1950, recognized the right to property as a fundamental right.

Speaking at The Economic Council for Asia and the Far East (ECAFE) or the Colombo Plan meetings or at the United Nations, Nehruji had quoted Euripides, a dramatist of classical Athens, to sum up his thinking, and I reproduce it here with delight and enthusiasm: 'What else is wisdom? What of man's endeavour, or God's high grace, so lovely and so great? To stand from fear set free to breathe and wait, to hold a hand uplifted over hate, and shall not loveliness be loved forever?'[13]

Even now, when I saw Rahul Gandhi unveiling the Nyuntam Aay Yojana (Minimum Income Scheme) or, in short, NYAY, launched shortly before the 2019 general elections, I felt good that Nehruji's great-grandson was essentially following the Nehruvian and Congress economic thinking of 'social Left and economic Right'.

From 2004 to 2014, Soniaji had successfully managed to communicate to the masses, even those who did not read newspapers or watch television, that the Congress's prime responsibility towards the poor did not stand compromised by Dr Manmohan Singh's thrust on economic reforms. It was not that Soniaji's and Manmohan Singh's economic thinking was not on the same page. Soniaji is not a firm believer in a state-controlled economy. In fact, her lengthy, freewheeling discussions with Manmohan Singh prior to 2004 had convinced her that a market-controlled economy, if properly guided, could benefit many, including those who were at the margins of society. Her understanding of the new world order and need for reforms contributed significantly to convincing the great Indian middle class and captains of industry that, under Manmohan Singh, reforms would continue and there would be further liberalization. As prime minister, Singh, too, made it clear that his government was not Sensex-driven, but functioned in a manner that was transparent, pro-industry and pro-entrepreneur.

At the numerous AICC sessions and CWC meetings, where I was privy to the discussions and deliberations, the Congress leadership constantly clarified and explained that its concept of socialism was not dogmatic or doctrinaire. In 1972, under Indiraji, the election manifesto prepared for upcoming Assembly polls read, 'Poverty must go. Disparity must diminish. Injustice must end.' At the Bombay AICC session around the same time, Jagjivan Ram had moved a resolution, saying: 'Modern man is the inheritor of all that is noble and good in human thought. And thus our democratic socialism is a synthesis of all that is best in the thinking of the East and the West and provides an ideology superior to other sectarian ideologies which are communalistic or communitarian.'[14]

As we know, the war with Pakistan that resulted in the creation of Bangladesh in 1971 had made Indiraji both popular and powerful. But even before the war, she had won the general elections earlier that year, riding high on her 'garibi hatao' (eradicate poverty) slogan.

Indiraji, who assumed charge as prime minister in January 1966, radicalized Congress policies, programmes and leadership through the nationalization of banks, the abolition of the privy purse and the presidential polls. The privy purse was a payment made to the former royal families of 565 princely states as part of their agreements to integrate with India in 1947 and later merge their territories with the Union.

I can never forget 19 July 1969, a red-letter day for us, when, as prime minister, Indiraji nationalized fourteen Indian banks by a special presidential ordinance. Among the leading banks that were nationalized, the biggest was Central Bank, controlled by the Tatas, with deposits of over ₹4 billion; the smallest was the Bank of Maharashtra that had deposits totalling ₹700 million. The other big business houses and financial institutions that suffered a blow included the Birlas, who operated the United Commercial Bank; the Dalmia-Jains who ran Bharat Bank and its 292 branch offices;

the Punjab National Bank, which was set up by Dyal Singh Majithia, Lala Harkishan Lal, Lala Lajpat Rai and others; and some Gujarati entrepreneurs who had big stakes in Dena Bank. An economic survey of twenty leading banks of that era showed that 188 people who served as directors were also directors of 1,452 companies.

In the larger context, party leaders handling economic issues reinforce the stand that, as an ideology, the party has been following the course of change with continuity. From its inception, the Congress has functioned as an amorphous organization. Describing the Congress at the Avadi session, U.N. Dhebar, president of the AICC in 1955, spoke extensively with a poet's flair in the presence of Nehruji, Indiraji and others, who nodded their heads in approval: 'What is the Congress? It is a tear, fallen from the sufferings and agonized heart of humanity in bondage, coming to life,' Dhebar said.

According to Nehruji, the Congress had always been something more than a party and capable of drawing allegiance from millions who were not formally with the party. Speaking in New Delhi at the 1951 AICC session, Nehruji had said, 'We have to retain something of that wider aspect of the Congress, but this should not lead to floppiness and loose thinking and accommodation of all kinds of contrary opinions within its fold. In regard to principles—social, economic and political—this must be clear. There should be no room for reactionaries in the Congress fold. Nor should there be any room in it for those who seek, through its medium, personal advancement and profit at the cost of the public good. We have to pull ourselves up from the narrow grooves of thought and action, from factions, from mutual recrimination, from tolerance of evil in public life and in our social structure, and become again fighters for a cause and upholders of high principles.'

22
Inclusive Growth and Economic Milestones

THE CULTURE OF HAVING A powerful, dominant leader and the tendency to change from time to time according to the political situation would give the Congress fresh ideological frames, helping it tailor its response to evolving circumstances. This was more a matter of policy than faith. Such compromises between various interest groups helped in the sharing of power and reflected the doctrinal pluralism of its leaders.

By the time the Congress under Soniaji met at Pachmarhi (1997), Shimla (2003) and Hyderabad (2006), the party had formally accepted the need for coalitions with parties of varying ideologies. The political resolution in Hyderabad said, 'At present, coalition of political forces and opinion is inevitable. Each political epoch needs a leader and a visionary who changes the traditional paradigm of society to face contemporary challenges.'

A milestone of sorts was reached on 24 July 1991, when my friend for decades, Dr Manmohan Singh, delivered a historic speech as finance minister in the P.V. Narasimha Rao government, and a budget that would change the face of the Indian economy. As I have stated before, it was Rajivji who had made the intellectual argument for reforms. Had Rajivji been alive and returned to power in 1991, India would have been different, not just as an economic power, but as socially cohesive, progressive, civil and a 'Vishwa Guru' in technology, spirituality and disarmament.

I must compliment Dr Manmohan Singh for his 1991 budget speech. The giant of an economist that he is, he made no attempt to hide the extent of the economic crisis prevailing then. 'The new government, which assumed office barely a month ago, inherited an economy in deep crisis. The balance of payments situation is precarious ... We have been at the edge of a precipice since December 1990 and more so since April 1991 ... The people of India have to face double-digit inflation which hurts most the poorer sections of our society. In sum, the crisis in our economy is both acute and deep. We have not experienced anything similar in the history of independent India,' Singh said in his speech in Parliament.

Dr Singh quoted the French poet and novelist Victor Hugo as he argued for reform. 'Nothing else in the world, not all the armies are as powerful as an idea whose time has come,' he said, adding that macroeconomic stabilization and fiscal adjustment alone would not suffice. 'They must be supported by essential reforms in economic policy and economic management, as an integral part of the adjustment process; reforms which would help to eliminate waste and inefficiency and impart a new element of dynamism to growth processes in our economy. The thrust of the reform process would be to increase the efficiency and international competitiveness of industrial production to utilize for this purpose foreign investment and foreign technology to a much greater degree than we have done in the past, to increase the productivity of investment, to ensure that India's financial sector is rapidly modernized, and to improve the performance of the public sector, so that key sectors of our economy are enabled to attain an adequate technological and competitive edge in a fast-changing global economy.'[15]

The economic reforms kickstarted in 1991 brought about the expansion of the services sector, helped largely by a liberalized investment and trade regime. They also increased consumer choices, and reduced poverty significantly. The share of services in India's GDP has increased 20 percentage points since 1991, reflecting a decisive change in the nature of the country's economic output. In the past thirty years, I am happy to note, our share of the global economy has tripled, from 1.1 per cent to 3.3 per cent. Moreover, as per the current value of the US dollar, our economy has multiplied eleven-fold; only China and Vietnam have done better. On key human development indicators (primarily life expectancy and literacy), we have done marginally better than the average of the countries in the 'medium development' bracket.

To my mind, Soniaji and Rahulji had both found Manmohan Singh's economic thinking to be on the same page as theirs. The Gandhis do not believe in a State-controlled economy.

Manmohan Singh became the prime minister in 2004 and, in his new role, focused on ensuring inclusive growth. The UPA government launched the National Rural Employment Guarantee Scheme (NREGS) in February 2006 in 200 of the most backward districts in the country. The scheme, later expanded to cover all rural districts, was aimed at providing at least 100 days of guaranteed unskilled manual work in a fiscal year to every rural household.

Following is a list of some of India's milestone achievements and important laws that were enacted during the UPA years:

- Launch of the 2010 census, one of the largest censuses in the world. The second phase, conducted in 2011, marked the first time biometric information was collected.

- The National Green Tribunal Act enacted in 2010, enabling the establishment of a special tribunal to handle environment-related cases.
- The Vivek Express—the longest route (4,286 km) on the Indian railway network—announced in the 2011 budget.
- The country launched its first intercontinental ballistic missile, Agni V, in 2012.
- Public Procurement Policy for Micro and Small Enterprises Order, 2012, to promote MSEs.
- Launch of the INS Vikrant, the first aircraft carrier built in India, in 2013.
- The Mars Orbiter Mission—also called Mangalyaan—launched in 2013. India became the first nation to reach the Martian orbit in its first attempt.
- India's first all-women commercial bank, Bharatiya Mahila Bank, started operations in 2013.
- The National Food Security Act, 2013, to provide food and nutritional security to all.
- Nirbhaya Act, 2013, a stricter law to deal with sex crimes against women.
- The Sexual Harassment of Women at Workplace (Prevention, Prohibition and Redressal) Act, 2013, to provide protection against sexual harassment of women at their workplaces.
- The Lokpal and Lokayukta Act, 2013, to provide for the establishment of the Lokpal and the Lokayukta to inquire into allegations of corruption against certain public functionaries.
- The National Mission for Empowerment of Women (NMEW), 2013, to coordinate women's welfare and socio-economic development programmes across ministries.

- The Land Acquisition Act, 2013, to regulate land acquisition and lay down the procedure for granting compensation to affected people and rehabilitating and resettling them.
- Companies Act, 2013. Corporate Social Responsibility (CSR) was made mandatory.
- India declared 'polio free' by the World Health Organization in 2014.
- Whistle Blowers Protection Act, 2011, to eliminate corruption in the bureaucracy and protect those who make complaints against public servants. The Act received presidential assent in 2014.
- Street Vendors Act, 2014, to regulate street vendors in public areas and protect their rights.

This list is by no means exhaustive but shows the UPA's all-round approach towards progress with a humane face. I can go on and on but would pause here and rewind—because others too have played their part in shaping the country's economic and political destiny.

Readers who have come this far might wonder why I didn't stick to a chronological order. I can, perhaps, justify that. I began this chapter with the Congress as an ideology—of change and continuity—and the rhythm of this narrative may have suffered, had I gone strictly by years. Some might counter this and say that Lal Bahadur Shastri too was a Congressman. My answer is that Shastriji deserves a separate section. Moreover, as I stated at the very beginning, I am no trained chronicler, but merely an accidental memoirist who wants to leave behind in words the impressions of a lifetime in politics. So I seek my readers' indulgence again as I go back a few decades and commence this new section with Shastriji, who helmed the country at a difficult time and left his mark despite his brief tenure.

A word about my siblings here. My eldest brother, Ziauddeen Mullah, was the manager of a tea garden in what was then East Pakistan. He lost his life during the struggle of the Bengalis for freedom from Pakistan. His family is now settled in Pakistan. My eldest sister, Husna, settled in Canada after her marriage. She has one daughter and two sons. Four of my younger siblings—two sisters and two brothers—are all settled in Pakistan with their families. One brother worked in Canada but took early retirement because of health issues and decided to return to India.

Lal Bahadur Shastri was a minister without portfolio in Nehruji's cabinet but assumed charge after Gulzarilal Nanda had helmed the thirteen-day transition period as a nightwatchman, to borrow a cricketing term, following Nehruji's death on 27 May 1964.

Shastriji's job was not easy after the war with China and India's precarious condition on the economic and strategic fronts. But the most onerous task before Shastriji was how to effectively deal with the twin problems of chronic food shortage and high inflation. Political capital, however, came in the form of India's victory over Pakistan in the 1965 war, enough for Shastriji to consider economic reforms. His approach was fresh and his resolve to revive the farm economy and strengthen the country's strategic capacity boosted India's image in the world.

Shastriji was behind two of India's finest economic experiments—The Green Revolution in agriculture and the White Revolution that established India as the largest milk producer in the world. The food shortage and near-mass famine of the 1960s had prompted Shastriji to make India self-reliant in terms of food production and save it from international pressure that was impacting the country's autonomy in framing policy. Geneticist M.S. Swaminathan, along with American agronomist Norman Borlaug and other scientists, stepped in with a high-yield variety of wheat seeds, setting off what came to be known as the Green Revolution.

Following the success of the Green Revolution, Shastriji worked to establish the organized dairy sector, particularly the cooperative movement in Gujarat's Anand, led by Verghese Kurien. He helped the Kaira District Cooperative Milk Producers' Union Ltd expand its work, ushering in the White Revolution. Many more cooperatives came into existence and helped the rural economy. Shastriji would, however, not live to see the successful launch of the dairy development programme. He died in Tashkent, Uzbekistan (in the then Soviet Union) on 11 January 1966, a day after signing a peace treaty to end the 1965 war between India and Pakistan.

Indiraji became prime minister on 24 January 1966, but since I have already dealt with her policies and some of her game-changing decisions, I'll skip the next eleven years of her rule and come straight to Morarji Desai, who assumed the reins on 24 March 1977, after the Janata Party had swept the Congress out in an anti-Emergency wave. Desai was independent India's first prime minister to ban currency notes. On 16 January 1978, he withdrew the legal-tender status of ₹1,000, ₹5,000 and ₹10,000 banknotes in a crackdown on illicit wealth—decades before Narendra Modi would announce his demonetization decision on one November evening in 2016.

Among other key economic highlights of the Janata Party government were the legalization of strikes, outlawed by Indiraji, and reinstatement of trade unions. Both affected economic activity.

Another highlight was that two multinational companies—IBM and Coca-Cola—shut their India operations during this time. That was after George Fernandes, the symbol of resistance during the Emergency but industry minister in the Janata Party government, insisted that the two companies comply with the Foreign Exchange Regulation Act (FERA). Under the provisions of that Act, which has since been repealed, foreign investors could not own over 40 per cent in Indian enterprises.

Desai resigned on 28 July 1979, as the Janata coalition imploded under the burden of its own contradictions.

In my assessment, Morarji bhai was inclined towards the Right, whereas Indiraji believed this country could never be run on such an ideology. I agree with her and that was why, in my view, she leaned towards the Left, which cherishes certain principles. On that basis, I don't consider the BJP a political party, because it has no principles; it thrives on RSS ideology. The RSS calls itself a cultural organization and does not enter the electoral arena. But those who fight elections on the BJP symbol are all adherents of RSS ideology. The BJP is only a label.

We in the Congress have many ideological, moral and ethical issues with our political rivals, particularly those belonging to ultra-Right wing. We often see how religion, emotions and religious symbols are manipulated to achieve electoral success. All while the Constitutional duty to promote liberal, scientific temper, eradicate poverty and championing the cause of the poor have not been prioritized.

If there are principle-based political parties, they are on the Left. They are cadre-based parties and, although we might not agree with their principles, they have certain values. I consider only the Left parties and the Congress as true political outfits. The rest are either religion-based parties or caste-based ones. Can such ideologies drive this vast country? This country can move forward only on the basis of Gandhi's ideology. Some changes in the system, in keeping with the times, may be desirable but the basic principles have to be the same, the values and ideology have to be the same.

I am unable to understand what exactly they mean by 'Hindu Rashtra'. I am not a social scientist but, from what I understand, is it not a repeat of the 'Gujarat pattern of 2002' to browbeat and intimidate the minorities or perpetuate hate? In Gujarat, I regret to say, a large number of Muslims seem resigned to their fate. They say they have to live in whatever condition that has been created for them. Is it the Gujarat Model of 2002 which the BJP says it will repeat at the Centre?

The Congress alone is not responsible for this sorry state of affairs. I had once asked Sharad Pawar what he was planning to do to combat communal forces. I told him that he should mobilize secular forces. All secular forces should come together, whether they are led by Lalu Prasad Yadav, Nitish Kumar or Mulayam Singh Yadav. But the determination of regional leaders is often not the same as that of a national party like the Congress and its leadership.

V.P. Singh, who succeeded Rajivji in 1989 as India's prime minister, will largely be remembered for implementing the Mandal Commission Recommendations that paved the way for reservation for OBC in government jobs. He introduced no real changes in the economic policy. Singh may also be reminisced for being a politician who provided legitimacy to the BJP's brand of mixing politics with religion. He had sought BJP's support against Rajivji and us, and ran the government for eleven months leaning on the BJP's support. The parliamentary elections of 1989 saw the BJP winning 89 seats, up from two in 1984. It was the first credible performance of the BJP after its formation in 1980.

By the time Chandra Shekhar took charge as prime minister (10 November 1990–21 June 1991) with the outside support of the Congress, signs were already evident that the Indian economy was hurtling towards a crisis. Chandra Shekhar's finance minister, Yashwant Sinha, was aware of the situation and, on 30 May 1991, the country, for the first time, had to sell 20 tonnes of gold to investment bank UBS to secure a $240-million loan. It pledged gold three more times after that sale, shipping 46.8 million tonnes of the yellow metal to secure $400 million in loans from the Bank of England and the Bank of Japan. All that gold was repurchased by December that year. By then, a new government was in place, headed by Narasimha Rao, who took over the reins on 21 June 1991, with Manmohan Singh as his finance minister.

The BJP's Atal Bihari Vajpayee succeeded Rao on 16 May 1996, but resigned on June 1 after the party failed to rustle up a majority. The country would see two more prime ministers over the next twenty-one months—H.D. Deve Gowda and Inder Kumar Gujral—before Vajpayeeji would return to power in March 1998. He would remain in the saddle till May 2004, focusing on the creation of infrastructure and divestment in PSUs, an idea his finance minister, Yashwant Sinha, had conceived in his 1990–91 budget.

I'll skip the UPA years, as I have already dealt with those previously, and come directly to the current government headed by Narendra Modi, who took over on 26 May 2014. Modi has chosen to discontinue with the Nehruvian legacy and one of the first steps he took was to replace the Planning Commission with the public policy think tank NITI Aayog in 2015. He also merged the railway budget with the main Union budget in 2017.

On 8 November 2016, Modi dramatically announced the demonetization decision, justifying the note-scrapping move as an effort to curb black money and terror financing but, in the process, ending up hurting the economy too. That was followed by the introduction of the Goods and Services Tax (GST), a uniform indirect tax regime for the entire country that disrupted businesses, initially.

The Modi government also introduced the Insolvency and Bankruptcy Code, 2016, which made it possible for lenders to oust errant promoters from a company and hand it over to financially sound owners.

Financial inclusion was already underway for the downtrodden, the elderly, weaker sections, women and adivasis, among others, when Prime Minister Modi went on a name-changing spree and sough credit for the Pradhan Mantri Jan Dhan Yojana (PMJDY). It was Prime Minister Dr Manmohan Singh's idea that over 36 crore new bank accounts should be opened to bring the vast majority of Indians within the ambit of a formal banking system, and the financial inclusion of those at the bottom of the income pyramid.

From 2014 onwards, a debate of sorts has begun on whether Gandhian and Nehruvian values were alien to India and Indian conditions. Nothing can be further from the truth. Gandhi's ideology has an international appeal. Some African countries have also been influenced by it. The core of Gandhian philosophy is non-violence. You will recall that the Swadeshi movement was at its peak when the Chauri Chaura incident happened. Some overzealous activists burnt twenty-two policemen alive in a police station, prompting Gandhiji to halt the movement. Nehruji and other leaders of the movement were aghast at the decision and criticized it, saying Gandhiji shouldn't have suspended the movement. But Gandhiji had remained firm. He said the means must be as pure as the goal and violence had no place in the movement.

Unfortunately, we have collectively failed to transmit Gandhian values to the young generation. This is where we have failed. However, a vice chancellor of a university recently told me not to lose hope, saying the young generation was more forward-looking, had their eyes fixed on the future and thought less about caste, temple, mosque or gurdwara. Let us hope he is proved right.

I'll end this chapter with an exhortation. It is our collective responsibility to rebuild the nation and the government has to play a major role in that effort. It needs to frame an education policy that would take India forward. The policy has to be compatible with the basic character of the country.

In our time, the emphasis would be on religious education. Children would imbibe sanskar [values] at home in what would be a joint-family system. But rebuilding the nation is not the responsibility of the government alone. No matter how hard it might try, a government cannot shape its citizens' individual character. If I am dishonest, the government cannot turn me into an honest person. That responsibility rests with the family and its sanskars. What we learn from our parents, we pass on to our children. It is like a relay race of sanskar.

Today, the family structure is broken. Parents scarcely have time for their children. The joint-family system has collapsed. Religious teaching has come to be seen as fundamentalism. Teachers don't recognize their pupils by face. If teachers scold their students, the parents get angry. These are the developments that have caused the deterioration in the society. No one seems to have honestly fulfilled their responsibility; neither parents, nor the government. Not even the society as a whole. This is what I strongly feel.

I recall an incident long back, that happened in a market in Barabanki, when a boy pulled the dupatta of a girl who was travelling by a rickshaw. The entire market had come to the defence of the harassed girl. Today, no one bothers even when a girl is molested in the open. In fact, such incidents are often given communal colours instead.

SECTION VI

MILESTONES ALONG THE JOURNEY

23

Meerut: My Parliamentary Karma Bhoomi

My parliamentary journey started on the dusty terrain of Azamgarh, but it would be the Lok Sabha constituency of Meerut I would represent for a longer period. Meerut, in Western Uttar Pradesh, was my karma bhoomi for nine years from 1980, two years after my by-election victory in Azamgarh showed that voters were willing to give Indira Gandhi another chance after the turbulent years of the Emergency.

Meerut was an unusual and difficult battle. For the record, I defeated Harish Pal of the JNP(S) by over 50,000 votes, but such figures of victory or loss are at best cold statistics; it was the underlying fundamentals that made this contest a different cup of tea. First, there was the distance between Azamgarh, my previous constituency in Eastern Uttar Pradesh, and Meerut; no less than 840 km apart. But it was not merely the physical distance that I had to overcome; culturally, demographically and politically, the eastern and western parts of Uttar Pradesh had little in common.

Despite development schemes and rising economic growth, a wide gulf still exists between the eastern and western regions of the state. Unlike Bahujan Samaj Party Chief Mayawati and a few others,

I am not for bifurcation of Uttar Pradesh; yet theoretically, there could always be two different states—a somewhat economically prosperous Western Uttar Pradesh and a relatively stagnant Eastern Uttar Pradesh. Western Uttar Pradesh's per capita GDP has always been higher, sometimes double that of the eastern part. The two regions seem decades apart but, having served both parts, I can say that humane feelings, sensitivities and the sense of belonging in both regions are the same, even though the articulation of these sentiments may be drastically different.

When Indiraji asked me to contest from Meerut, I was not so much concerned about my prospects or winning the hearts and minds of the different ethnic or caste groups, such as the Jats, Gujjars, Dalits, other weaker sections, Brahmins and Muslims, who made up the diverse electorate in this Lok Sabha constituency. Rather, it was General Shahnawaz Khan, who was in my thoughts.

Born in undivided India in Rawalpindi, Shahnawaz Khan was a freedom fighter, a former Union minister and a staunch Congressman. He had won from Meerut in 1952, 1957, 1962 and 1971, but, perhaps, the party doubted his ability to win again following his defeat in the 1977 elections. So it decided not to field him from Meerut in the 1980 elections. But it was only after I was told that General sahab would be given a ticket from Ghaziabad or Saharanpur that I agreed to contest from Meerut.

In 1956, in response to mounting public curiosity, Nehruji had set up a committee to look into the circumstances surrounding Bose's 'death' in a plane crash in Taipei on 18 August 1945. Shahnawaz Khan had headed the panel that also included Suresh Chandra Bose, Subhas Bose's brother, and S.N. Maitra, a nominee of the West Bengal government. While Suresh Bose had declined to sign the final report, Shahnawaz Khan and Maitra concluded that Subhas Bose had indeed died in the aeroplane crash. The committee declared that the ashes kept at Tokyo's Renkō-ji temple were those of Bose's and recommended that the government bring the ashes to India with due honour and erect a memorial to the freedom fighter.

When the Congress moved to 24, Akbar Road, our new party office, Shahnawaz Khan's services were requisitioned by Indiraji to train the party's youth wing. General sahab's constant thrust was on building a strong moral character and he would say that a nation was doomed if it was bereft of values.

Shahnawaz Khan had an adopted daughter, Latif Fatima, who was married to Taj Mohammad. Their son, actor Shah Rukh Khan, has outshone his grandfather in terms of fame and fortune. When Shah Rukh was young, Shahnawaz Khan would describe him as a 'true nationalist', since his mother's family had come to India from Rawalpindi at a time millions of Muslims were leaving India for Pakistan.

General sahab passed away in 1983 and was buried with full state honours near Lal Qila, the same place where he had erased his 'traitor' tag and emerged as a freedom fighter. By now, some of my readers must be wondering why I have dwelt at such length on Shahnawaz Khan, or brought up his actor grandson, after starting the chapter with my 1980 election from Meerut. Let me explain, since you have chosen to bear with me so far.

Shahnawaz Khan was a representative of an ideology of amity. That harmony has long ended; a series of communal conflagrations since the traumatic days of the Partition has only revealed how mistrust can be a potent tool in the hands of those out to further their own interests. The next few paragraphs will dwell upon the dangers of such communal polarization that claimed over 15,000 lives in fifty-eight major riots before the Godhara carnage of 2002 burnt itself forever into the collective consciousness of the nation.

While I would win from the city again in 1984, Meerut's tradition of peace had shattered in September 1982, a little more than two and a half years into my stint as MP from the constituency. By the time elections were held again in 1989, frequent riots had vitiated the atmosphere. My defeat in the Lok Sabha elections in 1989 had a lot to do with these incidents of violence that I tried to quell, while criminal elements and Right-wing Hindutva parties had a field day.

Let me say this upfront: communalism, majoritarianism, riots, arrest of innocent people on the charge of sedition and selective use of law have been blots on our otherwise vibrant and participatory democracy. Dissecting communal violence is always tricky, although most people blame district authorities for ignoring signs of an impending explosion. Meerut was no exception. The district administration failed to win the confidence of the two communities and was afraid to take unpopular measures.

The narrow lanes of Shahagasha in Meerut had a stainless record of communal harmony. Even when communal violence had broken out in Meerut earlier, the residents of Shahagasha had closed ranks. That concord ended in 1982. The violence that broke out was over a minor disagreement—a 200 sq. ft. property claimed by both communities. But the impact was huge—dozens of deaths and property worth crores of rupees was damaged.

'As always, in such conflicts, it was the poor and the underprivileged who had to bear the brunt of the violence. The conflict started as a religious one. It turned quickly into a confrontation with the Muslims on one side and the Scheduled Castes and Scheduled Tribes on the other. Then it developed beyond that into a stand-off between the district administration and the minority community,' a report published by *India Today* then had said.[16]

The biggest problem for the district administration, the report said, turned out to be the Provincial Armed Constabulary (PAC) that was pressed into service in different parts of the city. The PAC did not have the confidence of the people.

'More than twenty companies of PAC men were stationed around the town and as the riots progressed, there were allegations that they were terrorizing Muslim localities by resorting to unprovoked firings,' the magazine reported.[17]

I was then Union minister of state for labour and rehabilitation and, as an elected representative, did whatever I could, apart from briefing Indiraji and Union Home Minister P.C. Sethi. I ventured out against the district administration's directive and went on a door-to-door visit in the riot-torn areas. I regret to write that many local politicians were too intent on preserving their own positions and afraid of compromising themselves by taking what might have appeared to be a moderate stand.

I still believe that there was a political design behind the successive riots in Meerut. The constituency had always been a Congress stronghold and the entire episode had been engineered to defame the party and weaken Indira Gandhi's and then Rajiv Gandhi's following among the weaker sections and the minority population.

Meerut had started feeling a semblance of normality when communal violence erupted again on 14 April 1987, when the city's famous Nauchandi fair was in full bloom. It is said that a drunk, on-duty police sub-inspector, who had been struck by a firecracker, opened fire, killing two belonging to a particular community.

Another incident is also reported to have occurred on the same day, when members of a community had gathered for a religious sermon near the Hashimpura crossing close to a spot where a mundan (tonsure) ceremony was going on at Purwa Shaikhlal. Some people had objected to film songs being played on loudspeakers, which led to a quarrel and firing by private individuals. What followed was madness, as the violence snowballed, with shops and houses being burnt. Over the next three months, intermittent riots would leave many people dead and property worth crores of rupees destroyed.

Each time I visited hospitals, I heard the same complaint from survivors, '*Bahri log aaye the*' (outsiders had come). There was a design to the violence. The people behind the riots would bring in outsiders to Meerut to unleash violence, so that the victims would not be able to identify the thugs. Teams of rioters were reportedly swapped from one area to another, to mask their identities. It pains me to document these things.

I saw large-scale arson and looting in Hashimpura and Maliana. Often, I would not care about my own safety and try and visit the riot-affected areas in spite of the district administration's directive. Once, I was passing through the city when I noticed a stockpile of bamboo poles. I told the person who was with me, Mr Saxena, general secretary of the district Congress Committee that these bamboo poles could be potentially hazardous. On my way back from a round of the hospitals, where some of the victims had been admitted, I saw the bamboo poles had been set on fire.

I am grateful to Mr Saxena and a few others who often kept night-long vigil at Meerut's circuit house, where I stayed in May 1987. The district administration, the state's home minister and even the chief minister had advised me to keep away from Meerut and avoid staying at the circuit house. But I had a sense of duty and association with the citizens who were fighting a grim battle against mindless violence. I believe there were plans to physically attack me but, somehow, local people thwarted any such attempt. There was no police presence around me and even my own gunman was not allowed to stay.

Another aspect to the flare-up was that while the riots were at first a result of a confrontation between two communities, it ceased to be so after 22 May, when it became a Police-PAC violence against a particular community. Rajiv Gandhi, who was the prime minister then, was greatly upset by the riots. He had visited the narrow by-lanes of the riot-affected areas and ordered a CBI inquiry into the 22 May abduction and shooting of people at the Ganga canal. The allegation was that PAC personnel had rounded up dozens of Muslims and, instead of taking them to the police station, had driven them in a truck to the Ganga Canal in Muradnagar, Ghaziabad, where some were shot and reportedly thrown into the water body.

A Crime Branch, Central Investigation Department inquiry headed by Jangi Singh, DIG Police, Uttar Pradesh, began its probe into the Muradnagar canal incident on 4 June 1987. The report was submitted to the state government in October 1994 and it recommended prosecuting thirty-seven PAC personnel and police officers.

On 21 March 2015, after a long legal battle, the additional sessions judge at Tis Hazari Court, Delhi, acquitted all those eventually charged with the massacre. The court held that the evidence adduced by the prosecution was not sufficient to record guilt for the offences the accused had been charged with. It was painful for me to accept the verdict. So many innocent people had been traumatized, but the prosecution had failed to bring on record reliable material to establish the identity of the culprits.

Delhi High Court would eventually convict the accused in October 2018, after a retired police officer produced a police general diary as critical evidence in the case.

It is worth remembering that Meerut, throughout the 1980s, was one of the richest districts of Uttar Pradesh. One-third of the sugar produced in the state comes from this district and it was famous for its steel goods, too. Meerut is also known for its handloom industry that employs over 70,000 Muslim artisans. What the repeated incidents of violence did was explode the myth that economic prosperity and education reduce communal tensions in a society. Or was there something more sinister that kept the violence unfolding in the years to come? I leave that to the wisdom of this book's readers.

Looking back, 1987 was a difficult year for Meerut. If the riots shredded the veneer of peace, a massive kisan (farmer) agitation convulsed the city in January, that year. On 27 January, Bharatiya Kisan Union leader Mahendra Singh Tikait laid siege to the city with a charter of demands. Suddenly, the city was chock-a-block with tractor-trolleys, truck-tops, bullock carts, motorcycles and cars. Meerut city, with a population of six lakh then, had never seen such a congregation of humanity. The administration was in a quandary. Work was paralyzed at the commissioner's office; schools and colleges were closed, and even the judicial system came to a halt when lawyers went on strike in support of the farmers.

Food for the farmers came from far and wide, helping them sustain the agitation. Three-course meals arrived from Nainital, while tractor-loads of apples and gajar ka halwa came from other places. Some even felt that more than Tikait's personality, free food kept the agitation going. His charter of demands was as follows:

- Writing off loans, rent and electricity dues for the previous year because of drought, and concessions in electricity rates.
- Increase of sugarcane procurement price from ₹27 per quintal to ₹35.
- Reservation for farmers' wards in government jobs and pension for farmers.
- Representation of farmers in the Agricultural Prices Commission and local development bodies.
- Better payment for land acquired by the government and the right to cut trees for firewood.
- Waiver of criminal charges against farmers during agitations.

As a representative from Meerut, I had a difficult time persuading Union Home Minister Buta Singh, Finance Minister N.D. Tiwari and AICC General Secretary Ghulam Nabi Azad to ensure that the siege was lifted. But the damage had been done and I had to pay a political price for it.

The result of the 1989 Lok Sabha election left me disheartened as I realized that the communal divide that had set in, following the riots, was to a large extent responsible for my loss. It was all the more painful because, while I am a practising Muslim, I did not carry the tag of a Muslim representative in the governments headed by Indiraji and Rajiv Gandhi. Nor did I have what could be called a 'Muslim identity'.

But the riots, together with the Ayodhya movement and Mandalization (caste politics), restricted my appeal even as I moved back to Eastern Uttar Pradesh, to Domariyaganj (Siddharthnagar district), to seek the people's mandate in the 1991 elections. The district, situated on the border with Nepal, lacked development. But in the multi-corner electoral contest, what I saw was gross misuse of money, muscle power, caste and religion, as my political opponents violated every principle of propriety. To me, propriety is paramount in a parliamentary democracy like ours. As the seventeenth-century French author and moralist Francois de La Rochefoucauld had said, propriety may be the least of all laws, but most observed. I can say that I have tried to do my best to maintain propriety, even during the most testing times.

24
My Organizational Role

AFTER I HAD STOPPED CONTESTING Lok Sabha elections and had ceased to be a Union minister, I turned my attention to my original love, the Congress organization. To be honest, I enjoyed my stints as UPCC chief and AICC general secretary a bit more than my tenure as Union minister. Of course, that doesn't mean I wasn't comfortable as a minister—far from it—but perhaps I loved interacting with party workers from different parts of the country more and the pluralism they brought, a diversity the Congress has always epitomized. I still believe that only a robust Congress organization can bring back the 'good old days'.

I looked after party affairs in Punjab, Madhya Pradesh, Chhattisgarh, Bengal, Manipur, Assam, Meghalaya, Himachal Pradesh, Bihar, Jammu and Kashmir, Haryana, Karnataka and Kerala, and can say with pride and satisfaction that there was hardly a state or a region in the country where party workers were not in direct touch with me or I did not visit. It is a bond that I cherish.

Leaders, too, would acknowledge my efforts. One such endorsement came from Captain Amarinder Singh, who was the chief minister of Punjab till recently. The Congress veteran visited me on 17 July 2019, and tweeted minutes after the meeting, 'Met veteran leader Mohsina Kidwaiji in Delhi today. Had the pleasure of working with her during my first tenure as CM when she was General Secretary in-charge of Punjab. She has been a source of great strength and support all along.' I felt sad and disappointed the way things took shape in Punjab, six months before February 2022 state assembly polls. Without going into the specifics, I can say that many leaders from my party acted against the ethos and values that we had always stood for. Equally shocking was the degree of factionalism and groupism in the party. Some may argue that factionalism has been part of the Congress folklore but may I dare say that it was always within the Lakshman Rekha of party's interest. What happened in Punjab was suicidal and bizarre.

At times, I faced tricky situations too, such as in Bihar, where we got into an alliance with Lalu Prasad Yadav. I remember one of my early interactions with Laluji when he asked me if his hairstyle resembled that of actress Sadhna! I assessed that behind a comical face, Laluji was a shrewd politician who could charm both friends and foes. In 1997, he had to resign as chief minister in favour of his wife, Rabri Devi, when the CBI chargesheeted him in fodder scam cases. The Congress had faced a predicament of sorts in supporting Rabri, as some members of the Congress Working Committee were opposed to her. In 1999, the National Democratic Alliance (NDA) regime, then headed by Atal Bihari Vajpayee, dismissed Rabri Devi's government and imposed President's Rule after intercaste violence and massacre ensued. This was one move Vajpayee had to revoke within a month, because the NDA did not have the numbers in the Rajya Sabha to ratify the decision to impose President's Rule. In the subsequent Assembly elections that were held in Bihar, Lalu edged past the NDA led by his state rival Nitish Kumar.[18]

Within the Congress, opinion was again divided on supporting Rabriji. I told the working committee that the Congress should not abdicate its responsibility and should stand by Rabriji. I also argued that caste clashes had broken out even when President's Rule was in force. I accepted the fact that different views were being expressed within the Bihar Congress, but everyone was keen on keeping communal forces out. So we joined hands with Lalu's Rashtriya Janata Dal to keep the NDA out. We were committed to secularism.

Governor V.C. Pandey invited Nitish Kumar to take the first shot at forming the government. Both sides were almost equally poised. Nitish had 151 MLAs and Laluji, bolstered by our support, had the backing of 159 legislators. Technically, we had fought the elections on our own steam, although some MLAs had won on the strength of their individual standing and were apparently susceptible to local pressures to defy the high command's whip. But our party MLAs remained united and supported the RJD. The NDA was stunned. Laluji's party was home and dry.

Laluji had figured out that his first and topmost priority was to ensure that his Congress support remained intact. But matters were more complicated on the ground because eleven Congress MLAs were from south Bihar and Lalu had made his opposition to a Jharkhand–Vananchal state a prestige issue. I cannot divulge all the details even today, but can say that some deft political management by Soniaji ensured that the NDA's troubleshooters didn't even get a look-in. Prem Gupta, of the RJD, and Rajendra Singh, of the INTUC, the trade union wing of the Congress, played a significant role, too. Also, Laluji, I am glad to recall, readily accepted my proposal to make Congress veteran Sadanand Singh the Speaker of the Assembly. It sent the right feelers and, since then, Laluji and his RJD have been our trusted allies. Swapan Dasgupta, writing for *India Today*, had described me as 'the voice of the high command' who argued that 'support' to Laluji was a 'national imperative'.[19]

Modesty prevents me from saying more but I can look back with satisfaction that I and my team contributed for the party's success in Himachal Pradesh in 2003, Punjab in 2002 and Madhya Pradesh in

1998. In Himachal, my task was to forge unity between Virbhadra Singh, a veteran Congressman and leader of the legislative party, and Vidya Stokes, who headed the state Congress unit, and dispel perceptions that the Congress was a divided house in the hill state. Such was the situation that they would not even address public meetings together.

When I visited Shimla in 2002 and 2003, I insisted that there was no harm if Virbhadra Singh and Stokes addressed meetings separately as these rallies were also aimed at strengthening the party. Both of them finally decided to address a couple of meetings together. I also pointed out that there was no party that did not have internal differences.

I was looking after Rajasthan along with R.L. Bhatia when Rajasthan went to polls in November 1998. During this period, I came to know Ashok Gehlot very well, who excelled in micromanagement of polls and was made chief minister after the Congress defeated Vasundhararaje Scindia-led BJP in the state. Our mission had begun in June 1998 itself. We held many meetings and united the party leaders at state and district levels. Gehlot's easy manners, ability to take everyone along and understanding of local issues left a mark on me. He went on to win many elections and contributed immensely to the Congress organization, too.

The year 2002 would also be remembered as the year of the Gujarat riots. I remember criticizing Vajpayeeji then for shielding Narendra Modi and had remarked, 'It was unfortunate that the BJP was pursuing the two-nation theory of the RSS.'

I had never shied away from speaking my mind and was not going to change my habits, whatever the situation.

My brother, Ghayas, passed away in March 2005, and it took me long to get over the grief. Yes, French poet Jean Baptiste Legouve was right: 'A brother is a friend given by Nature.'

Exactly a year later, I received a call from Soniaji asking me to accompany her to Raebareli, where she was to file her nomination for a Lok Sabha by-election. Soniaji had just resigned, on her own accord, over an office-of-profit controversy. Soniaji was then Congress president and heading the National Advisory Council as its chairperson. While she was within her rights to continue as a Lok Sabha MP, she resigned and got re-elected after actress Jaya Bachchan of the Samajwadi Party was disqualified by the Election Commission for holding the post of chairperson of the Uttar Pradesh Film Development Corporation. According to Article 102(1)(a) of the Constitution, a person shall be disqualified as MP for holding any office of profit under the government of India or the government of any state, other than an office declared by parliament by law not to disqualify its holder.

Soniaji's gesture was in keeping with Indiraji's and Rajivji's personal warmth and affection for me. Looking back, I can say that these gestures have been far more rewarding for me than any high public office.

Other positives have accrued too, from my years as AICC general secretary, intangible gains that can never be measured, such as knowledge and insight, especially into the party organization, its strengths and weaknesses. While that would need a whole volume to express in words, let me make some observations for the benefit of my readers.

It is true that in many states there is a grave crisis of leadership in the Congress, Uttar Pradesh being a glaring example of that. But it is the state leaders themselves who are responsible for this crisis as they have abdicated their responsibilities when they should be beholden to the high command for guiding them.

Groupism within the organization or factionalism is another reason for our weakness. I understand personal ambitions but personal interest at the cost of the party often causes more damage than one could imagine. My request to the present and future generation of Congress persons is simple. Please keep the party's interest above personal gains.

We are all aware that Soniaji was reluctant to enter active politics and it was only after repeated requests that she took up leadership. When she finally agreed to become party president, there were hardly two or three states where the Congress was in power. Under her leadership, the Congress managed to come to power in seventeen states. The political atmosphere was the same, so were the organization and the people, but a lot changed under her leadership.

My grouse is against state-level leaders. The party gave them status and position, made them chief ministers or PCC chiefs, but they squandered the advantage by indulging in groupism and factionalism. Had the state leaders been more responsible, and not left it entirely to Soniaji, Priyanka Gandhi or Rahul Gandhi to revive the Congress, the party would not have landed in this situation.

Going back to what I have said earlier, the party won power in seventeen states after Soniaji assumed the reins in 1998, a remarkable turnaround, considering that the Congress ruled in only two or three smaller states when she took over. So who was responsible for the Congress losing those states? The state leadership, certainly.

Before Soniaji joined active politics, she would watch Indiraji and Rajivji tackle difficult problems facing the nation, but would avoid taking interest in matters of governance unless drawn into discussions by them. Indiraji used to respect her sense of aloofness, except in the last six months of her life, when she shared a lot of things with her bahu, who had become like a daughter to her.

The stamp of the Nehru-Gandhi family legacy was evident when Soniaji finally took over as the party chief in 1998. She took many decisions based on what she had learnt from her mother-in-law and her husband, but most remarkable was that she consciously avoided making mistakes. She did not disturb chief ministers of Congress-ruled states, a freedom these leaders should have utilized to take every faction along with them. Alas, that did not happen. Just to make things more complicated, AICC general secretaries began aligning with the chief minister concerned, the legislative party leader or the state PCC chief, instead of being a neutral observer. I think the role of an AICC general secretary as part of the party high command needs to be re-emphasized.

In my long and largely rewarding political career, I have one regret—that of not being able to retain Mamata Banerjee in the party fold. She left sometime in late 1997 to form the Trinamool Congress, when Sitaram Kesri was the Congress chief. It was around the time I had just returned to the Congress, following the merger of the Congress (Tiwari) with the parent organization, and had not been given any specific role in the new organization as yet. However, relying on my earlier experience of handling party affairs in Bengal, I can say that Mamata Banerjee was wronged by many, including those claiming to be Pranab Mukherjee's camp followers in the state politics. Pranab was my good friend and an exceptional Union minister. Somehow, I could not help noticing that when it came to Bengal party politics, Mukherjee had a rigid and unforgiving attitude towards some Bengal politicians. In his memoir, Pranab has sought to explain his ties with Mamata.

P.V. Narasimha Rao had assigned me the task of conducting party polls in Bengal soon after he took over as Congress president and the prime minister. I had then summoned all major leaders from the state, including Siddhartha Shankar Ray, A.B.A. Ghani Khan Choudhury, Priya Ranjan Dasmunshi, Somen Mitra, Pranab Mukherjee and others, for a meeting at my Bishambhar Das Marg residence. There was near unanimity that the views and strength of district Congress committee members would be ascertained to decide the new PCC chief. Clearly, Mamata had the majority but

Mitra went to court to disqualify certain voters. This was a tad unfair as intra-party matters should not be dragged to courts.

But in his book, *The Coalition Years*, Mukherjee has given his version of the events while terming Mamata Banerjee a 'born rebel'. The book, which came out in 2017, described how he was left feeling 'humiliated and insulted' after she once stormed out of a meeting where he was present. Mukherjee has, however, acknowledged in his book that there was an aura about Mamata that was 'difficult to explain but impossible to ignore', adding that she had built her career fearlessly and aggressively and that where she stood today was the 'outcome of her own struggle'.

Mamata was minister of state for youth affairs in Rao Sahab's council of ministers but would often be referred to contemptuously as 'that girl' by the Jyoti Basu-led Marxist regime in Bengal. But 'that girl' single-handedly created a lot of trouble for the then Left government in Bengal, hitting the Marxists where it hurt most—in their media image and in the public's perception of their policies. She would keep reminding people of Tagore's famous revolutionary words, '*Jodi tor daak shune keu na aase, tabe ekla chalo re* (Even if nobody responds to your call, go ahead alone)'. The louder she cried about 'the conspiracy to kill her', the more supporters would rally to her cause.

Digvijaya Singh was the Youth Congress general secretary when I was the UPCC president. He had come to invite me to a Youth Congress meeting to be held in Indore. I readily consented. He was a very promising young individual and extremely passionate about his work in the party. His daughter Mrinalini and my daughter Irum were classmates in school in Delhi. They are still good friends. He often refers to Irum as his fifth daughter. Over the years, when I became AICC general secretary and was given charge of the Congress-ruled state of Madhya Pradesh, Chief Minister Digvijaya

Singh and I worked closely on several matters. He held me in high esteem and I always found him to be an asset for the party.

When I was at the UPCC, Nirmal Khatri had come to meet me from Faizabad. I still remember my first conversation with him, 'Do you want to fight a by-election?' I had asked him. Surprised and overwhelmed, he hesitated at first. However, I encouraged him for the candidature and supported him. The electoral fight was a difficult one, as he was pitted against Anantram Jaiswal of the Janata Party. It was 1977 when the Janata Party was ruling at the Centre. Nirmal lost by barely 400 votes. When the next round of Assembly polls were held in 1979, I backed Nirmal Khatri again and this time around, he emerged triumphant. The politician in him has not looked back since, though he has remained extremely polite and gentle.

25
Chairperson, Central Haj Committee

> 'Whoever performs haj for the sake of Allah and does not utter any obscene speech or do any evil deed, will go back (free of sin) as his mother bore him.'
>
> (Bukhari; Muslim) Sahih al-Bukhari 1521

As we understand, haj is one of the five fundamental Muslim practices or pillars of Islam. The pilgrimage rite begins on the seventh day of Dhū al-Ḥijjah (the last month of the Islamic year) and ends on the twelfth day. It is incumbent on all Muslims who are physically and financially able to make the pilgrimage.

For every Muslim that I know, undertaking this sacred pilgrimage is a once-in-a-lifetime journey. It's definitely an unforgettable one and I can vouch for it. As a practising Muslim, I had performed haj along with my husband Khalil in 1986. I have also had several opportunities to visit Saudi Arabia, where I had consistently performed 'Umrah' or mini pilgrimage.

But on 10 March 2010, I suddenly and surprisingly found myself saddled with the gigantic task of haj management in India. I was AICC general secretary and a Rajya Sabha member from Chhattisgarh. As a new Haj Act was passed by the parliament in 2002, I was made a member of the Central Haj Committee. Established in 1927 for the purpose of haj management, the central haj panel did not have a woman head, except for 1989, when Anwara Taimur had discharged the responsibility for barely five months.

When I reached Parliament House and the chamber of External Affairs Minister S.M. Krishna, I saw many familiar faces, including Ahmed Patel, E. Ahmed and other Muslim parliamentarians, community leaders, among others. Ahmed quickly approached me and whispered that I should head the Central Haj Committee as it was desired by both Soniaji and Prime Minister Dr Manmohan Singh. I did not know how to react. Having been a cabinet minister and held several party posts, I had never fancied myself as a 'Muslim' politician or a community leader. However, circumstances and Soniaji's affection forced me to accept the job with full humility. I always believed I have a personal responsibility to make a positive impact on society. I often found myself in agreement with novelist Chuck Palahniuk's comment, 'Find joy in everything you choose to do. Every job, relationship, home … it's your responsibility to love it, or change it.'

This love and affection for haj management lasted for three years. When I look back, often eyes moist with a sense of gratitude towards the Almighty that my humble self was chosen for the gigantic task of haj management, I pray that some of my efforts pave the way for my salvation and please God in such a way that not me but my dear ones too benefit from His divine blessings.

The assignment was arduous one. The haj is one of the most complex organizational tasks undertaken by Government of India outside Indian borders. Although it is only a five-day long religious congregation, it virtually is a yearlong managerial exercise. Indian pilgrims constitute the third largest national group performing the haj after Indonesia and Pakistan. The broad norm followed by Saudi authorities is to indicate a quota of 1,000 pilgrims for every million of the Muslim population in a country. Consequently, a quota of 1,70,025 pilgrims was allotted to India for Haj 2013. Most travelers are first timers abroad and unaware of the protocols and customs of a foreign land. Food, stay, communication and sectarian practices pose multiple challenges.

Over 90 per cent of Indian hajis perform haj for the first time and almost all of them travel abroad for the first time. I felt it was our duty to make them comfortable and the pilgrimage a memorable experience. During my tenure, a special film was made explaining the practical aspects of haj, right from the time of arrival in Saudi Arabia to the departure, which is almost a forty-day affair. The film was uploaded to our website and on YouTube. We encouraged all state haj committees and private operators to screen it at their training and familiarization programme. We even got a survey done later on, where the findings revealed that 95 per cent of hajis found the film very helpful for haj.

We need to also remember that the contemporary ethnic India is an accumulation of several cultures, religions, languages and evolutionary histories, and Muslims are no exceptions. Since its introduction in the Indian subcontinent, Islam has had significant religious, artistic, philosophical, cultural, social and political influences on Indian history.

Muslim traders, mystics, preachers and invaders have shaped and influenced the Indian subcontinent for thirteen centuries, ensuing significant cultural diffusion of Muslim traditions among the ethnic Indian population till date. A majority of Muslims in India declare either Sunni Deobandi or Sunni Barelwi allegiance, while others follow Shia, Sufi, Salafi, Bohra and other smaller sects. For haj, while broadly all Islamic sects follow similar customs and traditions, familiarizing them with Saudi norms is an area of training.

As per the Central Haj Committee Act, in 2010, I was made chairperson of the Haj Committee of India and tasked to make arrangements for pilgrimage of Muslims not only for haj but for matters connected therewith. My mandate was to coordinate with senior officials from the Ministry of Minority Affairs, Ministry of External Affairs, Ministry of Civil Aviation, Air India, tour operators, state haj committee units and other stakeholders.

The haj quota, or the number of hajis going to Makkah and Madina, is fixed by the government. The state-wise quota of haj seats is distributed among the states and union territories on the basis of their Muslim populations. In case the state haj committees receive applications in excess of the quota, then the seats are confirmed to the intending pilgrims through draw of lots (qurrah). Once the permissible number of hajis have been selected, the Consulate General of India, Jeddah is tasked to make accommodation available at Makkah and Madina, allot flights and monitor the movement of the pilgrims.

The Indian hajis have special interest in bringing holy water known as Zam Zam to India. Since 2004, airlines ferrying hajis have permitted 10 litres of Zam Zam to all pilgrims at disembarkation points in India. We introduced safely wrapped PET bottles properly packed at the Zam Zam factory, which were handed over to every haji upon their return at the embankment point. Prior to this, hajis used to buy their own bottles to fill with Zam Zam—leading to incidents of breakage, causing loss of zam zam and damage to luggage. Similarly, during 2012, I had the satisfaction to see hajis receive neat and new bedsheets, pillow covers, buckets, mugs, etc. supplied by an agency, at their buildings. This ensured uniformity and quality of the items at no extra cost to the hajis. I guess being a woman helped me identify these seemingly small but significant reforms. The State Bank of India was most helpful when it introduced Vishwa Yatra Foreign Travel card to our hajis in 2011. This was a prepaid currency card which could be operated just like ATM cards in Saudi Arabia. Money could be added to the card by anyone in India.

I also introduced a system that applicants above the age of eighty should be automatically considered in the next year if they fail to get a chance to perform haj through the process of qurrah (drawing of lots) as mentioned earlier. This formulation helped many hopefuls to fulfill their dream of a lifetime.

I must mention the good work done by Faiz Ahmed Kidwai, a bright IAS officer who was posted as Consul General at Jeddah. Along with the Haj Committee Vice Presidents Hasan Ahmed and Aboo Bucker, we all worked together as a team. As I mentioned earlier, I received full cooperation from ministers S.M. Krishna and his deputy, E. Ahmed. With Saudis, we worked out quick settlement of cases of loss of cash and theft. Under the new system, the pilgrims were promptly compensated. There used to be 1,000–1,100 cases of cash loss, theft, among others, every year. We were also able to check a corrupt practice of sending beggars in the garb of pilgrims, which often maligned the image of our country. In 2011, we had detected 166 cases of beggars and subsequently eliminated the racket.

Please remember that in the port town of Jeddah, our Consulate General gets fully involved right from the airport, when the pilgrims arrive, and remains involved till the departure of the last pilgrim. A large contingent of seasonal local staff, supervisors, clerks, data entry operators, drivers and messengers, is appointed by Consul General of India to look after the pilgrims. In addition, doctors, nurses, pharmacists, lab technicians, coordinators, assistant haj officers, haj assistants and khadim-ul-hujjaj (or volunteers) are sent from India on short-term deputation basis to Saudi Arabia.

Apart from the Main Office-cum-dispensary, a fifty-bedded hospital in Makkah, eleven dispensaries-cum-branch offices are also set up in Makkah (two of these dispensaries also have provision for ten beds each; four in Madinah). Sixteen ambulances are deployed in Makkah and Madinah. Mobile teams of doctors keep visiting buildings housing Indian pilgrims. Translators are deployed in all Saudi hospitals in Makkah to assist Indian pilgrims. Medicines are supplied from India in advance of the haj period every year.

Accommodation as part of the Reserved Accommodation Scheme (RAS) is arranged under the supervision of the Consulate General. There are well-set procedures and norms to rent buildings. Help of Building Selection Teams (BSTs) sent by state haj committees is also taken. The buildings identified/measured by the BSTs are approved by members of the haj committee, who visit as Building Selection Committees (BSCs). We had hired 441 buildings in Makkah and Madina in 2013, while in 2012, the number of buildings hired were 479. I was very particular that we should accommodate families in rooms close to one another. By 2013, the figure went up to 39 per cent, from 17 per cent in 2011. We also had more data entry operators to ensure that all details of flight, accommodation of every haji was available online. Among the bureaucracy and haj committee, we had common mailing IDs and group mailing IDs. This led to seamless synergy. There were many more initiatives based on information technology. By 2011, we developed a quick lost baggage identification and location system and complete pilgrims' insurance management system. By 2013, I used to have a daily situation report at my table as well as on our website, complete flight-wise break-up and details of khadim-ul-hujjaj on the website.

In between 2010 and 2013, I had the satisfaction of supervising three haj with care and an eye for detail. We introduced many reforms that ranged from giving every haji a mobile chip and hot rotis (chapatis) along with their daily meals. For the first time, SIM cards with preloaded contact members of Saudi agencies and Indian haj offices were provided to pilgrims at embarkation points before their departure. The relatives of the hajis in India were also provided the contact number of pilgrims and their numbers were also uploaded on our website.

In 2011, we introduced remote city check-in during departure, which was a grand success. Under this system, the luggage of pilgrims was collected twenty-four hours before, from their residential buildings. It saved the hajis from facing overweight or oversized luggage, cut short delays during the return phase.

As the chairperson of the Central Haj Committee, I must acknowledge that Saudi officials, ministers and government were most helpful. As a woman, I faced no problem, neither was I ever expected to wear Abaya or any dress code. However, my own values and roots in faith always helped in according the highest respect to the holy places of Makkah and Madina.

Significantly, for the 2022 haj, the Saudi Ministry of Haj and Umrah said women did not need to have a male guardian to register and could do so along with other women. 'Those wishing to perform Haj will have to register individually. Women can register without a mahram (male guardian) along with other women,' the ministry had said in a tweet.

The landmark steps erode the longstanding guardianship system that renders adult women as legal minors and allows their 'guardians'—husband, father and other male relatives—to exercise arbitrary authority over them.

I may mention here that the issue of allowing women to perform haj on their own without a guardian was in discussion when I was representing the Indian Central Haj Committee. In 2014, Saudi

Arabia carried out the annual updating of haj guidelines where the rule on not allowing women without a male escort was changed, subject to the condition that they travelled in a group and were above forty-five years.

In 2017, Indian haj management recommended that women above forty-five years, unaccompanied by a man, should be allowed on haj pilgrimage in groups of four.

SECTION VII

MEMORIES AND IMPRESSIONS

26

Colleagues and Opponents

I HAVE FINALLY COME TOWARDS THE end of my narrative, the last section of this chronicle, immensely relieved, as well as surprised. Relieved because for a writer, an unexpressed thought is like an ache, a heavy burden that hangs heavy on my mind. And surprised because even a few months ago, I had doubts whether I could ever complete this book. One obvious reason for such misgivings was my advanced age; I have crossed ninety, an age where driving yourself to perform even routine tasks can sometimes be a struggle. Fortunately, my memories, my interactions with people, fellow politicians of different hues, go deep and far back—one reason the words did not dry up. Age has its own recompense, the unique privilege of reminiscence and the impressions of a lifetime.

So before I wrap up this memoir, I'd like to record some more impressions; basically, brief sketches of key leaders I came across in my long journey in politics, such as Mulayam Singh Yadav, Dr Manmohan Singh, Pranab Mukherjee, Farooq Abdullah of Kashmir and many others, who in their own way, for the better or worse, played a vital role in shaping the nation's destiny. As the word 'impression' suggests, these are entirely my own perceptions and my readers are free to disagree with what I have to say.

Sonia Gandhi

I met Soniaji several times on events and occasions across the span of my political and personal interaction with Indiraji and her family.

Indiraji would often talk about Soniaji and how well she had taken to the family. How she was such a caring and considerate daughter-in-law. When I complimented Indiraji on her beautiful selection of sarees, she had very proudly and pleasingly responded, 'Mohsina, Sonia often selects my sarees, aren't they so beautiful?' she had smiled.

Rajivji had introduced Soniaji to me once after my Azamgarh victory. He had proudly told her how my Azamgarh victory was such a proud moment for the Congress party and a catalyst to its comeback. After Indiraji's and Rajivji's tragic demise, Soniaji always upheld and respected our relationships. When she came to the helm of affairs and even before that, I would meet her often. Once she took on the responsibility of the Congress president and fought her first Lok Sabha election from Raebareli, I too had travelled there to join her when she went to file for the nomination papers. It was a very sentimental moment for me as well. I also joined in on Rahul's first nomination from Amethi, just like I would join Indiraji when she would file her nomination papers in her constituency.

This family and my association with them has been a constant parallel in my life. After we lost Indiraji, I felt a deep sense of vacuum. My loyalties and love for Indiraji and her family kept me close to them even after her loss. The love and emotions which cemented my association with Indiraji would always inherently make me reach out to her family, unwaveringly.

Just like Rajivji did, Soniaji too has, in all her capacity and predicament, upheld and honoured our relationship. So have her children, Rahul and Priyanka.

I want to emphasize here how difficult and truly unfathomable it is for any of us to understand her situation. In all that she has endured and suffered through all these years, after losing Rajivji, she has kept her entire life moving forward with such dignity and poise. From the very beginning of her marriage to Rajivji, she adapted and eased into all the Indian traditions and culture as her own. She seamlessly exudes the very Indian ethos she has imbibed and which she wholeheartedly lives.

The upbringing and values she has inculcated in both Rahul and Priyanka are absolutely incredible. A family that has suffered such grave personal loss and tragedy could have easily let go and moved on. But she chose otherwise. Her deep love for this country and its people is apparent and speaks volumes, and this is true for all of them, unequivocally. She has passionately held on to Indirajis and Rajivji's legacy and what they and their forefathers had stood for and fought for. She has carried it on with much humility, respect and responsibility. Her self-determination despite her own sacrifice and tragedy is to be admired and deeply respected.

It is very creditable how she has perfected her political acumen. She had always—in her life, in Indiraji's, and later on in her own household—been a passive onlooker at the very passionate political environment she was living in. She kept to her family and guarded very intensely their very private and personal spaces and time. However, at the time of calling for her responsibility toward her family's legacy, and to keep the Congress party together, tighter and alive, she stepped in with immense commitment and determination.

She was very sure of herself as she moved on, keeping all the heavyweights and loyal aides of the party close to her, on all political issues. She listened carefully and made her choices and decisions to the best of her own judgement, that she deciphered from her consultations and the advice she received from all her closely trusted leaders and workers. She did it very well and with immense success.

Her own strength as a strong leader surfaced in the continuous success that the Congress party saw in the years that followed her assumption of leadership, in the state elections and general elections. She was very clear that neither she nor her children would be behind the seats of power or position when she very categorically refused to take on the position of the prime minister.

Her selfless pursuit, despite her own personal struggles and anguish, of strengthening the Congress party at every step and level, is a commendable accolade in itself. Sometimes I wonder whether we as Congressmen failed to live up to her hardwork, commitment and dedication to the cause of the party. Once again, I wish to blame the ugly head of factionalism and personal ambition for the downfall of the Congress in post 2014 era. Sometimes for petty and personal benefits, Congress leaders indulged in acts and activities that not only weakened the great organization (the Indian National Congress) but allowed communal forces to consolidate their strangehold over the body polity of the country.

Mulayam Singh Yadav

I'll kick off this section with my impressions of the Samajwadi Party founder Mulayam Singh Yadav and, I'm afraid, this is not going to be too pleasant a read for his supporters. While I feel that nothing negative should be said about anyone, Mulayam Singh, I think, laid himself bare to criticism with the kind of political behaviour he has often exhibited. Opportunism has been the constant companion of this former wrestler and drawing teacher, who would eventually take up politics as his profession.

An example of how unreliable he could be came in early 1990. Mulayam had become chief minister the previous year. He and the Janata Dal had formed the government in Uttar Pradesh with the Bharatiya Janata Party's outside support. The BJP, however, withdrew its backing in 1990, after a confrontation near the Babri Masjid in Ayodhya between state police and kar sevaks. Mulayam had then sought the Congress's support, which was given, although I had, at internal party forums, opposed it.

But Mulayam had made some friends in the Congress who had worked out a tacit understanding with him. He then told Rajiv Gandhi that he would support the Congress at the national level if we backed him in the Uttar Pradesh Assembly. After Rajivji accepted the proposal, Mulayam resigned, forcing fresh elections in a stunning U-turn.

In some ways, Mulayam Singh owed his meteoric rise to Lalu Prasad Yadav. He saw how Lalu Prasad had united Muslims and Yadavs in Bihar and then replicated that approach in his home state of Uttar Pradesh, which has a large population of the historically underprivileged.

The Congress at that time had a strong united base, consisting of Brahmins, Muslims and Dalits and, if we look at the party's contributions, it has done a lot for the weaker sections. Above all, it gave them respect and dignity. The Scheduled Caste Act, for instance, that the party brought, acted as a deterrent against caste-based discrimination and I believe that it has helped a lot in suppressing such practices. After Bahujan Samaj Party leader Mayawati came into the picture, she ignited the fire of caste-based rivalry again. When Mulayam Singh saw how Mayawati had given the Dalits a powerful voice, he sensed an opportunity and started working towards uniting the Muslims and the backward classes. This widened the gap between Brahmins and Dalits in Uttar Pradesh.

My assessment of Mulayam Singh has been backed by well-known political commentators. I quote what Aditi Phadnis, Political Editor, *Business Standard*, wrote on 26 June 2012: 'Mulayam Singh has never been a reliable ally. Chandra Shekhar was one of his mentors. But when it came to choosing a prime minister on that fateful day in Central Hall, Mulayam Singh backed V.P. Singh. When he couldn't get along with V.P. Singh, he dumped him; the pretext being that V.P. Singh was negotiating with the Bharatiya Janata Party behind his back. He was then chief minister of UP. Then, he made common cause with Chandra Shekhar. And how did he describe the relationship? He told his biographers, '*Ham to experiment kar rahe hain. VP ko dekh liya ab Chandra Shekhar ki bari hai. Baat bahut saaf hai: jis taraf Mulayam rahega wohi mazboot ho jayega*' (I am experimenting. I have seen VP; now it is Chandra Shekhar's turn. Whoever Mulayam aligns with will become strong).[20]

That wasn't the last of Mulayam Singh's astonishing U-turns. In 1999, after the fall of the Atal Bihari Vajpayee government at the Centre, Mulayam Singh had told us he would support an alternative, coalition government to be headed by the Congress. It was on the strength of that assurance that Soniaji had declared that she had 272 MPs and more were coming over. Mulayam Singh later backed out. The BJP would then go on to form the government.

Aditi Phadnis also recalled Mulayam Singh's flip-flop during the 2002 presidential election. The Samajwadi Party was then a constituent of the People's Front, a coalition of non-Congress and non-BJP political parties. The BJP-led NDA, which was in power at the Centre, had floated A.P.J. Abdul Kalam's name as its candidate for President. The Left parties, which were constituents of the People's Front, had opposed Kalam and decided to field Captain Lakshmi Sahgal, a veteran freedom fighter from Netaji Subhas Chandra Bose's Indian National Army. The Samajwadis had then parted ways with the People's Front at the eleventh hour and supported Kalam's candidature. The Left had accused Mulayam Singh of betrayal, but the Samajwadi leader got political mileage by supporting a 'Muslim' for the post of president.[21]

Looking back, I have little hesitation in saying that Mulayam Singh's order to police to open fire on marching kar sevaks in

Ayodhya in 1990, and the excesses that were carried out under him, proved politically costly for all, including the minority community. Mulayam Singh claims his political guru was Ram Manohar Lohia, but I would say his support for the socialist political leader's ideology was also a convenient public façade.

For those not too familiar with India's political history, several parties had emerged from the freedom movement. While most of them emanated from the Congress, they lacked vision and often clashed with the Grand Old Party on policies. In the 1960s, for instance, Lohiaji had coined a slogan to press for scrapping the use of English, which he called a 'hindrance to original thinking'.[22] Had Lohiaji got his way, this country would have been reduced to a frog in the well.

Lohiaji would describe Marxism as the 'last weapon of Europe against Asia'. Propounding the 'Principle of Equal Irrelevance', he rejected both Marxism and capitalism. While nobody should have any objection to socialist thinking, the crude manner in which socialism was thus being promoted was wrong.

Coming back to Mulayam Singh, I have nothing against him personally, and we have maintained cordial ties. His personal conduct towards me has also been above reproach. I still remember what he told me one day when we were coming out of Parliament together: 'Mohsinaji, I have heard that when you were in UP, the politics there was very good,' he said.

I repeat, I have nothing against Mulayam Singh on a personal level, but I think the way he encouraged casteism in his state and increased the rift between communities has been harmful for Uttar Pradesh politics.

Mulayam Singh's son Akhilesh, a former chief minister, who now heads the Samajwadi Party, is a well-educated and smart individual, but has to understand that the need of the hour is to work towards a joint opposition against the present regime. Akhilesh, I must also say, has done a lot to develop Uttar Pradesh and whenever I travel down the Agra–Lucknow Expressway, considered to be his pet project, I think of him. Akhilesh, who assumed charge as chief minister in March 2012, inaugurated the 302 km, six-lane expressway in November 2016, a few months before he demitted office.

N.D. Tiwari

Narayan Dutt Tiwari was a very able man who, perhaps, did not get as much as he deserved in public life. A freedom fighter, Tiwariji had come from a socialist background and his thinking was grounded in socialism. As I have said earlier in this book, the old Socialist Party and the Congress were close, ideologically, a possible reason why Tiwariji fitted well in the Congress.

Tiwariji was born into a Kumaoni family, years after his father Poornanand Tiwari had resigned from his Forest Department job to join Mahatma Gandhi's non-cooperation movement in 1920–22. Two decades later, when Gandhiji launched the Quit India Movement in 1942, Tiwariji joined the movement and became a lifelong political activist thereafter. He was a member of the All India Student Congress till 1949, but after Independence, contested Assembly elections as a Praja Socialist Party candidate.

In 1952, Tiwariji won from Nainital to become an MLA in the Uttar Pradesh Assembly. The district is now part of Uttarakhand, following the bifurcation of Uttar Pradesh in November 2000. He retained the seat in 1957 and became the leader of the Opposition in the Assembly.

By 1963, Tiwariji had joined the Congress and, two years later, won from Kashipur (also in Uttarakhand now) to become a minister in the Uttar Pradesh government. He would eventually go on to head the Uttar Pradesh government thrice.

Tiwariji also held the distinction of handling two key portfolios at the Centre—first as the external affairs minister and then as the finance minister—during 1986–88, before returning to Uttar Pradesh as chief minister for the third and final time. He would later become the chief minister of Uttarakhand in 2002—the only Indian politician to have served as the chief minister of two states—and complete a full five-year term at the helm.

Always mild-mannered and polite, Tiwariji was a tough administrator who would brook no nonsense when it came to taking decisions. As chief minister of Uttar Pradesh, his top priority and life's mission was 'vikas' (development). I was a junior minister in his cabinet when the idea of Noida as a planned city was conceived. While it was actually a brainchild of Sanjay Gandhi, Tiwariji, who was considered to be very close to Indiraji's younger son, took that vision forward. Set up as part of an urbanization thrust under the UP Industrial Area Development Act, 1976, Noida came into administrative existence in April that year.

The idea behind Noida, part of the National Capital Region, was to reduce the rush in Delhi and encourage people to settle there. One area where the implementation of the project fell short was that people still had to travel to Delhi for work. Keeping this in mind, I had suggested that some offices should also be shifted to Noida, but the proposal was not implemented.

Today, I draw some comfort in learning that Noida city has the highest per capita income in the whole National Capital Region. Noida is also classified as a special economic zone and the Noida Authority is among the richest civic bodies in the country. I am now a resident of Noida myself.

Tiwariji had many of the qualities one would look for in a prime minister, such as tolerance and calmness, apart from being a learned man with an eye for development. To my mind, the most important quality to have in a prime minister is the breadth of mind to see everyone as an equal and from a similar lens, all the more so since we are a secular state. Tiwariji exemplified that quality.

Among the many memories that I have of Tiwariji, one stands out. That was the time MLAs and MLCs had been asked to choose the person they wanted to be the chief minister, and two AICC observers had come down to oversee the process. All the MLAs and MLCs had sat down together, and it was obvious that most of them preferred Tiwariji to the other person in the fray, Laxmi Shankar Yadav. I was then president of the Uttar Pradesh Congress and had asked the two observers to sit in a separate room, call the legislators one by one, find out who they wanted as chief minister, and then take a decision based on the feedback they got.

Finally, the result was declared: the majority was with Tiwariji. If that was not unexpected for a man of his popularity, Tiwariji's response was even less so. 'Not me, not me,' he said, in a manner typical of him, 'I am not worthy of this post.'

Before Tiwariji could say anything more, one of our MLAs from Eastern Uttar Pradesh had stood up. '*Ay Tiwariji*,' the MLA said, '*zada hichir bichir na karo; agar hichir bichir kariyo to is khidki se neeche phaink dewa*' (do not please stray from the subject or change your mind; if you do so, we may be forced to take some drastic measure). Everyone had a good laugh.

It is said that comparison is the thief of joy, but Tiwariji and H.N. Bahugunaji, another former chief minister, were often compared. I had the privilege of working with both and in my opinion, Tiwariji, unlike Bahugunaji, was not a shrewd politician. Also, Bahugunaji had strong likes and dislikes and promoted groupism within the Congress organization.

Tiwariji, on the other hand, was considered a soft politician and a darling of the bureaucracy. As chief minister, he was never harsh on bureaucrats, no matter what decisions they had taken. But he was a bit credulous and that was his weakness. Besides, he had blind faith in Sanjay Gandhi and did whatever Indiraji's younger son told him to do. Another drawback of his was the inability to take quick decisions on his own.

Tiwariji was a fiery freedom fighter and had been shackled by the British police when he was barely fourteen. Not only that, his eardrum suffered permanent damage, apparently, after his prison jailor had slapped him on the ear.

Among his administrative and technical qualities, Tiwariji's understanding of finance was sharp. So was his memory, and those who know him say that he could tell even after years which village had which bridge built during his time. Most of the roads, bridges, culverts, parks and stations in Uttar Pradesh were constructed when Tiwariji headed the state government.

Dr Manmohan Singh

History will be kinder to Dr Manmohan Singh than the contemporary media has been. Or, for that matter, the Opposition parties in Parliament, which did not miss any opportunity to run him down. But few would dispute that, as the Prime Minister of India, Dr Singh did some wonderful work during his ten-year rule from 2004, implementing economic schemes and keeping everyone together. Taking into account the circumstances and the compulsions of coalition politics, Dr sahab, I think, did the best he could under the circumstances.

Earlier, in the 1990s, as P.V. Narasimha Rao's finance minister, Manmohan Singh did a lot of work for the economy. Economic reforms, he would say, were not an event but a process and a well-thought-out plan of action. As long as the Congress was in power, it continued to push for reform wherever there was scope for it, and whenever circumstances permitted it to press forward.

Personally, I have a great equation with Dr Singh and his wife, Gursharan Kaur, both wonderful people, well-mannered and polite, who had imbibed the good old tradition of giving respect and, in turn, commanding respect through their conduct.

It is true that Dr Singh was never a politician in the real sense of the term. He is an economist and a scholar, so I think it would be unjust to him if he is labelled a political leader, though as a prime minister, he carried out all his responsibilities with the utmost dignity and the seriousness they demanded.

While I don't think Dr sahab can be called a weak person, some people did take undue advantage of his reserved nature. The Congress as a party was also partly to blame for this perception battle. It didn't do enough to channel social media as a political tool, which the Opposition utilized fully to target Dr Singh.

I remember Dr Singh addressing this charge of being a 'weak' prime minister at a press conference and in an interview to *The Hindu*: 'The BJP and its associates may say whatever they like,' Dr Singh had said. 'But if by "strong prime minister" you mean that you preside over a mass massacre of innocent citizens on the streets of Ahmedabad, that is the measure of strength, I do not believe that sort of strength this country needs, least of all, in its prime minister.'[23]

Coming back to the utilization of social media as a political tool, I remember a conversation I had with Pranab Mukherjee when petrol prices were rising. Mukherjee was the finance minister and I had told him that the hike should be explained to the public.

'When such a thing happens and you have to increase petrol prices, you should explain to the public why this is happening and it should become apparent to people that you have had to do this because of the situation and not because of personal want or desire,' I had said.

The Opposition had pounced on the price hike and targeted the administration through the social media, weaponizing it as a political tool. But we were lacking in that. So while we cannot particularly blame Manmohan Singh for this inability to use the social media as a tool for dissemination of information, this was an aspect where his administration as well as the Congress, as a party, fell short. We failed to reach out to the people with our message and vision.

When Dr Singh became the prime minister, there was a perception in certain quarters that he might not be able to run a coalition government. However, we showed that the Congress could successfully manage coalitions and complete not one, but two terms in power. In the process, there may have been some compromises made, but Dr Singh ensured that these compromises remained confined to peripheral areas and the Congress's ideology and principles remained intact.

On the personal front, both Dr Singh and Gursharanji were gracious hosts. Whenever I went to meet Singh Sahab at his residence, Gursharanji and he played the perfect hosts. There were gestures that were so gracious yet earthly, that left a deep mark on me. I can say with confidence that these courtesies were extended to every guest who had visited them.

Pranab Mukherjee

Whatever his differences with Rajiv Gandhi, later, Pranab Mukherjee was someone Indiraji respected a lot. She trusted him, too. Not only was he an extremely able minister, he was also highly educated and had a phenomenal memory.

'Dada, your memory is so amazing and you never forget anything,' we used to tell him often.

After Indira Gandhi's assassination, Pranabji had left the Congress. Everyone has their faults and his grudge was that he should have succeeded Indiraji as the prime minister, a matter I think he has dealt with in his memoir. As it turned out, Rajiv Gandhi was the popular choice for prime minister. People preferred him to Pranabji, and I think it was the right choice, as I believe that the amount of work Rajivji did before being cut short in his prime could not have been replicated by anyone else.

Pranabji's autobiography, *The Turbulent Years: 1980–1996*, has some candid admissions where he has addressed all the issues relating to him and Rajivji.[24] He has also pointed out that the age difference between him and Rajivji was only nine years. I am taking a liberty of sorts to quote him extensively from his memoir but it is for accuracy's sake. When Pranabji was dropped from the Rajiv cabinet, he was not even fifty years old. Pranab wrote,

> Rajiv was a reluctant politician. He was forced by circumstances to become prime minister at the age of forty. He was ahead of his times. He wanted rapid change and saw the old guard in the Congress as an obstacle to his vision. He was forward-looking, tech-savvy and welcomed foreign investment in India as well as an enlargement of the market economy. In contrast, I was a conservative, conventional political leader who favoured the public sector, a regulated economy and wanted foreign investment only from NRIs.

I think this sums up whatever differences he had with Rajivji. To Pranabji's credit and also Soniaji's, they got along very well.

Personally, I had a great equation with Pranabji and addressed him as Dada, which means elder brother in Bengali. Once, on our way to Assam by bus on one of those trips Indiraji used to send Antonyji, Pranabji and me together. You can imagine the state of Assam buses at that time. It was a long journey and the weather, too, was hot. I was sitting by the window and the sun was directly on my face. Pranabji must have seen that my face had turned red, because he asked me to come and sit next to him.

Pranabji would often recount this incident to my kids. 'Mohsinaji was sitting in so much pain but still did not say a word or move from her seat until I asked her to,' he would tell them.

We finally reached our destination, where a room had been reserved for Pranabji. For party workers, a big hall had been booked so that they could sleep there. I was the only woman worker who had arrived then and it was an awkward situation for me. When Pranabji noticed this, he offered me his room and went to sleep with the party workers in the hall.

Ahmed Patel

Ahmed Patel's passing has left a huge vacuum in the Congress and in politics in general. I don't think the void that he has left behind can be filled easily.

Among the many qualities that Ahmed possessed, the one that stood out was his ability to bring everyone together. He was also on good terms with people from other parties, which contributed to his rise in the Congress, as well as politically.

As political secretary to Sonia Gandhi, he would advise her on all matters and often explain to her the facts of an unfolding situation. But what made him a truly wonderful asset to the party was that he stayed away from any sort of groupism; in other words, he was someone who could offer unbiased advice. Needless to say, Soniaji depended upon him a lot.

As a person, Ahmed was extremely helpful and there are countless needy people who benefitted from his big heart when he was the party treasurer. He could never see anyone in trouble.

Ahmed had helped me, too, after my Rajya Sabha term ended in 2016. I did not have a house to live in and would stay as different people's guest (fellow MPs'). In the end, when I had no options left, I approached Ahmed. I told him my house was still under construction and I had nowhere to go. He listened to what I had to say and then came up with the solution. 'I myself seek a guest accommodation, and you stay as my guest,' he told me. That's how I managed to stay for some time at an apartment on Baba Kharak Singh Marg, New Delhi.

Ahmed passed away in November 2020. He was seventy-one.

Lalu Prasad Yadav

Behind his rustic ways, ready wit and tomfoolery, Lalu Prasad Yadav is a serious and astute politician who has the ability to size up people and not concede too much ground.

The Rashtriya Janata Dal boss could be charming when he wanted, often disarming stern-faced politicians with his humour. Take, for instance, what he said once in a room full of people when I had gone to Bihar ahead of an election to the Legislative Council. 'Everyone says my hairstyle is Sadhna cut. You tell me, Mohsinaji, is this true?' he asked me suddenly, as we all sat in his room.

Lalu cut his political teeth under Jayaprakash Narayan and is a contemporary of Ram Vilas Paswan's, the late Lok Janshakti Party leader, and Nitish Kumar, Bihar's current chief minister. But personally, as well as politically, Lalu, I think, matured better than his contemporaries from the Janata Party and the socialist movement. He is also secular in his approach, which is vital in today's politics.

I feel that the Congress–RJD alliance was fruitful for both of us and we should have continued it.

Arjun Singh

Arjun Singh, with whom I shared a very good relationship, truly belonged to the Nehruvian tradition. Committed to the Congress ideology, he remained a staunch opponent of the RSS and the Sangh parivar throughout his life. As chief minister, AICC functionary and Union human resource development minister, Arjun Singh never missed a chance to ask successive governments to cleanse the administration of people owing allegiance to the Sangh. He would also often publicly accuse them of being responsible for the events that led to the assassination of Mahatma Gandhi.

The two-time chief minister of Madhya Pradesh was forthright in his belief that our first duty was to detect fascist forces. 'Today, the government administration is in the grip of the RSS; we have to cleanse it,' he told a national convention on secularism in August 2004.

As union human resource development minister under P.V. Narasimha Rao and Dr Manmohan Singh, he would often remove academics close to the BJP and the RSS from panels tasked with drafting school textbooks. 'Men having sympathies with the Sangh parivar were appointed (by non-Congress governments) in key positions,' he would say. Likewise, he did not shy away from calling out and exposing those in the government who had links with the Sangh.

The veteran leader would also caution that there was not one but hundred different fronts of the RSS that were receiving crores of rupees through donations and diversion of government funds in the guise of NGOs.

As I have mentioned earlier in this book, I had thrown in my lot with Arjun Singh when he broke away and formed the Tiwari Congress in May 1995. Now that I reflect and look back, I feel that when our party was going through a tough situation, we should not have broken away and instead, sought to rebuild unity and questioned the leadership from within. So I feel it was a wrong decision. But the situation then was such that I felt if we did not break away, we wouldn't be able to bring Sonia Gandhi to the front, which was one of the motivating factors for me.

The lead up to the split also coincided with a particularly tense phase in my life. I was in Jeddah then with my brother, who had suffered a heart attack. After I returned, M.L. Fotedarji had come over one day. 'Either you can leave Congress or you can leave Sonia Gandhi, wherever Sonia Gandhi is, that's where Congress is,' he told me.

That won me over. But, looking back, I feel that I should have first spoken to Soniaji directly, which I was unable to do because of my prevailing circumstances. I did not like the decision, which I was part of myself, and I still regret it. I strongly believe that we should have remained in the party and tried to strengthen it from within.

I can neither comment on why Arjun Singh broke away from the party nor the circumstances that made him do so, but, speaking for myself, I feel that the decision was not right at my end.

Arjun Singh was an accomplished politician. There can be no doubt about that and there can be no doubt also that he was secular-minded to the core. This, I feel, was a great quality he had. When the Babri Masjid was vandalized in December 1992, he had even offered to resign from the P.V. Narasimha Rao government.

Arjun Singh was the chief minister of Madhya Pradesh when deadly methyl isocyanate gas, leaking from the Union Carbide factory in Bhopal, instantly killed over 3,000 people on the intervening night between 2 and 3 December 1984. It was a major human tragedy which could have been handled better.

Madhavrao Scindia

Madhavrao Scindia was a very good boy—I call him a 'boy' because he was like that to me and, as I write these lines, I can imagine Madhavrao's face lighting up with a boyish grin.

He was polite, courteous to a fault and had all the qualities that a good human should have. Let me recall an incident that had moved me deeply. It was the day I left the transport ministry, which then included railways, civil aviation and surface transport. Madhavrao, who was the minister of state for railways, told the bureaucrats and everyone present at Rail Bhawan that day, that even though Begum Saheba (that was how he addressed me) was leaving, 'we will still consider her as a head of the ministry and do everything she says or suggests'. I was deeply touched by this gesture.

Madhavrao ran the railway ministry extremely well. There is a difference between staying on in a ministry or organization and running it with passion. This is what Kiichiro Toyoda, the late founder of Toyota Motor Corporation, had once said: 'The ideal conditions for making things are created when machines, facilities, and people work together to add value without generating any waste.'[25] Madhavrao strongly believed in that philosophy and practised it, too.

We, as ministers, generally think that a ministry can be run with the help of bureaucrats, but Madhavrao was a master at this; he ran his ministry very well, guiding and taking everyone along. He was good with ideas as well as their execution and, suffice it to say, his work and achievements require a whole volume, if one were to do justice to him.

His son Jyotiraditya's exit from the Congress has left me saddened, all the more as I have known him since his childhood and have fond memories of him as a little boy. Another reason I feel sad about Jyotiraditya's exit is because he has many good qualities, apart from the fact that he is polite like his father, whose life was cut short in his prime.

I feel our party needs a strong leadership at the state level and it is young people with the potential to lead who can provide the necessary impetus.

In this context, let me compliment Rahul Gandhi for the step he had taken to groom young leaders. We used to do this as well, in our time. We would be on the lookout for young people with the potential for leadership. In every election, we would give young boys field work to do and involve them in various committees and other tasks. Rahulji, too, has tried to do this.

Rajesh and Sachin Pilot

Just like it is with Madhavrao Scindia, I have many fond memories of Rajesh Pilot who, too, left us early. Rajesh died in a road crash when he was only 55, around the same age as Madhavrao. I knew him from Indiraji's time, when she told me about a beautiful blue-eyed boy who had come asking for a ticket from Baghpat, Uttar Pradesh. I remember asking Indiraji if she wanted him to win, because Charan Singh was contesting from there.

'If you want him to win, give him a ticket from somewhere other than Baghpat,' I had told Indiraji.

'I want him to win,' Indiraji had replied.

Rajesh was eventually fielded from Dausa, Rajasthan.

I had a very cordial relationship with Rajesh and his wife Rama; they both respected me a lot and we visited each other often. Rajesh was someone who could develop a good relationship with people easily, which is what I liked about him.

Sachin Pilot is proving to be a worthy son of his father's. I consider him as my own son and perhaps words are failing me in describing my feelings for him. I have a word of advice for Sachin. Dabbling in state politics is not easy, and I speak from experience. All I can say without prejudice is that the current era for the Congress is a difficult one with seemingly insurmountable challenges. This is not the time to fight among ourselves. Rather, it is the time for each of us in the Congress to realize our responsibility towards the party and the people of this country, and come together to fight the communal forces that are on the rise in this country. Unity within the party should be the priority at this juncture of Indian politics.

Sachin has a pan-Indian appeal and comes from a very good family. Power and position are temporary but the quality of leadership stays forever. Only ethical politics can save our country and bring it back on track.

Jitendra Prasada

Jitendra Prasada, former Raja of Shahjahanpur, Uttar Pradesh, came from a very good background. His father, Jyoti Prasad, was an MLC when I, too, was a member of the state's Legislative Council. Because of that, I had very good relations with both, and called Jitin, Prasada's son, Jiti. Another reason we shared a rapport was that we both looked up to Rajiv Gandhi as our leader.

Cultured, affable, soft-spoken and reflective, Jitendra Prasada was initially considered loyal. But, after Rajivji's death, I feel that Narasimha Rao often fired bullets on his shoulders to encourage factionalism within the Congress parivar. I found it both disturbing and disappointing to note that Jitendra Prasada, as political secretary to the Congress president (Rao), himself indulged in faction politics and encouraged groupism in the party's Uttar Pradesh unit. I feel this kind of politicking has been fatal for both Uttar Pradesh politics and the Congress. At this point, I don't want to say who mislead whom, whether it was Rao who mislead Jitendra Prasada or the other way round, but, overall, it has been a sad chapter.

Jitendra Prasada, who used to be Rajivji's political secretary, too, would often come to me for advice. Once, he sought my opinion on a matter relating to the Rajya Sabha. I had told him that when all the MLAs were with N.D. Tiwari, the party should bring him to the Rajya Sabha.

'Why are you hesitating,' I had repeatedly asked him, 'when all the Congress MLAs are agreeing on this?'

I still remember his reply. 'Begum Saheba,' he said, 'how can I make two power centres, since Tiwariji is also capable of prime ministerial-level leadership?' Rao was the prime minister then. Readers can gauge what Jitendra Prasada was all about.

So as I mentioned a few paragraphs earlier, it cannot be said who misled whom in Uttar Pradesh, but there surely was groupism, which proved detrimental to the Congress.

Whenever I think of the past, it brings back so many memories. During the 1996 alliance with the BSP, Prasada and Sitaram Kesri had played a vital role. Personally, I was against the alliance. It created space for identity politics in Uttar Pradesh and it led to the Congress losing its image as an all-encompassing umbrella party, which it was.

Many years later, Rahulji would term the Congress–BSP alliance a 'sell-out' and I am glad that he has said there would be no such 'blanket alliances' in the future. 'The 1996 alliance was a sell-out and a blanket one,' Rahulji had told journalists in March 2007, when he was touring Muzaffarnagar to campaign for Assembly elections.[26] He also emphasized that the Congress's downfall in Uttar Pradesh in 1996 was due to an organizational problem and I fully endorse his point of view.

M.L. Fotedar, R.K. Dhawan, Vincent George

I had a long association with M.L. Fotedar, R.K. Dhawan and Vincent George, three men who became the trusted aides of successive Congress leaders, often acting as their eyes and ears. Both Dhawan and George were like Indiraji's shadows, her confidants, although they were vastly different in the way they functioned, especially when it came to communicating something to her.

For example, if you asked Dhawan to convey a message to Indiraji, he would add his own bit before the communication reached her. George, on the other hand, would pass on the message as it is, without editing or adding anything to it. He would report to Indiraji whatever you told him. George also worked with Rajiv Gandhi as his private secretary and later, with Sonia Gandhi.

Fotedar was the person who informed me that I had been given a ministry when Indiraji had, for the first time, included me in the Union council of ministers. Fotedar was a Kashmiri who had settled in Delhi for a long time. He gave a lot of service to the Gandhi family but I don't think he could achieve what he had desired.

After the Emergency, Dhawan and his father had endured third-degree torture by the intelligence agencies, but never said a word against Indiraji. This was loyalty, a quality he had, that is all I have to say.

V.P. Singh

Vishwanath Pratap Singh was an ambitious politician. Long before 1989, the year he assumed charge as the prime minister, he had said of himself: 'The day I become prime minister, I will be a disaster for the country.'

I think he turned out to be right. I have no hesitation in recording that as a Congress chief minister, he gave a lot of encouragement to caste and communal politics and did everything that went against the party's ideals.

When the Janata Party was formed, V.P. Singh had one day come over to UP Niwas, where I was staying. 'Mohsinaji,' he told me, 'I'm giving you my resignation.' I was president of Uttar Pradesh Congress Committee then.

He was general secretary then and was among several Congress stalwarts from Uttar Pradesh whom I had appointed to party positions. I thought he was joking but asked him why he was handing in his resignation. He kept on saying, 'I just can't do it.'

When I realized he was serious, I requested him with folded hands to stay on. 'Indiraji,' I told him, 'is already in trouble and we are all dealing with that. If you resign now, there will be headlines for many days about this; why do you want to cause such trouble? I'm imploring you to reconsider your decision.'

I asked him again why he wanted to resign and these were his words: '*Main apni jayedad dekhunga ya apki general secretaryship karunga*' (Should I look after my ancestral property or the UPCC general secretary's post)? He seemed concerned that the new Janata regime would hound him or highlight some alleged wrongdoings surrounding his ancestral property.

I still pleaded with him and did not accept his resignation. He stayed on but never attended any meetings. Even as prime minister, I think, V.P. Singh was the most unsuccessful for this country.

When I won from Meerut in 1980, youths from there had said they voted for me but voiced a common complaint they had: 'When we go for selection in Police, we always fail in interviews,' they said.

I told Indiraji about their complaint and she asked me to seek the help of V.P. Singh, who was chief minister of Uttar Pradesh then. I had gone and met V.P. Singh and told him what the youths in my constituency had said.

V.P. Singh listened to what I had to say and then turned to Rajendra Tripathi, State Home Minister then, who was also in the room. 'Look,' he said, 'Mohsinaji is here to talk about minorities.'

I was furious and told him that not one of these youths was from the minority community. V.P. Singh then picked up the phone and spoke to Dixitji, who was IG police, and the matter was resolved.

Chandra Shekhar

Chandra Shekhar became prime minister with the Congress' support. Personally, a good human being whom I respected and shared a cordial relationship with, I can't say much about his short tenure as I did not get to meet him in person often after he moved to the Centre.

The socialist leader (born as Chandra Shekhar Singh, a Rajput) got an opportunity to form the government just after the eleven-month-old National Front coalition, led by Prime Minister V.P. Singh's Janata Dal Party, fell on a vote of no-confidence. The Janata Dal had split just before the confidence vote after Chandra Shekhar, one of its members, formed a splinter group to challenge V.P. Singh and got the backing of the Congress, led by Rajiv Gandhi.

According to Harivansh, the Rajya Sabha deputy chairman and Janata Dal (United) leader, Chandra Shekhar did not hesitate to take some of the boldest initiatives to reduce the overt belligerence between the purported leaders of the Hindu community (Vishwa Hindu Parishad) and Muslims (the Babri Masjid Action Committee).

In his book, co-authored with Ravi Dutt Bajpai, *Chandra Shekhar: The Last Icon of Ideological Politics*, Harivansh says, 'Chandra Shekhar managed to get both the groups of claimants to sit across the negotiating table and explore avenues for mutual agreements to bring about a peaceful solution to the issue.'[27]

Chandra Shekhar was an unassuming and kind-hearted man, who would often serve tea to Special Protection Group personnel at his residence. Similarly, at any location of his visit, whether in India or abroad (he went on only two overseas trips as prime minister), he would make sure that his security complement was served the same menu as him.

Generous, caring and bold, Chandra Shekhar maintained friendships with all—family, friends and even political adversaries—

even if some of them had a tainted reputation. He never abandoned a friend in good or bad times. Other qualities that stood out, rare for a man of his stature, were his simplicity and straightforwardness. Glamour, the sheen that public life often bestows, was not something you associated with Chandra Shekhar.

Chandra Shekhar was earlier in the Congress where he was part of a small radical group called the 'Young Turks' that supported Prime Minister Indira Gandhi at first, but turned against her in the 1970s. This was a period when Indiraji faced many challenges and saw the radicalization of Congress policies, programmes and leadership, followed by its fall.

Indiraji had inherited powerful factions within the Congress which opposed her policy of bank nationalization and abolition of privy purses. On the one hand was the old guard, represented by Morarji Desai, Y.B. Chavan, S.K. Patil and S. Nijalingappa; on the other were the Young Turks, young socialist leaders such as Chandra Shekhar, Mohan Dharia, Krishan Kant, C. Subramaniam, Chandrajit Yadav and others.

The Young Turks had caught the imagination of an entire generation when they ensured the removal of Raja Kamakhya Narain Singh from the then Bihar cabinet. The zamindar from Ramgarh had been appointed through the offices of the then chief minister, Hari Har Singh, in violation of an earlier decision that feudal lords, who were not part of the Congress, should not be inducted as ministers in party-ruled states.

C. Subramaniam, who was then Tamil Nadu Congress chief, resigned from the CWC in protest against the appointment of Kamakhya Narain. On 14 May 1969, the CWC asked Subramaniam to withdraw his resignation and the Bihar government to remove Kamakhya Narain from the Bihar ministry, in a victory for Subramaniam and other Young Turks like Chandra Shekhar.

H.D. Deve Gowda

Luck had smiled on H.D. Deve Gowda soon after the exit of the P.V. Narasimha Rao government in May 1996. The Congress had lost the mandate, getting only 140 Lok Sabha seats, and the BJP, with 161 MPs, had hurriedly staked claim to form the government. It didn't even last a fortnight. Atal Bihari Vajpayee had to step down as prime minister within thirteen days as he failed to prove his majority.

It was in such a situation that many non-Congress and non-BJP leaders swung into action and formed United Front. This rainbow coalition of fourteen parties, such as the Janata Dal, Telugu Desam Party, DMK, Samajwadi Party, the Left and a range of regional players, sought the Congress's support from outside to cross the magic figure of 272 in the House.

But more than the numbers, the United Front struggled to find a prime ministerial nominee. The Front, stitched together carefully by V.P. Singh and CPM veteran Harkishan Singh Surjeet, first offered the post to Jyoti Basu, who was the chief minister of Bengal then. Basu, a towering and principled CPM leader, was open to the idea of taking charge at the Centre but his party vetoed the suggestion. Many, including a section of the CPM, would later describe the party's rejection of the proposal as a 'historic blunder'.

What followed was a spell of one-upmanship, trust deficit and realpolitik, that saw aspirants like Mulayam Singh Yadav and Lalu Prasad Yadav fall by the wayside. Andhra Pradesh Chief Minister N. Chandrababu Naidu then proposed his Karnataka counterpart Deve Gowda's name. Deve Gowda had no experience of Delhi politics but the Congress, under Sitaram Kesri, decided to support him from outside, sealing the unexpected elevation of a man who had earlier been with the party.

Deve Gowda had joined the Congress in 1953 and remained in the party till 1962. He was then president of the Anjaneya Cooperative Society of Holenarasipura, Karnataka, and later became a member of the Taluk Development Board of Holenarasipura.

When Indiraji contested from Chikmagalur in 1978, Deve Gowda was the Karnataka state president of the Janata Party. Congress MP D.B. Chandre Gowda, who had won from Chikmagalur in 1977, vacated the seat so that Indiraji, routed in the post-Emergency general election, could contest again. Indiraji won the bypoll by more than 77,000 votes, her victory over the Janata Party's Veerendra Patil kicking off a chain of events that would see her return as prime minister in 1980.

A farmer's son, Deve Gowda served as prime minister for ten months, from June 1996 to April 1997, heading a government that had CPI leader Indrajit Gupta as home minister, P. Chidambaram in charge of finance, and Mulayam Singh Yadav as defence minister.

In spite of internal pressures and contradictions, Deve Gowda championed the cause of the have-nots, farmers, landless labourers and slum-dwellers, and initiated a series of measures aimed at improving their lot and providing basic minimum services to all sections of the society. He started a set of reforms that led to the country's economic revival, culminating in Chidambaram's epoch-making budget of 1997–98 that many corporate leaders and economists felt was a dream budget.

Deve Gowda's initiatives in resolving problems in the insurgency-torn Northeast led to a significant improvement in the situation there, including a firm foundation for the peace process. In Jammu and Kashmir, his efforts at normalization resulted in an elected government after eight years.

On the external affairs front, he signed a water-share agreement with Bangladesh, ending a long dispute. Another water treaty the Deve Gowda government was involved in, was with Nepal—the

Mahakali Treaty that it ratified. India also resumed talks with Pakistan during his prime ministership.

I don't want to go into the reasons behind Sitaram Kesri's decision to withdraw support to the Deve Gowda government, leading to its fall, but here's an anecdote that I must mention before I wrap up this section on reminiscences and impressions.

It was 30 March 1997. An official banquet was being held where watermelon had been served as a dessert item. At one of the tables, Narasimha Rao sat chatting with his old friend, Atal Bihari Vajpayee, then leader of the Opposition in the Lok Sabha, when the BJP veteran suddenly said the 'tarbooz' was 'khatta' (lacking in sweetness and colour). Vajpayee wondered why watermelon had been served when it was not the right season for the fruit.

'If we can have withdrawal of support in the budget session of Parliament,' Rao is said to have commented, 'why cannot we have watermelon served off-season?'

I.K. Gujral

Just like Chaudhary Charan Singh, Chandra Shekhar and H.D. Deve Gowda, his immediate predecessor, Inder Kumar Gujral served as prime minister for a very short time. Gujral was sworn in as India's twelfth prime minister in April 1997 and remained in office till March 1998. But Gujral is assured of his place in India's history, and not least because of his civility, unblemished record and probity in public life.

While I can't comment much on Gujral's tenure as prime minister, it can surely be said that he had all the qualities needed to be one. He did not do anything during his term that was very wrong and, I think, he became a victim of politics.

Gujral will be remembered for two significant contributions to India's foreign policy. One, he propounded what has been termed as the 'Gujral Doctrine' when he was the Union minister for external affairs in the Deve Gowda government. The doctrine, basically a set of principles for the government's neighbourhood policy, notably relations with Pakistan, is considered a milestone in India's foreign policy. Two, despite international pressure, Gujral had refused to sign the Comprehensive Test Ban Treaty (CTBT) in October 1996.

In or out of government, Gujral, a well-educated man, ran a 'Saturday Club', a group of mostly retired policy wonks, that traditionally met at New Delhi's India International Centre.

Gujral used his Urdu skills to strike up good equations with many Pakistani leaders, including Prime Minister Nawaz Sharif, with whom he shared a relationship of trust and warmth. The two had a summit meeting at Kurumba Village, an island resort close to the Maldivian capital, Male, where Gujral kept reciting Ali Sardar Jafri's famous line, '*guftagu bandh na ho, baat se baat chale*' (may our conversation never end, may one thing lead to another). Nowadays, it's rare to find men like Gujral, especially in politics.

Arvind Kejriwal and Aam Aadmi Party (AAP)

Delhi Chief Minister Arvind Kejriwal owes his political success to the Anna Hazare movement. Kejriwal and former top cop Kiran Bedi were Hazare's key spokespersons when the then septuagenarian activist took Delhi's political class by storm with his 2011 movement against corruption.

While Kejriwal has possibly been the biggest beneficiary of the Hazare movement, the IIT-educated-engineer-turned-politician deserves praise for two reasons. One, the Mohalla Clinics (primary health centres) that his party, the AAP, set up to provide good healthcare to the poor; the other is the wonderful work he has done to strengthen Delhi's education system. These are two basic needs of an underprivileged person and Kejriwal has delivered on both.

Coming back to Hazare, I think his movement was fully backed from the shadows by the RSS and the BJP. Such a huge movement cannot be sustained without such support. The RSS and the BJP gained, too, from the movement, which eventually led to the BJP's spectacular triumph in the 2014 parliamentary elections. This is why I feel that the BJP had extended full support to Hazare's movement.

I had an opportunity to interact with Hazare's team when the UPA was in power. They were then demanding a Lokpal bill for the creation of an anti-corruption institution to investigate cases of graft. I think some people were genuine but the movement was politically motivated. Its political agenda, which looked attractive, particularly to the young, is still unfolding. A number of people left the AAP party when they failed to deliver their original agenda—the Lokpal appointment.

Acknowledgements

I HAVE TOO MANY PEOPLE TO thank—numerous political workers, leaders and people of India—who gave me so much affection and joy. I have seen misery, poverty and helplessness. I have been fortunate to see growth and development at such a magnitude that it brought smiles on teeming millions.

My daughters, Irum, Farida, Seema, my son-in-laws—Javed, Arif and Razi—kept pressurizing me to pen my memoir. Razi, in particular, did a lot of running around and always remained a call away. Razi, Farida and Seema often read written passages with me and offered valuable inputs and suggestions. My tech savvy grandson Aariz was always around extending his full time assistance and support in addition of his rigorous work from home schedule. Adil too remained insistent that I find time to record, write, go through the manuscript over and again. Thank you Faraz, Rida, Kulsum, Saad, Asra, Omar and Zehra for keeping me smiling and laughing. My grandchildren were a constant source of support and joy and individually gave some useful inputs too.

My husband remained my rock throughout my political journey. It was his wish that my autobiography was written, for he felt it was worth writing. I have therefore dedicated the book to late Khalil Ur Rahman Kidwai, without whom I would not have achieved anything in public life.

A special word of thanks to Azra Kidwai, my cousin, friend, confidante, sister-in-law, all rolled into one. Blessed with elephantine memory and scholarship, Azra was ever helpful. Here, I am tempted to transgress a bit and recall how Alex Gendler and Avi Ofer, in their TED-Ed talks had remarked on elephant memory and I quote them, 'Unlike many proverbs, the one about elephant memory is scientifically accurate. Elephants know every member of the herd and are able to recognize thirty companions by sight or smell. They also remember and distinguish particular cues that signal danger and can recall important locations long after their visit. But it is their memories unrelated to survival that are most fascinating.' I am also indebted to her husband and my cousin, Sadiq Ur Rahman Kidwai, an acclaimed literary critic and their son Jamal, my nephew Asad ur Rahman Kidwai, and numerous others. Usha Prasad of the Nehru Memorial Museum and Library (NMML) was most helpful in interviewing and transcribing some of my thoughts.

This work would not have been completed had Rasheed Kidwai not prodded me all along and helped me shape this memoir. His experience as an author and journalist came handy with dates, events and references becoming readily available.

No words of appreciation would be enough to thank my literary consultant Atul K. Thakur, who reached out to the publishers and stitched up everything. Atul gave me some useful suggestions and inputs. Always attentive and smiling, young Mohammad Omar, Oxford-SOAS scholar, was also part of their team.

A special word of thanks to my friend and well-wisher Shobhna Bhartiya, editorial director of the Hindustan Times group who readily and generously donated the photographs for this book. R Rajagopal, Editor, The Telegraph and Sakti Roy, chief librarian of the ABP, Calcutta were most helpful.

A big thank you to Swati Chopra, Udayan Mitra and his team at the HarperCollins India. I also wish to thank Sunetra Choudhury and Rakesh Dixit for their assistance.

Notes

1. Rhea Charles, 'Muslim Women in Indian Politics', *Indian School of Democracy*, 15 June 2021, https://www.indianschoolofdemocracy.org/post/muslim-women-in-indian-politics
2. J.C. Johari. *Indian National Congress* (Lotus Press: New Delhi, 2007).
3. Rana Al Khouli, 'Analyzing Part of Rousseau's Confessions on the Role of History in Art and Influencing People', Research Gate (June 2016).
4. Sunil Sethi and Arati Jerath, 'Azamgarh Lok Sabha By-election: Janata Party's Waterloo?', *India Today*, 15 May 1978, https://www.indiatoday.in/magazine/indiascope/story/19780515-azamgarh-lok-sabha-by-election-janata-partys-waterloo-818362-2015-01-03
5. Sethi and Jerath, 1978.
6. I have written this with a sense of full responsibility and to illustrate how party leaders of that era were expected to make sacrifices. It also tells a story of the difficulties in building the party virtually from scratch after the 1977 debacle.
7. As per Maulana Abdul Majid Daryabadi (tr.), *Tafsir ul Quran*, a 4-volume translation and commentary on the *Holy Quran* (Ulama, Lucknow Uttar Pradesh: Academy of Islamic Research and Publication, Nadwatul, 2019).
8. Emma Tarlo, *Unsettling Memories: Narratives of the Emergency in Delhi*, University of California Press, 2002.

9. As quoted in Sunil Sethi, 'Family Planning Emerges as Priority Number One for Rajiv Gandhi Government', *India Today*, 31 July 1985, https://www.indiatoday.in/magazine/living/story/19850731-family-planning-emerges-as-priority-number-one-for-rajiv-gandhi-government-770261-2013-12-28

10. *Times of India*, 'Lesser-Known Facts About India's Second Prime Minister', 2 October 2017, https://timesofindia.indiatimes.com/india/lal-bahadur-shastri-lesser-known-facts-about-indias-second-prime-minister/articleshow/60910884.cms

11. Ajay Singh, 'I Am Completely Disappointed With the Janata Party's Performance: Jayaprakash Narayan', *India Today*, 31 March 2015.

12. Prabhash Ranjan, 'Barring Select Sectors, Nehru Was Not Opposed to Foreign Investment', *The Wire*, 27 May 2018.

13. Euripides, *The Bacchae* (UK: Vintage Classics, 2016).

14. Rasheed Kidwai, 'Rahul Gandhi's NYAY Reflects Congress' Flexible Economic Ideology', 26 March 2019.

15. Dr Manmohan Singh, 'Budget 1991–92 Speech of Shri Manmohan Singh, Minister of Finance', delivered on 24 July 1991, https://www.indiabudget.gov.in/budget2021-22/doc/bspeech/bs199192.pdf

16. Prabhu Chawla, 'Meerut Burns in Communal Fire Ignited by Squabble for 200 sq ft Property', *India Today*, 26 August 2013.

17. Prabhu Chawla, 'Meerut Burns in Communal Fire Ignited by Squabble for 200 sq ft Property', *India Today*, 31 October 1982, https://www.indiatoday.in/magazine/special-report/story/19821031-meerut-burns-in-communal-fire-ignited-by-squabble-for-200-sq-ft-property-772302-2013-08-26

18. Javed M. Ansari and Ashok K. Damodaran, 'Bihar Massacres: Centre Push for Dismissal of Rabri Government, President Agrees', *India Today*, 22 February 1999, https://www.indiatoday.in/magazine/states/story/19990222-bihar-massacres-centre-push-for-dismissal-of-rabri-government-president-agrees-825019-1999-02-22

19. Ansari and Damodaran, 1999.

20. Aditi Phadnis, 'Mulayam Singh Yadav: The King of U-turns', 26 June 2012, rediff.com
21. Phadnis, 2012.
22. India Today Web Desk, 'Remembering Ram Manohar Lohia: 10 Interesting Facts About the Freedom Fighter', 12 October 2016.
23. Interview with Manmohan Singh, 'History Will be Kinder to Me Than the Media, says Manmohan', *The Hindu*, 23 May 2016, https://www.thehindu.com/opinion/interview//article61451665.ece
24. Rupa Publications, India, 2016, p. 101.
25. '25 Toyota Production System', https://global.toyota/en/company/vision-and-philosophy/production-system/#:~:text=Kiichiro%20Toyoda%2C%20who%20inherited%20this,for%20eliminating%20waste%20between%20operations%2C
26. Staff, '1996 Cong-BSP Alliance in UP Was a "Sell-Out"': Rahul', *One India*, 20 March 2007, https://www.oneindia.com/2007/03/19/1996-cong-bsp-alliance-in-up-was-a-sell-out-rahul-1174334364.html
27. Rupa Publications, India, 2019.

Short Bibliography

Adams, Jad and Whitehead Philips. *The Dynasty: The Nehru-Gandhi Story*. London: Penguin Books, BBC Books, 1997.

Alexander, P.C. *My Years with Indira Gandhi*. New Delhi: Vision, 1991.

Chadha, Kumkum. *The Marigold Story: Indira Gandhi and Others*. Westland: Tranquebar, 2019.

Frank, Katherine. *Indira: The Life of Indira Nehru Gandhi*. London: HarperCollins, 2001.

Gill, S.S. *The Dynasty. A Political Biography of the Premier Ruling Family of Modern India*. New Delhi: HarperCollins India, 1996.

Jayakar, Pupul. *Indira Gandhi*. New Delhi: Penguin India, 1992.

Johari, J.C. *Indian National Congress since Independence*. Lotus Press. New Delhi.

Kidwai, Rasheed. *24 Akbar Road: A Short History of the People Behind the Fall and Rise of the Congress*. New Delhi: Hachette India, 2011 and 2013.

Kidwai, Rasheed. *Sonia: A Biography*. New Delhi: Penguin-Viking, 2009.

Masani, Zaheer. *Indira Gandhi: A Biography*. New Delhi: Oxford University Press, 1975.

Mukherjee, Pranab. *The Turbulent Years, 1980–1996*. New Delhi: Rupa, 2016.

Mukherjee, Pranab. *The Coalition Years: 1996–2012*. New Delhi: Rupa, 2017.

Paul, Swaraj. *Indira Gandhi*. London: Robert Royce, 1985.

Rao, P.V. Narasimha, *Ayodhya 6 December 1992*. New Delhi : Penguin Books, 2006.

Tully, Mark and Satish Jacob. *Amritsar: Mrs Gandhi's Last Battle*. UK: Random House, 1987.

Index

Aam Aadmi Party (AAP), 232–233
Abdul Kalam, A.P.J., 208
Abdullah, Farooq, 203
Abdullah, Sheikh Mohammad, 76–77
Adil (grandson), 97
Advani, Lal Krishna, Ram Rath Yatra and, 148
Ahmad, Begum Abida, xxiv
Ahmed, E., 194, 197
Ahmed, Hasan, 197
Ahmed, Mofida, xxiv
Ahmed, Sajda, xxiv
Ahmed, Ziauddin (elder brother), death of, 135
Akali Dal, 45
Akarbai, Chavda Zohraben, xxiv
Ali, Hafiz Shaikh Asghar, Raja of Gandara (Barabanki) (maternal grandmother's father), 71

Ali, Nafisa, xxiv
Aligarh Muslim University (AMU), 8, 70, 76–77, 79, 98; as the Oxford of the East, 71
All-India Anna DMK, 66
All India Congress Committee (AICC), xxvii, 45–46, 64, 89, 124, 158–159
Ambedkar, B.R., 39, 147
Amethi, 125, 204
Anandamayi Ma, 143
Anantram, 23
Ansari, Hamid, 104
Anthony, Frank, 44
anti-Emergency wave, 166
Antony, A.K., 216
Aquila (sister-in-law), 79
Arif (son-in-law), 95, 109
Asaf Ali, Aruna, 119
Atomic Energy Commission, 152
Ayesha (maternal aunt), 72

INDEX

Ayodhya movement, 183, *see also* Advani, Lal Krishna, Ram Rath Yatra and; Babri Masjid, demolition of
Azad, Abul Kalam, xxvi, 57, 107, 111, 136
Azad, Ghulam Nabi, 183
Azamgarh, xxiv, xxvi, 3–14, 58–62, 64, 69, 108, 120, 175, 204

Babbar, Raj, 54
Babri Masjid, demolition of, 207, 220
Bachan, Ram, 10
Bachchan, Jaya, 188
Bahuguna, H.N., 5, 27, 84, 90, 103, 212
Bahujan Samaj Party, xxv, 207
Bajpai, Ravi Dutt, 227
Banerjee, Mamata, xxv, 190–191; leaving Congress, 190
Bangarappa, S., 125
Bangladesh: formation of, 135; war 1971, 137
banks, 159; nationalization of, 158
Barabanki, 4, 10, 22–24, 52, 69–71, 73–74, 79–80, 99, 101, 104, 171
Barooah, D.K., 45
Basu, Jyoti, 191, 229

Battiwala, M.N., Capt. 49–50
Battle of Buxar, role of Kidwais in, 72
Bhagat, H.K.L., 121
Bharatiya Janata Party (BJP), 140, 146, 148–149, 167–168, 187, 206, 208, 214, 219, 229, 233; two-nation theory of, 148–149, 187
Bharatiya Jana Sangh, 24, 84
Bhatia, R.L., 187
Bhushan, Shashi, 89
Bhutto, Begum Nusrat, 121
Bhutto, Benazir, 121
Bohra, 195
Borlaug, Norman, 165
Bose, Subhas Chandra, 176
Bose, Suresh Chandra, 176
Brahmananda Reddy, K., 46
Brēze, 96
British Empire, 21, 70; 'divide and rule' objective of, 130; role of Kidwais in, 72
Brunei, 119–120
Bucker, Aboo, 197
al-Bukhari, Sahih, 193
by-election, 3, 6, 58–9, 61, 108, 175, 192; Azamgarh Lok Sabha, 3–5, 7–8, 13–14, 58–63, 69, 175; Chikmagalur, 63–64; Raebareli Lok Sabha, 188

capitalism, 156

INDEX

castes, upper, 11, 23; *see also* Dalits; Other Backward Castes (OBCs); Scheduled Castes (SCs)
census, 2010, 162
Central Drug Research Institute (CDRI), 79
Central Haj Committee Act 2010, 193, 196
Centre for Development of Telematics (C-DOT), 145
Chandrababu Naidu, N., 229
Chandrasekhar, Maragatham, 45, 150
Chandre Gowda, D.B., 230
Chauri Chaura incident, 56, 170
Chavan, Y.B., 45, 87, 228
Chidambaram, P., 230
Chisti, Khwaja Ghareeb Nawaz Hazrat Moinuddin, 72
Colombo Plan, Nehru on, 157
communalism, xxvi, 148, 153, 177–179
Communist Party, 23
Comprehensive Test Ban Treaty (CTBT), 232
Congress: Barabanki victory of, 24; and coalitions, 160; factionalism in, 82–84, 185, 188–189, 206, 223; as Grand Old Party, xxvi–xxvii, 151, 209; ideology, xxvii–xxviii, 20; leadership crisis in, 188; Nehru on, 159; new office at 24, Akbar Road, 177; Trinamool, 190
Congress (Indira), 3, 5, 9, 13, 46, 52; formation of, 46
Congress (Ruling) or Requisitionist, 89
Congress (Tiwari), 124, 219; merging with Congress, 190
Congress–BSP alliance, 224
Congress Parliamentary Board, 86
Congress–RJD alliance, 218
Congress Socialist Party, 83, 136
Congress Working Committee (CWC), 45, 86–87, 89
Constitution (Seventy-third and Seventy-fourth) amendment, 146
Constitution of India, 56–57, 149
Contemporary Arts and Crafts (CAC), 96
Contraceptive Marketing Organization (CMO), 114
cooperative movement in Anand, 166
Crossette, Barbara, 150

Dalits, 7, 10–11, 176, 207, *see also* castes
Daryabadi, Abdul Majid (great-uncle), 70, 76
Das, Banarasi, 83

Das, Bindumati, 24
Das, Thakur Mahant Jaganath Baksh, 22, 24
Dasgupta, Swapan, 186
Dasmunshi, Priya Ranjan, 190
Dastkar, 96
demonetization, 166, 169
Desai, Morarji, 4–5, 45, 50, 65, 84, 87–88, 144, 228; as Prime Minister to ban currency, 166; resignation of, 167
Dev, Acharya Narendra, 83
Deve Gowda, H.D., 169, 229–231
Devi, Rabri, 185
Dey, G.V., 49
Dharia, Mohan, 89, 228
Dhawan, R.K., 4, 44, 224–225
Dhebar, U.N., xxvii–xxviii, 159
Dikshit, Sheila, 102, 104, 123
Dikshit, Uma Shankar, 47, 89
DMK, 66, 229
Doordarshan, 115
Do Ya Teen Bas campaign, 115
drought in 1987, 115

Eastern Uttar Pradesh, 59, 175, 183, 212
East Pakistan. *See* Bangladesh
Economic Council for Asia and the Far East (ECAFE), 157
economy of India, 144, 152, 156, 160, 168; gold pledging for loan, 168–169; liberalization, 144; reforms, 123, 144–145, 157, 162, 165, 213
Election Commission, 7, 188
elections, 4, 7–8, 23–28, 59, 61, 63, 86–87, 90, 131, 140, 158, 176–177; 1942 Constituent Assembly, 19–20; 1960 Legislative Council, 18; 1966, 27–28; 1967 UP Assembly, 23–24, 84; 1969 UP Assembly, 89; 1977, 3, 11, 13, 32, 35, 37, 58, 142, 176; of 1979, 192; 1984 Lok Sabha, 113; 1991, 183; BJP in parliamentary, 168; Lok Sabha, 3, 5, 113, 178, 183–184; and lowering the voting age, 145; panchayat, 116, 145; religion for successes of, 167
Eleventh ASEAN–India Summit, 120
Emergency: during 1962 war, 137; during 1971 war, 137; in 1975, 3–4, 31–32, 43, 45, 49, 106, 111, 114, 136–140, 142, 225, 230
extremism, 148

Fabian Society, 155
family planning programme, 31–32, 114–115, 139–141;

and international media, 140;
propaganda against, 141; in UP,
140
Farida (daughter), 93–96, 99;
engaged with Arif, 109
Fatima, Latif, 177
Fernandes, George, 9, 11, 45,
64–65, 141, 166
financial inclusion, 170
financial institutions, 158, *see also*
banks
Firangi Mahal, 19
Five Year Plan, Sixth (1980–85),
117
fodder scam cases, 185
foreign investment, 156, 161, 216;
Nehru on, 156
Fotedar, M.L., 123–124, 220,
224–225
freedom movement, 17, 56, 82,
136, 209
fundamentalism,
institutionalization of, 148

Gadgil, Vithal, xxvii
Gajapathi Raju, Uma, 150
Gandhi, Indira, xxiv, xxvi, 3–10,
13–14, 17–18, 27–39, 41–47,
52–55, 59–66, 86–89, 94, 99,
101–103, 109, 150–151, 158,
175, 179; as 'amma,' 65; arrest
of, 42–45, 50; assassination
of, 110–111, 122, 144, 215;
contesting from Chikmagalur,
230; elected as party president,
46; expulsion from party, 45;
floating Congress (I), 46; on
her death, 110; 'garibi hatao'
(eradicate poverty), 158; on
her security, 109; interview
with Ustinov, 110; loss in
Raebareli, 32–33; resignation
of, 136; returning to power,
144; tour of Western Uttar
Pradesh, 38–40; and 'Young
Turks', 228
Gandhi, Mahatma, xxvii–xxviii,
20–21, 80, 82, 84, 107, 111,
115, 130, 134, 141, 170, 210;
assassination of, 141, 219
Gandhi, Maneka, 42; in *Surya*
magazine, 44
Gandhi, Priyanka, 110, 154, 189,
204–205
Gandhi, Rahul, 155, 157, 162,
189, 222, 224
Gandhi, Rajiv, xxiv–xxv, 43–44,
112–114, 116, 121–124, 144–
147, 149–151, 154, 160–161,
168, 179, 181, 183, 188–189,
204–205, 207; 215–216, 223,
225, 227; assassination of, 122,
125, 146, 150; and economic
reforms, 145; as Father of

Information Technology and Telecom Revolution, 145; 'PCO revolution' of, 145; as sixth Prime Minister, 111
Gandhi, Sanjay, 4, 13, 30–31, 44–45, 138–139, 211, 213; arrest of, 13; death of, 143; 5-point programme of, 31, 141; losing parliamentary seat, 32
Gandhi, Sonia, xxviii, 44–45, 104, 122–125, 154–155, 157, 160, 162, 186, 188–189, 194, 204–206, 208, 216–217, 220, 225; AICC chief, 124–125
Gandhian values, 97, 167, 170
Gehlot, Ashok, 187
George, Vincent, 224–225
Germany, 119–120, 152
Ghayas (brother), 73, 123; death of, 187
Giri, V.V., 86, 89
Goods and Services Tax (GST), 169
Gopal, Neena, 150
Gowda, D.M. Putte, 66
Green Revolution, 165–166
groupism, 185, 188–189, 217, 224
Gujarat Model, 168
Gujarat riots, 149, 187
Gujral, I.K., 120, 169, 231–232
Gujral Doctrine, 232
Gupta, C.B., 5, 26–27, 83–85, 90

Gupta, Indrajit, 230
Gupta, Pradeep, 150
Gupta, Prem, 186

Haj, 193–199; special film on, 195; Zam Zam, 196
Haj Act. *See* Central Haj Committee Act 2010
Hakeem-ul-Ummat, 70
Harivansh, 227
Hashimpura, 179–180
Hazare, Anna, 232–233
Hindu Rashtra, 167
Humaira (maternal aunt), 72
Hungary, 120
Husain, Zakir, 86
Husna (elder sister), 73, 165

Iffat Un Nisa (grandaunt), 70
iftars, 103–104
Imam, Aziz, 60
inclusive growth, 131, 162, 165, 167
Indian Airlines plane, hijack of, 49–51
Indian Constitution, xxvii, 39, 86, 136, 147, 156
Indian Institutes of Management, 152
Indian Institutes of Technology, 152
India–Pakistan relations, 132
Indo-Tibetan Border Force, 110

Insolvency and Bankruptcy Code, 169
Integrated Rural Development Programme (IRDP), 117
Irum (daughter), 48, 62–63, 93–95, 101–103, 191
Irwin, Terri, 105

Jaffrelot, Christophe, xxiii
Jafri, Ali Sardar, 232
Jahan, Begum Akbar, xxiv
Jahan, Nusrat, xxiv
Jain, L.C., 116
Jaiswal, Anantram, 23, 192
Jaitley, Priyadarshni, 61
Jakhar, Balram, 6, 108
Janata Dal, 116, 124, 146, 206, 227, 229
Janata Party, 3–7, 10, 31–32, 34, 43, 50, 53, 58–60, 64–66, 144, 166, 192, 230; coalition with, 13, 167; government, 43, 47; and multinational companies., 166
Jauhar, Mohammad Ali, 70
Javed (son-in-law), 95
Jawahar Navodaya Vidyalayas, 146
Jerath, Arti, 9
JP Movement, 24, see also Narayan, Jayaprakash (JP)
Jyotiraditya, 221

Kaira District Cooperative Milk Producers' Union Ltd, 166
Kaisar Jahan, xxiv
Kamaraj, K., 84, 87–88
Kant, Krishna, 89, 228
Kapoor, Yashpal, 4, 55
Kareem, Mufti Mazhar, 70
Kashmir, 148; militancy in, 148
Katara, M., 114
Kaur, Gursharan, 214
Kejriwal, Arvind, 232–233
Kesri, Sitaram, 190, 224, 229; withdrawing support to Deve Gowda, 231
Khalida (first cousin), 78
Khan, Shahnawaz, Gen., 176–177
Khan, Shah Rukh, 177
Khan, Sultan Alam, 27
Khan, Syed Ahmad, Sir, 77
Khan Choudhury, A.B.A. Ghani, 190
Khatri, Nirmal, 192
Khilafat movement, 70, 131
Kidwai, Atiq Ur Rahman (maternal uncle), 72
Kidwai, Basheer Ur Rahman, 71
Kidwai, Faiz Ahmed, 197
Kidwai, Fazal Ur Rahman, 71
Kidwai, Hasan Ur Rahman (maternal grandfather), 71, 78
Kidwai, Imran (brother-in-law), 102

Kidwai, Jalil Ur Rahman (brother-in-law), 79
Kidwai, Jameel Ur Rahman (father-in-law), 14, 17–26, 43, 52, 56, 79–83, 106–108, 131; death of, 52, 108
Kidwai, Khalil Ur Rahman (husband), 22, 25, 73, 77, 104, 193; death of, 104
Kidwai, Khaliq Ur Rahman (maternal uncle), 72
Kidwai, Mohsina: as AICC general secretary, 184, 191; arrest of, 48; birth of, 73; as cabinet minister for small-scale industries, 90; as chairperson of district Social Welfare Board, 79–80; education, 74–75; first Assembly speech, 25; first meeting with Indira, 18; as Haj Committee chairman, 196; hit by stone, 108–109; introduction to politics, 17; marriage, 77–78; as member of Central Haj Committee, 194; as minister of state for food and civil supplies, 90; minister of state for labour, 112, 179; as MLC, 25, 81–82; passion for social work, 80; as Union minister of state, 106; as union transport minister, 135; as UPCC president, xxvi, 6, 14, 30–31, 33, 37, 46–47, 51, 53, 55, 59, 62, 94, 108, 139, 212; urban development minister, 115, 119–120
Kidwai, Maghfoor Ur Rahman, 71
Kidwai, Mubashir Hussain (uncle), 78
Kidwai, Mustafa Kamil, 90
Kidwai, Nawazish Ur Rahman, 71, 74
Kidwai, Nisar Ur Rahman (parents' maternal great-grandfather), 71, 74–75
Kidwai, Rafi Ahmed, 83
Kidwai, Shafiq Ur Rahman (maternal uncle), 72–73, 131
kisan (farmer) agitation, 182
Kripalani, Jivatram Bhagwandas, 84
Kripalani, Sucheta, 84
Krishna, S.M., 194, 197
Kumar, Nitish, 168, 185–186, 218
Kurien, Verghese, 166

Ladies' Club, 79
Lal, Bansi, 45
Lal, Lala Harkishan, 159
Le Monde, 44
Lohia, Ram Manohar, 209
Lokpal bill, 233

INDEX 253

LTTE suicide bomber, 150
Lucknow University, 79

Madani, Hussain Ahmed, xxvi, 70
Mahakali Treaty, 231
Mahmoodabad, Raja, 74–75
Maimuna Sultan (maternal aunt), xxiv, 72
Maitra, S.N., 176
Majithia, Dyal Singh, 159
Maliana, 180
Malviya, K.D., 4
Malviya, Madan Mohan, 83
Mandal Commission Recommendations, 146, 168
Mandalization, 183
Mandela, Nelson, 56
Masood Uz Zaman (father's uncle), 7, 71
Masoomnoor, xxiv
Mateena (sister), 73
Mathai, John, 156
Maurya, Budh Priya, 45
Mayawati, Bahujan Samaj Party Chief, 175, 207
medicine distribution scheme, 115
Meerut, xxiv, 39, 55, 109, 175–176, 178, 180, 182, 226; Lok Sabha constituency, 175; Lok Sabha elections defeat, 178; Shahagasha violence, 178

Members of Parliament (MP), xxiii, xxv, 23–24, 32, 87–88, 108, 178, 188, 208, 229
Merton, Thomas, 55
Mian, Jamal, 19
Ministry of Health and Family Welfare, 115
minorities, 57, 168, 226
Mishra, Jaganath, 13
Mitra, Somen, 190–191
Modi, Narendra, 149, 169; demonetization of, 166, 169
Mohammad, Taj, 177
Momina (sister), 73
Moopanar, G.K., 45, 150
Mrinalini, 191
Mufti, Mahbooba, xxiv
Muhammad Ali Zati Diary, 70
Muhammadan Anglo-Oriental College, 77
Mukherjee, Pranab, xxvii, 43, 64, 66, 190, 203, 214–217; on Mamata Banerjee, 191
Mukhtar Un Nisa (maternal grandmother), 71
Mulla, Qutubuddin Ahmad (father), 69
Mullah, Ziauddeen (brother), 165
Mumtaz Jahan Begum, 76
Muradnagar canal incident, 181
Muslim League, 19–20

Muslims, xxiii–xxiv, xxvi, 6–7, 9–11, 19–20, 23, 72, 176–178, 193, 195–196, 207; education of, 77; societies, 95

Muslim women, xxiii–xxiv, 27; education of, 76–77; elected to Parliament, xxiii; Jaffrelot on, xxiii; rights of, 95; Verniers on, xxiii

Muslim Women's College, 76

Nadwatul Ulama, 70
Nagarpalikas Bill 1989, 115
Nanda, Gulzarilal, 165
Narah, Ranee, xxiv
Narain, Raj, 33
Narain, Yogendra, 48
Narasimha Rao, P.V.: as Congress president, 122–125; as Prime Minister, xxvii, 113, 160, 190–191, 213, 219–220, 223, 229, 231
Narayan, Jayaprakash (JP), 144; 'Sampoorna Kranti' of, 136–137
National Democratic Alliance (NDA), 186; dismissing Rabri Devi government, 185
National Front coalition, 227
nationalism, xxvi, 106
National Policy on Education (NPE), 146

National Rural Employment Guarantee Scheme (NREGS), 162

nation rebuilding, as collective responsibility, 170

Natwar Singh, K., 121, 123

Nehru, Jawaharlal, 14, 17–21, 79, 82–84, 86–88, 107, 111, 124, 129–130, 134, 151–155, 157, 159; and committee for Bose's death, 176; death of, 87, 131, 165; Industrial Policy Resolution, 156; Motilal, 74–75, 83; peaceful co-existence, 154; and Public Sector, 152

Nehru-Gandhi family legacy, 189
Nehru Report of 1928, xxvii
new party headquarters, 108
Nijalingappa, S., 89, 228
Nisa, Ateef Un (paternal grandmother), 70
Noida, as planned city, 211
Non-aligned Movement, 124, 154
non-cooperation movement, 56, 210
non-violence, 170
Noor Begum, xxiv
Nyuntam Aay Yojana (Minimum Income Scheme -, NYAY), 157

Operation Blue Star, 109

Other Backward Classes (OBCs), 23, 147, 168

Pakistan, 57, 74, 87, 121, 132–133, 158, 165–166, 177, 194, 231–232
Pal, Harish, 175
Palahniuk, Chuck, 194
Panchayati Raj system, 115, 146
Pande, Kedar, 13
Pandey, V.C., 186
Pandit, Tilakdhari, 11
Pant, Govind Ballabh, 83, 85
Patel, Ahmed, 194, 217–218
Patel, Sardar Vallabhbhai, 111, 141
Patil, S.K., 87, 228
Patil, Vasant Dada, 45
Patil, Veerendra, 64–66, 230
Pawar, Sharad, 168
People's Front, 208
Phadnis, Aditi, 207–208
Phool Patti craft, 95–96
Pilot, Rajesh, 112, 222–223
Pilot, Sachin, 222–223
Planning Commission, replaced with NITI Aayog, 169
Pradesh Congress Committee (PCC), 46, 81, 108
Pradhan Mantri Jan Dhan Yojana (PMJDY), 170
Praja Socialist Party. *See* Socialist Party (India)

Prasada, Jitendra, 223–224
privy purses, abolition of, 158, 228
Provincial Armed Constabulary (PAC), 178–179; and Ganga canal shooting, 181

Qasim, Syed Mir, 45, 59, 64
Qidwa, Qazi (Muizuddin Kidwai), 71–72
Quit India Movement, 119, 136, 210

Raebareli, 33, 188, 204
Rai, Kalpnath, 59, 61
Rai, Lala Lajpat, 159
Ram, Jagjivan, 5, 87, 158
Ramachandran, M. G. (MGR), 66
Ramsewak, 22–23
Rashtriya Janata Dal, 186, 218
Rashtriya Swayamsevak Sangh (RSS), 31, 141, 148, 167, 187, 219, 233
Ray, Siddhartha Shankar, 190
Razi (son-in-law), 95, 109
Reddy, K. Brahmananda, 45–46
Reddy, Neelam Sanjiva, 89
riots, 177–178, 180–183; Bombay, 148; in Meerut, 179; outsiders behind, 180
Rochefoucauld, Francois de La, 183
Roosevelt, Franklin D., 55

Rourkela steel plant, 152
Royal Asiatic Society, London, 70
Rubab Syeda, xxiv

SAARC summit, 119, 121
Sabiha, 96
Sahgal, Lakshmi, Capt., 208
Salafi, 195
Salahuddin (brother), 73–74
Samajwadi Party, xxv, 188, 206, 208–209, 229
Sampurnanand, Dr., 83
Samyukta Vidhayak Dal, 85
Sanatkada, 96
Sanghamita, Mamtaz, xxiv
Santap, 6
Sathe, Vasant, 65
Saudi Arabia, 120, 123, 193, 195, 197
Saxena, 14, 180
Scheduled Caste Act, 207
Scheduled Castes (SCs), 23, 64, 118, 151, 178
Scheduled Tribes (STs), 118, 138, 151, 178
Scindia, Madhavrao, 112, 125, 220–222
Scindia, Vasundhararaje, 187
Second Round Table Conference, xxvii
sectarianism, 139

secularism, xxvi–xxvii, 111, 124, 153, 186
Seema (daughter), 79, 93–97, 99–101, 106, 109; married to Razi, 109
Sehra, Gulab, 39
Sen, A.K., 49
Sethi, P.C., 4, 179
Sethi, Sunil, 9
Sewa Dal workers, 41
Shahab (brother), 73–74
Shah Bano Begum, xxv
Shah Commission, 4
Sharif, Nawaz, 232
Sharma, A.P., 45
Sharma, Chaturbhuj, 81
Sharma, Shankar Dayal, xxiv, 13
Shastri, Lal Bahadur, 87–88, 130–131, 133–135, 164–165; and 1965 Pakistan war, 132; and Ariyalur accident, 134; death of, 87, 166; 'Jai Jawan, Jai Kisan' by, 133; setting up National Defence Fund, 133; success of, 166
Sherwani, M.R., 8, 27
Shia, 195
Shukla, Chandra Bhushan, 107
Shukla, V.C., 45
Singh, Amarinder, Capt., 184–185
Singh, Arjun, xxvii, 123–124, 218–220

Singh, Beant, assassin of Indira, 110
Singh, Buta, 12, 45–46, 108, 183
Singh, Chandra Shekhar, 5, 89, 149, 207–208, 227–228, 231; as prime minister, 168
Singh, Chaudhary Charan, 3–6, 43–44, 84–85, 222, 231; and caste-based politics, 85; defected from Congress, 85
Singh, Digvijaya, 191–192
Singh, Dinesh, 27
Singh, D.P., 39
Singh, Ghanshyam, 23
Singh, Hari Har, 228
Singh, Jangi, 181
Singh, Kamakhya Narain, 228
Singh, Karan, 45
Singh, K.N., 123
Singh, Manmohan, 104, 123, 157, 160–162, 169–170, 194, 203, 213–215, 219; as Prime Minister, 162; on 'weak prime ministership', 214
Singh, N.K., 44
Singh, Rajendra, 186
Singh, Ramchandra, 23
Singh, Sadanand, 186
Singh, Satwant, assassin of Indira, 110
Singh, Swaran, 37, 45
Singh, Virbhadra, 187

Singh, V.P., 146, 168, 208, 225–226; fall of, 149
Singh, Zail, 104
Sinha, Dharam Bir, 49
Sinha, Tarkeshwari, 6
Sinha, Yashwant, 168–169
Sitaramayya, P., xxvii
Sixty-second Amendment Act of the Constitution, 145
socialism, 156, 158, 209–210
Socialist Party (India), 23, 84, 136, 210
Socially and Educationally Backward Classes Commission (SEBC), 146–147
Soni, Ambika, 45
State Bank of India, Vishwa Yatra Foreign Travel by, 196–197
Stokes, Vidya, 187
Subramaniam, C., 228
Sufis, 72, 195
sugarcane protest, 47, 49
Sughra (Apa), 79, 101
Sunni Barelwi, 195
Sunni Deobandi, 195
Surjeet, Harkishan Singh, 229
Swadeshi movement, 170
Swaminathan, M.S., 165
Switzerland, 120

Tabbasum Begum, xxiv
Tafsir Majidi, 70

Taimur, Anwara, 194
Tashkent, 87, 134, 166
Telugu Desam Party, 229
Tewari, Narayan Dutt, 29
Thakur, Karpoori, 147
Thanwi, Ashraf Ali, 70
Tihar Jail, 42–43, 45
Tikait, Mahendra Singh, 182
Tiwari, N.D., 12, 29–30, 37–39, 47, 54, 123–124, 142, 183, 210, 223
Tiwari Congress. *See* Congress (Tiwari)
Toyoda, Kiichiro, 221
Tripathi, Kamalapati, 5, 12, 30, 37, 39, 46–47, 55, 59–62, 83–84, 89–90
Tripathi, Rajendra, 226
Tully, Mark, 9
The Turbulent Years, 216
20-Point Programme, 31, 117, 138, 141; land patta for landless, 141
Tytler, Jagdish, 112

UAE, 97, 121
union budget, merged with railways, 169
Union Carbide gas leak, 220
union health ministry, 114
United Front, 148, 229

United Nations General Assembly, 120
United Progressive Alliance, 104, 162–164
United States, of Stop-go policy, 133
untouchability, xxviii, 56
Upadhyay, Muneshwar Dutt, 26
UP Industrial Area Development Act, 1976, 211
Urs, Devaraj, 9, 13, 66
USSR, 119–120, 134
Ustinov, Peter, 110
Uttar Pradesh Congress Committee (UPCC), 14, 30, 53, 55, 59, 62, 83, 192, 225–226; new office, 54

Vajpayee, Atal Bihari, 11, 149, 169, 185, 187, 208, 229, 231
Vajpayee, Rajendra Kumari, 90
Venkataraman, R., 149
Verma, Jairam, 85
Verniers, Gilles, xxiii
Vietnam, 119, 133, 162
Vishwa Hindu Parishad (VHP), 148, 227

Waziruddin (paternal grandfather), 69
White Revolution, 165–166
women Lok Sabha MPs, xxiv

INDEX

World Peace Conference, USSR, 119

Yadav, Akhilesh, 209
Yadav, Chandrajit, 3, 6, 11, 228
Yadav, Lalu Prasad, 168, 185–186, 207, 218, 229
Yadav, Laxmi Shankar, 212
Yadav, Mulayam Singh, 85, 168, 203, 206–210, 229–230
Yadav, Ram Bachan, 4, 6, 10
Yadav, Ram Naresh, 3, 5, 12, 50, 58
Yadav, Ramsewak, 22, 24
'Young Turks,' 89, 228. See also under *separate names*
Youth Congress (I), 50

Zaheer, Syed Ali, 83
Zahra Khatoon (mother), 71–72
Zaidi, Gufran, 61
zamindari system, 73; abolishment of, xxviii, 56, 151, 181
Zia (brother), 73
Zubaida (maternal aunt), 72–73

About the Authors

Mohsina Kidwai is a leader of the Indian National Congress. From Barabanki in Uttar Pradesh, she has been a member of the Lok Sabha and the Rajya Sabha, holding several offices in the Congress Working Committee as well as the All India Congress Committee. In the 1970s and 1980s, she served as union cabinet minister in several ministries including health and family welfare, transport, urban development and tourism.

Rasheed Kidwai is a journalist, author, columnist and political analyst. He is a visiting fellow with the Observer Research Foundation. A former associate editor of the *Telegraph*, he is a graduate from St Stephen's College, New Delhi, and holds a master's degree in mass communications from the University of Leicester, United Kingdom. He also contributes to numerous television channels, including CNN-News18, ABP News, NDTV, India Ahead News and India Today TV.